Hamlet in His Modern Guises

✣

Hamlet in
His Modern Guises

✣

ALEXANDER WELSH

PRINCETON UNIVERSITY PRESS

PRINCETON AND OXFORD

Library of Congress Cataloging-in-Publication Data
Welsh, Alexander.
Hamlet in his modern guises / Alexander Welsh.
p. cm.
Includes index.
ISBN 0-691-05093-7 (alk. paper)
1. Shakespeare, William, 1564–1616. Hamlet. 2. Shakespeare, William,
1564–1616—Influence. 3. Fiction—19th century—History and criticism.
4. Fiction—20th century—History and criticism.
5. Moderism (Literature) 6. Heroes in literature. I. Title.
PR2807.W39 2001
809′.93351—dc21   00-038563

This book has been composed in Janson

www.pup.princeton.edu

Printed in the United States of America

1 3 5 7 9 10 8 6 4 2

"Character," says Novalis, in one of his questionable aphorisms—
"character is destiny." But not the whole of our destiny. Hamlet,
Prince of Denmark, was speculative and irresolute, and we have a
great tragedy in consequence. But if his father had lived to a good
old age, and his uncle had died an early death, we can conceive
Hamlet's having married Ophelia, and got through life with a
reputation of sanity, notwithstanding many soliloquies, and some
moody sarcasms towards the fair daughter of Polonius, to say
nothing of the frankest incivility to his father-in-law.
(George Eliot)

✢ *Contents* ✢

❖ Preface and Acknowledgments ❖

HAMLET BECAME a modern hero, I contend, as soon as Shakespeare put his hands on him four hundred years ago. At least, the only other Hamlets who have come down to us are distinctly medieval, even ancient, if folk and classical analogues are taken into account. The leading difference between *Hamlet* and the earlier narrated adventures of the same hero is the introduction of a close-knit family. Indeed Shakespeare underlined the difference by creating two families, the second fashioned around the nameless friend of the hero's stepfather who would come to be called Polonius. With two families in hand, the playwright constructed his superb model of filial relationships, the resonance of which is attested by the fame of his play. By the later eighteenth century *Hamlet* became a stronger cultural force than in the days of its first performances, and its influence thereafter increased. To stay in the forefront of this growth industry, Hamlet had to be modern.

In a laboratory for the study of filial relations, if there were no troublesome rules about the use of human subjects, one would presumably kill off a few fathers and watch what happened. Fortunately, we have various verbal and miming techniques called plays, in which lethal injections (say into the ear) can be performed quite harmlessly and the reactions of sons directly imagined. Of course Shakespeare did not set out to study any human behavior in the abstract, but unquestionably the death of Hamlet's father puts the young man and their relationship, and the relationship with the mother and the girlfriend, to the test. About twenty years ago, after conducting an undergraduate seminar on *Hamlet* and during a painful time in my own life, I wrote an essay on Hamlet's task in mourning the loss of his father. The essay endorsed, in passing, the notion that Shakespeare adapted the story with the knowledge of his own father's death, or impending death, in 1601. I still find myself pondering what the play meant to its author. Shakespeare did not have to behave like Hamlet or even especially to feel like Hamlet in order to put his experience, and that of so many other sons and fathers, to good use in the theater. He did what he could do sympathetically for Hamlet. He needed no laboratory for his experiment. But the resulting play, in its accommodating texture, has provided ample work room for later writers great and small.

The present book is far from a survey of later writers' uses of *Hamlet*. For one thing, I do not even touch on the vast stage history of the play. I do discuss a group of sixteenth-century revenge tragedies in support of the argument that revenge—especially brooding about revenge—is a function of mourning. These guides are the best we have to what Shakespeare thought he was doing with and for the audiences of his own time. When I turn to the period of *Hamlet*'s ascendancy in Western culture, however, I treat of novels and become highly selective. In the nineteenth century the novel, rather than drama, was dominant in the literary marketplace and the genre of choice for studies of character. By selecting a few well-known novels, I can hope to show in some detail how Goethe, Scott, Dickens, Melville, and Joyce responded to Shakespeare's play. A major purpose of this book is to let such later writers help us see why Hamlet is a distinctly modern hero.

I hasten to add that each of the novels discussed here would have taken one shape or another had *Hamlet* never existed. These are works by strong writers with agendas of their own: the use they make of *Hamlet* is gratuitous, as it were, and thus affords all the more remarkable commentary on the possibilities inherent in the play. Goethe's *Wilhelm Meisters Lehrjahre* in effect delivers the hero from allegiance to the older generation, while at the same time it enlarges on the possibility that he could write for the theater as well as patronize it. By enlisting *Hamlet* for his autobiographical novel, Goethe accepts the idea that it is Shakespeare's signature work. He celebrates Hamlet's intellect and learning process by making his own work a bildungsroman. His novel has come to be seen as an important event in literary history, and it says something about perceptions of Hamlet that each of the novels I examine here is in some sort a bildungsroman and in some degree autobiographical.

A younger contemporary of Goethe's, Scott wrote many more influential novels, all in the last third of his lifetime. As he himself would admit, his heroes proper were much of a sameness; but their sameness follows from their representativeness. They stand for a new polity of the present and future generations; and the past—the ancien régime, let's call it—can be mourned for as dead and over with. One novel, *Redgauntlet*, engages more than the others with *Hamlet*: it is recognized as one of Scott's autobiographical fictions and it owes something, almost certainly, to Goethe as well as Shakespeare. The hero of Dickens's *Great Expectations* is also representative (he could virtually be anonymous as well). Pip's outward story is that of a working-class lad from the provinces who manages to reach the city and get a hold on gentility, which he keeps hold of by eventually emigrating to the colonial world. His inward story is a dream of the same, at once more aggrandizingly pleasurable and nightmarish in its criminal associations: a drawn-out story of guilt, notwithstanding the hero's inno-cence. *Hamlet*, it seems, is never far from Dickens's instinctive feelings about this novel and its probing of unconscious guilt. *Great Expectations* is something of an event in the history of psychological narrative. The novel strikingly anticipates twentieth-century psychoanalytic criticism of Shake-speare's play for which Hamlet rather than the criminal Claudius is the guilty party. For all its differences, the novel is perhaps the closest replica of the play imaginable in another era. In *Great Expectations* as in *Hamlet*, the portentous events and unraveling mysteries are finally to be understood as outward dramatizations of states of mind.

Since these particular novels by Scott and Dickens are to a degree auto-biographical, they too are tangentially about writers. Melville's *Pierre* takes up several *Hamlet*-like actions—most notably it becomes suffused with mourning—and more than halfway through the novel the reader learns that Pierre *is* a writer. Because of Hamlet's vulgar reputation for inaction, Pierre consciously strives to be unlike him, but he ends his days very much in the pattern of the last scene in Shakespeare's play. He is nothing if not a Romantic writer, bent on relating autobiographically for humanity truths too deep to tell. He is, in truth, a Titanic failure and therein embodies certain extremes of nineteenth-century Hamletism. Though published in 1852, *Pierre* is also a surprisingly modernist work. In what is often thought of as *the* modernist novel, Joyce adopts another nineteenth-century model that pairs Hamlet as the modern type against some ancient hero—in this case Ulysses. Joyce's *Ulysses* takes from Shakespeare a more trammeled re-lation of father and son than could be found in Homer, and therefore Ste-phen Dedalus is more Hamlet than Telemachus. In modernist texts, that the Hamlet connections are only half-serious is par for the course.

Hamlet's melancholy ironizes rather than condemns the world. His tol-erance for clowning and penchant for ridicule arrive at a pitch when he is nearest his own death. For most of the play he mourns and is unsparing of himself, but the jarring of disgust and constraint results in a heightened consciousness. Mourning, I suggest, is partly what we mean by modern consciousness, for which Hamlet would not seem nearly as representative if it were not for his youth. Modernity assumes the loss of some priority—always in the novels examined here the loss of fathers, whether still living or not, but it may be of prior customs, allegiances, governments, or literary conventions as well. The sincerity of youthful mourning nevertheless re-mains in question. With the notable exception of Melville's Pierre, modern Hamlets seem on the whole contented to be the youthful survivors. In a long essay William Empson once speculated that *Hamlet* was Shakespeare's parody of the existing revenge tragedy by that name. These famous novelists are surely parodists of sorts, and their idea of *Hamlet* is that of a tragicomedy of modern consciousness.

. . . . .

The present book owes many insights to the long tradition of Shakespeare scholarship as well as to criticism of the novelists treated here. My footnotes, the best I can do to register this indebtedness, have been set down with felt gratitude. Many students have shared their thoughts with me over the years, and I also take pleasure in recalling the introduction to Shakespeare provided by two of my earliest teachers, Harry Levin and Alfred B. Harbage. The former, whose short book *The Question of Hamlet* (1959) can still hold its own, is perhaps best known for his lifetime's work as a comparativist and student of the novel. The latter devoted his wit and scholarship mainly to Renaissance English drama: yet Harbage's lectures for the American Philosophical Society, published as *A Kind of Power* (1975), deserve to be known for the striking analogy they draw between the creative gifts of Shakespeare and Dickens. I feel fortunate in having had such teachers and in encountering many others as colleagues over the years. Robert Newsom, in a review of an earlier book of mine, first protested the importance of *Hamlet* for *Great Expectations* in particular. Jonathan Bate, Lawrence Manley, and David Quint have kindly read the typescript of this book, offered thoughtful suggestions, and corrected not a few mistakes. Ruth Bernard Yeazell, less of a Shakespearean but my best loved and most necessary reader for all that, has also performed her part: if the argument is not perfectly clear, it is my own perverse fault.

I thank Mary Murrell of the Princeton University Press for her help; Diane Repak, Kris Kavanaugh, and Imraan Coovadia for their expert handling of the final draft; David Allen for his copyediting. Some pages of chapter 2 originally appeared in the *Yale Review*, and I thank the present editor, J.D. McClatchy, for permission to use them here. The greater part of chapter 3 appeared recently in *Modern Language Quarterly*, whose editor Marshall Brown, together with Jane Brown, proved especially helpful on Goethe. Legions of textual editors, of Shakespeare and of our other writers, deserve thanks. The text of *Hamlet* quoted throughout this book is that of Philip Edwards (1985) for the New Cambridge Shakespeare.

Hamlet in His Modern Guises

✜

Medieval Hamlet Gains a Family

IGNORANCE ABOUT the lost play that was performed on the English stage some years before Shakespeare's *Hamlet* makes it all the more imperative to compare his play—traditionally the conflation of two texts, the quarto of 1604 and folio of 1623—with the still earlier narrative versions of the hero's story that do survive. This procedure at least apprises us of features not wholly original to Shakespeare, even if it leaves us only with intelligent guesses as to the intervening contributions of an *Ur-Hamlet*.[1] Comparison with the earlier narratives also yields a positive understanding of ways in which the play is modern, and particularly why Hamlet's family—a little more than kin, if less than kind—seems to us so modern. For good measure, Shakespeare built into his play a second family, that of Polonius, posed novel-like for intermarriage with the younger generation of the first. The word "family" in our sense of parents and children was new in the sixteenth century. Shakespeare rarely uses the word at all, and never in its modern sense. Yet his *Hamlet* reads like a textbook on the conjugal and patriarchal family.

The present study is concerned with Hamlet in history, more especially Hamlets of the last four centuries. Was there, in the other direction of time, a historical Hamlet with a mother and father who lived and died a violent death six centuries prior to Shakespeare's time? The difficulty of answering this question—apart from my difficulty of collapsing a millennium into a few pages—is that very old histories defy modern belief. Thus when Amleth, in the earliest extant chronicle of Hamlet's story, travels to England and somehow intuits the English king's secrets (without recourse to magic), we seem to be reading of an exercise of wit that never was, though the chronicle does not distinguish between this feat and others more plausible. Like speculations about the *Ur-Hamlet*, the quest for the historical Hamlet is bound to be frustrating compared to the experience of suspending disbelief in the play, for Shakespeare is among those artists chiefly responsible

---

[1] Harold Bloom, *Shakespeare: The Invention of the Human* (New York: Riverhead, 1998), 395–401, contends that the earlier play must also have been by Shakespeare. The evidence for the *Ur-Hamlet* consists of a satirical allusion to it by Thomas Nashe in 1589, the record of a performance in 1594, another allusion by Thomas Lodge in 1596, and lesser matter. For a succinct summary see *Hamlet*, ed. Harold Jenkins (London: Methuen, 1982), 82–85.

for our (high) standards of verisimilitude. Notoriously, it is Shakespeare's Hamlet who so unmistakably lived that we can engage in long debates about his character. Even the ghost in the play, who does not arise in the old story, seems all too human—though I for one do not believe in ghosts any more than I believe in Amleth's extraordinary intuitions.

The chronicle in question, Saxo's *Historiae Danicae*, written in Latin at the end of the twelfth century and printed in 1514, was most likely never seen by Shakespeare; but its elaboration in François de Belleforest's *Histoires tragiques* had been available in five French editions since 1570.[2] Thus the medieval history is the source of the sixteenth-century narrative most likely consulted by Shakespeare along with the *Ur-Hamlet*. If the French version or an unpublished translation of it had not been familiar to some English playwright, obviously, there would have been no *Ur-Hamlet* or any *Hamlet* at all.[3] Saxo's history is both a better read and closer to folklore, whether it be fact or fiction; Belleforest's version, over twice as long but without more action or incident than Saxo's (and a faithful translation in that sense), is already a Renaissance text, with explanations, political and religious reservations, and moralizing, some of which matter is reflected in the play. Even if one refuses the quest for a historical Hamlet and isn't much interested in which details Shakespeare may have lifted from Belleforest, both earlier narratives are important for the perspective they throw on Hamlet in his modern guises.

Saxo's story is compelling in its own right, and not merely dependent—as might be charged of Belleforest's—on the fame of its Shakespearean sequel. There are few wasted words; in the style of northern saga, interest and suspense are characterized throughout by the unspoken, a withholding of explanation that enhances each demonstration of the hero's cleverness. The unspoken irony, in fact, offers a foretaste of the ambivalences of Shakespeare's hero. But though Amleth suffers as a boy—roughly, until he slays the uncle who has murdered his father and married with his mother—his suffering and madness are not pitiable as such, but rather disguise his motives and sustain the suspense. Nor is the uncle, Feng, particularly wicked or expressive of something wrong so much as he is simply dangerous. Saxo, called Grammaticus, is proud of his Latin, as his allusions, proper names—

[2] Information on these two sources can be found in Jenkins, 85–96; also *Narrative and Dramatic Sources of Shakespeare*, ed. Geoffrey Bullough, vol. 7 (London: Routledge; New York: Columbia University Press, 1973), 5–25.

[3] An English translation of Belleforest, apparently prompted by the success of Shakespeare's play, was published anonymously as *The Hystorie of Hamblet* in 1608. This is given nearly in full by Bullough, 7:81–124.

Amlethus, Horwendillus, Gerutha, Fengo, Vigletus—and a few incidents show; yet his overt summary or commentary is still very spare, with moralizing confined to the end of each book:

> O valiant Amleth, and worthy of immortal fame, who being shrewdly armed with a feint of folly, covered a wisdom too high for human wit under a marvelous disguise of silliness! and not only found in his subtlety means to protect his own safety, but also by its guidance found opportunity to avenge his father. By this skilful defence of himself, and strenuous revenge for his parent, he has left it doubtful whether we are to think more of his wit or his bravery.[4]

Amleth's ingenious revenge, plotted all along by means that are eventually disclosed in the acting but never confided in advance to the reader any more than to Feng, is thus said to merit eternal fame; but this fame boils down to that of a man both tough and smart, *fortis* and *sapiens*.

The triumph over Feng completes book 3 of *Historiae Danicae*, and just about here (with a very different action) terminates the experience of Hamlet dramatized by Shakespeare. For the chronicle, however, the rest is not silence: book 4 commences with the notation "Amlethus rex" in the margin; the prince becomes king in Jutland and enjoys further successes in England and Scotland before his eventual defeat at the hands of another uncle at home. The marked differences between the play and the chronicle, therefore, are the truncation of the career and the alteration of the first triumphant return to tragedy, in which the principal actors *all* die.[5] Omitted along with the remainder of Amleth's career, significantly, is a long stump speech by which the latter defends his action and calls for his election to the throne: Shakespeare's tragedy, by no means apolitical, is less political and less historically situated than its source, more focused on the personal and familial clash of its antagonists. But the chronicle is not so naïve as to offer mere triumph and congratulation where its famous redaction supplies

---

[4] "Fortem virum, aeternoque nomine dignum: qui stultitiae commento prudenter instructus, augustiorem mortali ingenio sapientiam admirabili ineptiarum simulatione suppressit: nec solum propriae salutis obtentum ab astutia mutuatus, ad paternae quoque ultionis copiam eadem ductum praebente pervenit. Itaque et se solerter tutatus: et parentum strenue ultus: fortior, an sapientior existimari debeat, incertum reliquit." From *The Sources of "Hamlet*," ed. Israel Gollancz (1926; rpt. New York: Octagon, 1967), 130, with Oliver Elton's translation on the facing page. Elton's translation is also given by Bullough, 7:70.

[5] Famously, the tragedy is also presaged by a Senecan ghost. That the *Ur-Hamlet* too featured a ghost, crying "Hamlet, revenge," is one of the few things we know about it: see *Hamlet*, ed. Jenkins, 83; and Bullough, 7:24.

tragedy. With the play's ending one ought to compare the irony of Amleth's second homecoming in book 4 and his death.

When in England for the first time, Amleth disposes of the two companions bearing a letter begging the favor of his death just as Hamlet disposes of Rosencrantz and Guildenstern, but he scores one better than Hamlet by marrying the king's daughter there. On his second visit, when he has told his father-in-law what has become of his uncle back in Jutland, the king inwardly recalls his pact with Feng and—in spite of this marriage—sends Amleth off on a dangerous mission to court on his behalf the queen of Scotland, known for putting to death every suitor to date. Hermutrude the queen is only opposed to older husbands, however; Amleth she embraces with all her kingdom, and after an ingenious victory over the English king his father-in-law, the hero returns to Jutland with much plunder and two wives. Of the (apparently) younger English wife, who has borne him a son, backed him against her father, and put up with Hermutrude, nothing more is told. Amleth dotes on Hermutrude, and meanwhile a new threat has arisen against his mother Geruth—this time from her own brother Wiglek. In the swiftly told end of his days, and now more concerned for Hermutrude's future than for his own life, according to Saxo, Amleth nonetheless cannot shun battle with Wiglek: he loses, and in the last sentence of book 4 this maternal uncle weds Hermutrude. Belleforest, it has to be said, weakens this irony in his version by moralizing and claiming that Amleth's second wife planned in advance her widowhood and remarriage. Given the way Hermutrude proposed to Amleth in Scotland earlier, Saxo's few words suffice to make the point: to Wiglek "she yielded herself up unasked to be the conqueror's spoil and bride."[6]

Amleth's death is not tragic; as with many heroes of northern saga, when his violent life has run out, it is over with. Saxo's two books neatly divide the hero's life course into two parts, in which first a paternal uncle murders the father and marries the mother and then, after the hero copes well with this emergency, a maternal uncle kills the hero himself and marries his widow. There is something about Amleth's choice of women—more nearly their choice of him—that leads to trouble with uncles, in short, while the design of the whole seems to make an ironic statement about clever young men. The moral Saxo has to offer is one long sentence of misogyny—the quod erat demonstrandum, so to speak—which parallels his praise of Amleth at the end of book 3:

---

[6] "Ultro in victoris praedam, amplexumque concessit" (Gollancz, 160–61). For Belleforest's French with the 1608 English translation on the opposite page, see Gollancz, 302–3. The respective translations may also be consulted in Bullough, 7:79, 122.

Thus all vows of women are loosed by change of fortune and melted by the shifting of time; the faith of their soul rests on a slippery foothold, and is weakened by casual chances; glib in promises, and as sluggish in performance, all manner of lustful promptings enslave it, and it bounds away with panting and precipitate desire, forgetful of old things, in the ever hot pursuit after something fresh.[7]

About ten times longer, Belleforest's restatement of this moral is relieved only by a quaint apology for being so carried away by the subject. Shakespeare evidently was impressed by the whole of Amleth's history and not merely the first half. The irony of Amleth's eventual destiny could be said to reappear in the repeated poisonings of the play, or indeed in the difficulty so many critics have experienced in determining what if anything Hamlet finally achieved. On the playwright's side, it might be said that at least he assigned the misogyny dramatically to the deceased father and to the son rather than endorsing it outright.[8]

That Saxo is closer in spirit to northern saga than is the moralizing Belleforest no one would deny. He is still far from modeling himself on the sagaman, and it seems doubtful that his narrative is a faithful translation from old Danish originals, even if the hazards of translation might account for some of the story's baffling details.[9] Saxo is too much the classicist; he most likely emulated the Roman historians, for it has long been observed that he borrows Livy's account of Junius Brutus seeking vengeance upon *his* uncle, Tarquin.[10] Homer and Virgil offer famous precedents for such details as the intricate history of his exploits that Amleth has painted on

---

[7] "Ita votum omne foemineum fortunae varietas abripit: temporum mutatio dissolvit: et muliebris animi fidem lubrico nixam vestigio fortuiti rerum casus extenuant: quae sicut ad pollicendum facilis, ita ad persolvendum segnis; variis voluptatis irritamentis astringitur atque ad recentia semper avidius expetenda, veterum immemor: anhela, praeceps cupiditate dissultat" (Gollancz, 160–63). For Belleforest's outdoing of Saxo in this vein, see Gollancz, 304–10; translations also in Bullough, 7:79, 122–23.

[8] For the case that the play itself bears the misogynist burden, see Janet Adelman, *Suffocating Mothers: Fantasies of Maternal Origin in Shakespeare's Plays, "Hamlet" to "The Tempest"* (New York: Routledge, 1992), esp. 11–37. The subtext that Adelman creates may be more persuasive than the one offered by Freud, but her method and evidentiary claims are thoroughly Freudian.

[9] See William F. Hansen, *Saxo Grammaticus and the Life of Hamlet* (Lincoln: University of Nebraska Press, 1983), 125–34.

[10] Shakespeare's Brutus, sometimes thought to be a prototype for his Hamlet, alludes to Junius Brutus in *Julius Caesar*, 2.1.53–54: "My ancestors did from the streets of Rome / The Tarquin drive when he was call'd a king." See also 1.2.159–61; and *The Rape of Lucrece*, 11.1807–41. Quotations from Shakespeare's works other than *Hamlet* are from *The Riverside Shakespeare*, ed. G. Blakemore Evans (Boston: Houghton Mifflin, 1974).

his shield. While Saxo could not have known the carefully orchestrated return to Ithaca of Homer's Odysseus, Amleth's recourse to his former filth-covered self when he returns to Jutland is similar to Odysseus's disguise as a beggar; so too is the scale of the slaughters carried out by the two heroes, which extend beyond their immediate enemies or practical needs. Most of these resemblances to classical epic are generic in the oral tradition. Thus we would expect long set speeches rather than dramatic dialogue: the longest, Amleth's political justification and appeal to the people, fills about one-eighth of the total number of pages of Saxo *or* Belleforest. That speech Shakespeare has no use for; but another, heralded in Belleforest by a part title, "Harangue d'Amleth a la Royne Geruthe sa mere," supplies many of the verbal borrowings that persuade one that the playwright consulted the French, or an unpublished translation of the French, firsthand. The corresponding scene in *Hamlet* is by far the longest confrontation of the hero and another character and notoriously, in the closet scene he does most of the talking. Finally, classical allusions appear in Saxo only less frequently than in Belleforest. Possibly the studied comparisons of Amleth to Hercules (twice in Belleforest) provoked Hamlet's wry disclaimer: "My father's brother, but no more like my father / Than I to Hercules" (1.2.152–3).[11]

Amleth's tricks and self-abasement seem closer to folktale. It may be claimed that the wily Odysseus is also a famous trickster, but his ruses are so well advertised and prolonged in the return to Ithaca that the pleasure they afford is quite different. Homer invests Odysseus's disguise as a beggar with high dramatic irony, whereas Saxo provides a low and less certain irony: at times we can only surmise that Amleth knows what he is doing. As a mere youth, he has no heroic past to build our confidence in the part he has to play. To Feng, certainly, the threat arises from below, in the regressive and apparently witless behavior of the younger adversary. The name Amleth appears to derive from a word meaning fool,[12] and the stunts and riddling of this fool afforded Shakespeare material that still baffles but

[11] Quotations identified by act, scene, and line number in parentheses are from *Hamlet, Prince of Denmark*, ed. Philip Edwards (Cambridge: Cambridge University Press, 1985). Like many recent students of *Hamlet*, I am more indebted to Harold Jenkins's edition (note 1 above) than to any other; but while Edwards too includes all lines from the second quarto, he makes it easier to view the first folio text as a later version of the play. For an excellent account of the issues involved, see R. A. Foakes, *Hamlet versus Lear: Cultural Politics and Shakespeare's Art* (Cambridge: Cambridge University Press, 1993), 78–97, 146–80.

[12] See Kemp Malone, *The Literary History of Hamlet: The Early Tradition* (1923; rpt. New York: Haskell, 1964), 52–58; also Hansen, *Saxo Grammaticus and the Life of Hamlet*, 6 and 161–62n.

seldom fails to please an audience, material that doubtless fuels the warmth and even exultation that *Hamlet* inspires, notwithstanding the doubt and cruelty and bloodshed. Shakespeare had already designed high and low scenes for Prince Hal, and he would unforgettably put King Lear through an even greater range of experience and styles, but the creation of Hamlet *as* clown owes something to the northern saga material.[13] Saxo may afford grounds for answering one famous question about the play: if Amleth's strategy supplied the precedent, Hamlet was not mad but invented his "antic disposition" (1.5.172). Yet the source provokes a similar question: it is not possible to tell where strategy leaves off and madness begins, since Amleth seems not fully in control of himself.

Near the heart of Amleth's seeming madness is his riddling. Notably, when anyone tries to trap him into revealing himself, he speaks the truth but in such a way that his antagonist cannot understand it. The riddling creates a special kind of dramatic irony, since the reader or listener to the story is able to glimpse both meanings while the antagonist is only able to sense that he is being put on. Belleforest feels he needs to gloss the practice as a sort of Aristotelian virtue—"as a generous minde is a mortal enemie to untruth"[14]—but the hero's way is really to tease with the truth, to risk giving himself away without quite doing so, to reply to a challenge with the counterchallenge of a riddle, and to enjoy the upper hand that riddling confers (much as children love to riddle). Language is the medium most used for conveying truth; and language can be used to baffle those who demand the truth. To lie outright forgoes wit and fails to exploit language to the fullest. Shakespeare's Hamlet may be closer to Saxo's filthy child in this respect than he is to Belleforest's generous spirit. Then, too, in the play riddling assumes its modern role of masking the hero's genuine ambivalence, as if he were playing with words from despair of expressing himself. Telling the truth in riddles keeps the game fair; and the sincerity of Hamlet's Montaigne-like doubts is faithful to an aspect of his own story that goes back to Saxo and to folklore.

---

[13] The early reactions to *Hamlet* surveyed by Paul S. Conklin, *A History of "Hamlet" Criticism, 1601–1821* (1957; rpt. New York: Humanities Press, 1968), 7–26, suggest that the play was indeed popular but not always taken with complete seriousness. The few surviving remarks about the *Ur-Hamlet*, in fact, tend to laugh at it; and William Empson, in "*Hamlet* When New," *Sewanee Review* 61 (1953), 15–42, 185–205, speculates that Shakespeare addressed this state of affairs in his revision by staging theatricality itself. Hamlet "walks out to the audience and says 'You think this is an absurd old play, and so it is, *but I'm in it*, and what can I do?'" (189).

[14] "Comme aussi tout esprit genereux est mortel ennemy de la mensonge" (Gollancz, 228–29). Also Bullough, 7:101.

The prominence of mourning and funeral rites in *Hamlet* derives mainly from Elizabethan revenge tragedy. Belleforest's uneasiness about using pre-Christian Danish lore, however, may have moved him to omit a long speech on proper burial in Saxo. In the medieval account, when Amleth's father Horwendil proposes single combat to Coller, the Norwegian king, the latter agrees but counters with the proposal that the combatants mutually guarantee a dignified burial for the loser—the speech represented by a single clause in Belleforest's translation. Coller, of course, is the one who wins the funeral so desired, but these are the terms with which Saxo commences the story of Amleth's inheritance. Of a funeral for Horwendil after his brother Feng's treachery, nothing is told (and not much more in Shakespeare). Presumably there was scant ceremony. When Amleth triumphs in turn over his uncle, according to Saxo, he vehemently directs that Feng not be buried at all: "Let no trace of his fratricide remain; let there be no spot in his own land for his tainted limbs; let no neighbourhood suck infection from him; let not sea nor soil be defiled by harbouring his accursed carcase."[15] Belleforest renders this speech more or less faithfully yet softens the thrust of the nephew's words. No exact equivalent exists in *Hamlet*, but denying burial is a common enough idea in other revenge tragedies including *Titus Andronicus*; and Hamlet's jokes about dead bodies keep them in view regardless—just as his parrying of questions about Polonius's body creates an intertextual joke about what happened to the adviser whom Amleth killed, cut in pieces, boiled, and fed down a drain to the hogs. When Amleth returns from England the first time, a funeral is being held for him in absentia; in the play this becomes Ophelia's funeral, a tragic rather than an ironic turn. There is no graveyard scene in the chronicles, either at this point or upon the second return. In his world of violence the saga hero needs no skull to contemplate, no momento mori.[16]

This is not to deny that Belleforest's French is the nearest text we have to an actual source for *Hamlet*.[17] With his cautions and allusions, moralizing and justification, Belleforest has done his best to transform the matter into a "histoire tragique." Without adding any characters, his treatment creates

[15] "Nullum parricidii vestigium maneat: nullus contaminatis artibus intra patriam locus existat: nulla contagium vicinia contrahat: non mare, non solum damnati cadaveris hospitio polluatur" (Gollancz, 134–37). Also Bullough, 7:71–72.

[16] Roland Mushat Frye, *The Renaissance Hamlet: Issues and Responses in 1600* (Princeton: Princeton University Press, 1984), 205–53, fills in the rich iconographical background of Shakespeare's graveyard scene.

[17] Besides the summaries of opinion in Jenkins and Bullough (notes 1 and 2 above), see A. P. Stabler, "King Hamlet's Ghost in Belleforest?" *PMLA* 77 (1962), 18–20, and "Melancholy, Ambition, and Revenge in Belleforest's Hamlet," *PMLA* 81 (1966), 207–13.

the impression of Hamlet surrounded by a small Renaissance court. The hero is substantially pacified and civilized, without deviating from his original bloody deeds. Amleth has become "le Prince" and "le Prince Danois." Instead of being merely crafty and strong, he possesses "la modestie, continence, et courtoysie" and is devoted to "l'honneur" and "la vertu." Not Ophelia, to be sure, but Hermetrude of Scotland declares him to be "le Prince plus accomply," one who "par son excellence et lustre, surpassa l'humaine capacité."[18] (In Saxo this same queen talks mainly of herself and her desirability for a hero.) Most important, in a passage that has no equivalent in Saxo's history, Belleforest has already in principle checked the immediate impulse to vengeance and qualified the proper means for achieving it. His Amleth advises Geruth that he will avenge his father in due time but trusts that Feng will be the instrument of his own death somehow, rather than simply being killed by him. Thus "I shall not dye without revenging my selfe upon mine enemie, and that himselfe shall be the instrument of his owne decay, and to execute that which of my selfe I durst not have enterprised."[19] Here speaks the modern rather than the medieval Hamlet. The scenario is for the end of Shakespeare's play rather than the action that its author is engaged in translating from a twelfth-century history of the Danes. Thus Hamlet will vow, "Let it work, / For 'tis the sport to have the engineer / Hoist with his own petar" (3.4.206–8). The point is not that a handful of words supplied by Belleforest inspired Shakespeare's management of a suitable ending for his Claudius but that his Amleth's expressed intention, or self-hoisting of the villain, reflects a common sentiment about just vengeance in the sixteenth century.[20] The audience of the play will be privileged to overhear the plan to kill Hamlet in a fencing match, will know of the poisons provided by Laertes and by Claudius in case this plan fails, and will then watch the attempt take place before them on the stage—"And in this upshot, purposes mistook / Fallen on th' inventors' heads" (5.2.363–4). Claudius and Laertes will have brought about their own deaths; especially Claudius, who will thus doubly deserve his. This formula was already given in the speech Belleforest assigns to Amleth.

---

[18] Gollancz, 310–11, 288–91; also Bullough, 7:124, 119 (though Bullough omits a portion of the speech).

[19] "Que je ne mourray ja, sans me venger de mon ennemy, et que luy mesme sera l'instrument de sa ruine, et me guidera à executer ce, que de moymesme je n'eusse osé entreprendre" (Gollancz, 226–29). Also Bullough, 7:101.

[20] Cf. Helen Gardner, *The Business of Criticism* (Oxford: Clarendon, 1959), 41–44. Gardner cites *Titus Andronicus*, Kyd's *The Spanish Tragedy*, and Cyril Tourneur's *The Revenger's Tragedy* as instances from the theater.

The histories have no equivalent to Laertes. He is the most important entirely new character in Shakespeare's *Hamlet*, others being the gravediggers and Osric and Fortinbras, who appear only in act 5. The ally who is Horatio, for example, distantly compares to the unnamed friend of Amleth who helped him avoid Feng's first trap. Similarly, Ophelia and Polonius can be traced back through Belleforest to Saxo's history of Amleth. All of the characters in the play seem larger to life than their originals, partly because—as Harold Bloom keeps reminding us—Shakespeare set so many of our standards of what it is to be a character. Yet the members of Laertes' family are so nearly made out of whole cloth as Laertes himself that it is worth paying special attention to them.

Though Polonius figures very importantly in the play and instigates, as I shall argue, a popular modern method for interpreting the hero's behavior, he appears only as one of Feng's friends in Saxo—elevated to counselor by Belleforest but still unnamed—in a single episode of the story. He has no family in these narratives and no ready explanation for Amleth's madness; but he is suspicious as Polonius is, and the latter's character can already be glimpsed—"gifted more with assurance than judgment," according to Saxo.[21] As in the play, he suggests that a spy be placed where he can overhear Amleth's interview with his mother, volunteers for the job, and suffers the consequences (except that Amleth disposes of the body immediately, before resuming the interview). The Ophelia part in Amleth's adventures, quite unrelated to this of Polonius's prototype, is sketched so minimally as to make one doubt whether the shadowy young woman in the chronicle was at all necessary to Shakespeare's conception. Yet on the theory that a healthy sexual impulse, if present, will give the lie to any pretended insanity, an unnamed female acquaintance of Amleth's childhood is deployed to tempt him into lovemaking, and this device is too much like the crudeness with which Ophelia is used—the idea in *Hamlet* further credited to Polonius—to be overlooked. And I would add another hint of Ophelia's role from the second part of Amleth's history: his young English bride, similarly without a name, is torn between loyalties to her father and to the hero, sides with the latter, but is so completely overshadowed by Hermutrude that she drops unnoticed from the story.

With these few possibilities afforded by the medieval story and rehearsed by Belleforest, Shakespeare has done a great deal. He has developed two unnamed participants from the portion of the story that he dramatizes, he has related them as father and daughter, he has added the son and brother

---

[21] "Praesumptione quam solertia abundantior" (Gollancz, 110–11). Also Bullough, 7:65.

Laertes—and has thrown Osric into the ways of this family for good measure. In so doing he domesticates and makes familiar the love test, provides a foolish opposite for the hero's fool's antics, and connects the two clinical examinations of Hamlet in the presence of women, his girlfriend and his mother, by having Polonius direct both. He thus introduces a second two-generation family to the play and creates his subplot, the second family serving in a number of ways to reflect Hamlet's own. In the represented action Hamlet relates to the Polonius family that Shakespeare has created for him as to a series of potential in-laws: a father-in-law, brother-in-law, and bride—for a wife is an in-law, too, not a blood relation but a contractual one. The matter is best put schematically thus because the crisis in Hamlet's immediate family—the one that has existed in story at least since the twelfth century—is already that of the hero's relation to an in-law, his father-in-law Claudius, as a stepfather could be called in Shakespeare's time.[22] The problem of this father-in-law—irrespective of poison, incest, and the rest—is the problem of becoming intimate, or being thrust into intimacy with someone who is not of one's own family but suddenly becomes so and will remain so. Conceivably, the second family presented to Hamlet in the play—his less mind-numbing but not less lively set of possible in-laws—Polonius, Laertes, and Ophelia—could previously have been staged by the *Ur-Hamlet*; yet what we know of the sources of *King Lear* argues that the Polonius family is Shakespeare's contribution.[23]

Since, unlike the *Ur-Hamlet*, the anonymous play *King Leir* has survived, it is perfectly clear that it was Shakespeare who determined to make parallel to the action of Lear and his daughters a second action of Gloucester and his two sons. The introduction of the subplot redoubles the plight of old age and suggests that Lear's predicament has not more to do with kingship than with something as commonplace as family. As in *King Lear*, the main result of introducing a subplot in *Hamlet* is to generalize the relations of parents and children, to make it less possible to view the hero's situation as unique. In certain respects Polonius actually resembles Gloucester in the later play. The fathers in both subplots are old, a little foolish, and distinctly out of touch with their children. But Gloucester suffers terribly for being foolish and trusting, and he is allowed that natural death that only seems to intensify the painfulness of *King Lear* as a tragedy. Polonius, suspicious rather than trusting, and far more interfering, dies the swift

---

[22] Shakespeare uses "father-in-law" with this meaning in *Richard III*, 5.3.81.

[23] Or it might be the Corambis family, for in the first quarto Polonius is called Corambis. If anything, the subsequent change of the name suggests a newly developing role.

unnatural death that his prototype died in the *Historiae Danicae* and is largely unlamented—except by his newly provided children, whom he has systematically distrusted. Polonius and his son and daughter are weaker creations than Hamlet, his uncle, and his mother, in the same sense that Gloucester and his sons are weaker than Lear and his daughters: that is, their behavior, even in extreme, is more commonplace and less finely strung. By that very secondariness, the subfamilies in the two plays fulfill the audience's expectations and bring home a sense of the main action. Both are tragedies with marked points of view, one with pity for the old and the other for the young. *King Lear* shows that to be old and repudiated is virtually to be dehumanized before death, and *Hamlet* shows how wretched it is to await power that accrues only from the death of parents.[24]

In *Hamlet* the older generation is oppressive throughout. Even if one makes allowances for the poor ghost, the living representatives of that generation are bad enough. Given the supernatural frisson of the first scene, in fact, and the remarkable account of murder soon to follow, the domestic emphasis of most of the first court scene is all the more remarkable. Polonius clearly provides an additional mark for the youthful bias of the play: while much of what Claudius says to his nephew is already more parental than governmental, retaining Polonius as his principal henchman in the state makes the bad uncle still more one of the company of tiresome parents. Once that manipulating father has been lost, Claudius takes over the manipulation of Laertes in act 4 and pits one young man against the other. Ophelia and Laertes have no mother, of course, but therein the Polonius family is also more typical, more recognizable because more literary, than the Hamlet family itself. Gertrude is the great exception to rule, for she is not only a surviving mother but stands in powerful relation to her son; the only mother of comparable development in Shakespeare is Volumnia in *Coriolanus*, and that play at least affords the relief of a third generation to come.[25] Present in the background of the old story of Amleth and his

[24] On the youthful aspect of the hero I am indebted to Barbara Everett, *Young Hamlet: Essays on Shakespeare's Tragedies* (Oxford: Clarendon, 1989), 14–34; also to Harold C. Goddard, *The Meaning of Shakespeare*, 2 vols. (1951; rpt. Chicago: University of Chicago Press, 1967), 1:331–86. Everett recalls the role of Shakespeare's play in Goethe's *Wilhelm Meisters Lehrjahre*, Dickens's *Great Expectations*, and Joyce's *Ulysses* and reflects that "*Hamlet*, the first great story in Europe of a young man growing up, in a sense originates the *Bildungsroman* itself" (28–30).

[25] The policy of extirpating mothers from literary plots would persist in the English novel: Jane Austen made fun of the habit at the beginning of *Northanger Abbey* (1818), but in practice did little to resist it. Memorable mothers in classic English novels tend to be made fun of; only a handful carry the weight that Gertrude does in *Hamlet*, her rather spare language notwithstanding.

mother and uncle is Amleth's maternal grandfather Rorik, to whom the local kingship owes fealty. It is Rorik's death, in fact, that precipitates the hero's eventual fall. But *Hamlet* dramatizes conflicts of the strictly conjugal family, and Shakespeare increases the sense of oppression by confining the action to Elsinore.[26]

To realize how the design of the original story has been transformed it is useful also to remember how determinedly Shakespeare introduces and integrates his subplot. The play begins with the sentinels, with Horatio and the first appearance of the ghost, followed by the exposition of the court scene and Hamlet's soliloquy. The third scene, however, suspends the exciting prospect of an appearance of the ghost to Hamlet himself in favor of introducing Ophelia, at first with Laertes and then with Polonius at home. Linking this scene to the main plot, besides the new theme of Hamlet's courtship, is a repeat of the parental advice giving in scene 2, buffed to a higher sententiousness by Polonius. By comparison with the all-knowing yet all-suspecting—and forgetful—father of this family, Hamlet's mother and stepfather seem more, not less than kind. "A green girl," "a baby," Polonius calls his daughter, and characterizes Hamlet's addresses to her as "springes to catch woodcocks" (1.3.101,105,115).

Then again, after the tremendous visitation and words of Hamlet's deceased father's ghost and the son's near hysterical reaction, the scene shifts still more deliberately to Polonius's supervision of his family. Reynaldo, a bit player unheard of before or after this scene, receives instruction from the father on how to spy on the son in Paris. So filled with anticipation and possible scenarios are the instructions that we gather Polonius would carry them out himself if he could. Reynaldo seems to have been on this mission or received these instructions before, but his chief is a stickler for detail and overfond of method: "thus do we of wisdom and of reach, / With windlasses and with assays of bias, / By indirections find directions out" (2.1.62–4). Except for Polonius's fuss and forgetfulness, the substance of these seventy lines would answer English notions of an Italian rather than a Danish court, but the play is being faithful to the greater *praesumptio* than skill of the original adviser to Feng (Saxo's characterization comes to seem more and more laconic), with the result that this spy master seems less the Machiavel and more like some old boy of the MI or CIA.

Hamlet proceeds thus far by the alteration of plot and subplot. At the same time the plots begin to move toward one another, mainly by playing

[26] Students, players, and ambassadors come and go, and Hamlet starts for England; but unlike Shakespeare's usual practice the stage action remains close to one place. Harley

15

on the question of courtship. The scene with Reynaldo continues with Ophelia's report of Hamlet's odd behavior and the establishment of Polonius's fond theory (directly opposite to his presumption in the first interview with his daughter) that "This is the very ecstasy of love," and that Ophelia's rejection of that love (in accordance with her father's orders) "hath made him mad" (2.1.100,108). Without the surprising instructions of the father to Reynaldo, the next succeeding scene of the play might seem odd: the king and queen, in only their second appearance on stage are in the midst of introducing Rosencrantz and Guildenstern to the mission of befriending and spying upon their son. The greater politeness and tone of concern from these parents and the greater unction of these playfellows put Polonius's frank instructions and enjoyment of the game in proper perspective. The scene, and for that matter the entire play through to the fatal breakup of the fencing match, is notable for its atmosphere of a well-to-do family's worries in stunning conjunction with Polonial crassness and mistake. We know little of Feng's family life, but Claudius might be any uxorious husband and hard-pressed stepfather of a certain class, rather than a royally got-up fratricide, incestuous lover, and usurper. Polonius "tells me, my dear Gertrude, he hath found / The head and source of all your son's distemper" (2.2.54–5). Much later he seems genuinely moved by Ophelia's insanity: "O Gertrude, Gertrude, / When sorrows come, they come not single spies, / But in battalions" (4.5.76–8). The part may be performed by the actor as one of consummate hypocrisy; but it reads (to me) as some much more ordinary mix of amorality and confidence not unlike Polonius's, with at least the attractiveness of being colored by desire rather than officiousness. The worst that can be thought of Claudius is thought for us by his victims, Hamlet and the ghost; the play's criminal stepfather would nearly win sympathy if it were not for his manipulation of Laertes and fresh use of poison.

In his eagerness to interpose between Hamlet and his mother and uncle, Polonius becomes an easy target of the hero's back talk and impertinence. The constraint that youth usually feels in the presence of its own elders is absent: besides, in the earlier domestic scenes the playwright has portrayed a father-in-law-to-be who deserves to be taken down. Now in his "fishmonger" and "old Jephtha" exchanges (2.2.172,374), the hero blatantly attacks Polonius's age, the very ground of his bossiness and manipulation of his children. The book that the younger man pretends to be reading spells

---

Granville-Barker speculates that in *Hamlet* the playwright dramatized inactivity by this means: *Prefaces to Shakespeare*, 2 vols. (1930; rpt. London: Batsford, 1958), 1:38–39.

out the insult: "for the satirical rogue says here that old men have grey beards, that their faces are wrinkled, their eyes purging thick amber and plumtree gum, and that they have a plentiful lack of wit, together with most weak hams. All which, sir, though I most powerfully and potently believe"—like Amleth, Hamlet will speak truth—"yet I hold it not honesty to have it thus set down" (2.2.193–8). Conversely, these are sentiments that Polonius's own children might feel: actors playing Laertes and Ophelia today sometimes express themselves by grimacing out of their father's sight, since their lines betray no impatience. It takes an inspired naughtiness like Hamlet's to stall Polonius's ingrained hypocrisy by taking words out of his mouth, or to stump his powers of observation with rudeness. And though Polonius and Hamlet are not father and son, the intrusiveness of the one and withdrawn state of the other generate much of the humor in the play, until the death of the old man starts the humor off on a different track.

The greatly expanded role of Feng's adviser provides popular, if one-sided, theater. As Shakespeare approaches the action supplied by Saxo and Belleforest, he proceeds more soberly and repeatedly stresses rather than alters the original adviser's responsibility. No sooner does Claudius reject the theory that Hamlet's madness is caused by love—"Love? His affections do not that way tend" (3.1.156)—than Polonius proposes a new experiment, this time from the narrative sources of the play and completely divorced from the seemingly boundless authority as a father that he has acquired. Audiences and readers of *Hamlet*, concentrating on the hero's plan to catch the conscience of the king by means of a play, mostly fail to notice how determinate Polonius's moves continue to be in act 3. He gives in to the entertainment but is impatient to resume afterward the routine he understands best.

> My lord, do as you please,
> But if you hold it fit, after the play,
> Let his queen mother all alone entreat him
> To show his grief. Let her be round with him,
> And I'll be placed, so please you, in the ear
> Of all their conference.   (3.1.174–9)

In each scene of the act to follow, Polonius seizes his chance to forward this scheme, whether by summoning Hamlet to the interview or by diplomatically crediting the king with his idea and its premise (mothers are more subject to nature than are fathers):

17

And as you said, and wisely was it said,
'Tis meet that some more audience than a mother,
Since nature makes them partial, should o'erhear
The speech of vantage. (3.3.30–33)

Thus Shakespeare fixes the responsibility of the adviser for his own death more thoroughly than Saxo or Belleforest. The closet scene of *Hamlet* is Polonius's idea, and he next appears on stage to introduce it. "Look you lay home to him," he tells the queen—"Pray you be round" (3.4.1,5); and he promises to be silent himself. Unfortunately, Hamlet is round with his mother; Polonius fails to hold back three monosyllables—"What ho! Help"—and manages to utter four more after he is stabbed. Then he falls silent at last.

Around the stopping of that voice for good turns a wide difference in the dramatic irony of the play. Right up to the moment of Polonius's death, Hamlet may be partially ignorant of the spying routine against him; yet overall, he shares with the audience, to the exclusion of all other characters, a knowledge of what his father's ghost has revealed. The sharing of this superior vantage, in fact, makes us confident that Hamlet must be able to see through the watch that has been placed upon him and to guard against it. Once Polonius is slain, however, Hamlet loses his superior vantage, for the brief reappearance of the ghost yields nothing but conjecture, and during act 4 the audience shares knowledge of the plans of Claudius and Laertes that the hero does not possess—which awareness makes us see him as a very cool character indeed, if not foolhardy, in act 5. Something like this shift occurs in the medieval story as well: precisely when the young Amleth is not in control, we expect that his policy is to achieve control; but once he is king and nearing his end, the motions of his Hermutrude and of Wiglek are closed to him. Again Shakespeare seems to draw upon Amleth's full career and not merely the portion he dramatizes and alters to tragedy.

The killing of Polonius in *Hamlet* also coincides with some striking mental alterations in the person who kills him—including a new attitude toward death and dead bodies, a discovery of the part played by accident in human undertakings, and an apparent end to his melancholy and return to social life. The graveyard scene could be said to commence right here with the play's first undeniably dead body. The tone of Hamlet's few words covering the disposal problem, both on stage and in the represented action—"This man shall set me packing," and "I'll lug the guts into the neighbour room" (3.4.212–3)—may at first be lost on the audience, but not after the game of go-seek-the-body and his series of wisecracks on the consumption of kings and beggars at the beginning of act 4. It was similar meat that the medieval Amleth chopped and washed down a drain to the pigs; in the play, Polonius favors us with the ineluctable dead body, a gift that eventuates in the clowning of the sexton and his sidekick, together with Hamlet and Horatio, before the burial of Ophelia in act 5. At the end the hero still has no express plan for dealing with Claudius. In the "interim" before the business in England becomes known, he seems confident that some opportunity will present itself, for twice in recounting his adventures to Horatio he explains how quick thinking has served him. "Our indiscretion sometimes serves us well / When our deep plots do pall," he remarks, and "Or I could make a prologue to my brains, / They had begun the play" (5.2. 8–9, 30–31)—a play sealing death for Rosencrantz and Guildenstern. This new attitude, like his humor of the dead body, can reasonably be traced to Hamlet's "rash and bloody deed" in the queen's chamber, which he has angrily defended as the destruction of a "wretched, rash, intruding fool" (3.4.27,31) and then more calmly as justifiable homicide:

> For this same lord
> I do repent; but heaven hath pleased it so,
> To punish me with this, and this with me,
> That I must be their scourge and minister.   (3.4.173–6)

Note the demonstratives, which merely point at the formerly voluble counselor. The only calm utterance from anyone in the closet scene is thus directed at the corpse and anticipates the hero's trust in providence at the end.

In the short run, at least, the family Shakespeare has bestowed on Polonius survives him. The disparate reactions to the death by Laertes and Ophelia thrust the subplot unforgettably to the center of the stage in act 4. In fact the emotions generated by these scenes—especially the unexpected and haunting music of Ophelia's madness and her reported death but also the blustering return of Laertes with sword drawn—tend to overcome the intellectual burden of the analogies and comparisons that Shakespeare has constructed overall. Laertes and Ophelia divide between them the two impulses of mourning that tease Hamlet from the time of his own father's death: that is, revenge in the one case and suicide in the other, reactions to the loss of a father now differentiated as male and female respectively.[27] Act 4 easily traps an audience into excited approval of Laertes'

---

[27] Laertes' "cause" and Ophelia's are both Hamlet's cause, as he comes to recognize in the brother's case. And who shall say what a Hamlet who was forced to witness Ophelia's part in

storming of the gates and, because he first demands satisfaction from Claudius, almost makes us forget that Hamlet should be the object of this vengeance. Yet the swift-following action shows Laertes to be wrong and wrong again: ignorant of how his father's death came about, mistaken either to accuse or to trust Claudius, obtusely eager to cut somebody's throat in the church, treacherous in his offer to use poison, and above all easily manipulated by a more experienced poisoner of the older generation. Notwithstanding these sad mistakes, critics of the play often suppose that Laertes' behavior is designed to put Hamlet's in a bad light. To the contrary, Shakespeare distributes the action in act 4 so as to qualify plotting and revenge once more, by punctuating each of Laertes' reactions with those of his sister: first the reentrance of Ophelia insane and thereafter word of her suicide. Here too, as in the closet scene, he might have stressed Hamlet's responsibility, but instead he works toward analogy and comparison. Before this, Claudius—the play's most vocal authority on mourning— has explained that Ophelia's derangement "is the poison of deep grief, it springs / All from her father's death" (4.5.74–5). Just so Laertes' angry action also springs from his father's death, and the entire play from Hamlet's father's death.

The two male representatives of the younger generation in mourning now draw closer to one another even as they posture over Ophelia's grave or cross and then exchange swords at the end. The brother's love for his sister, though accompanied by a curse, stirs Hamlet to a more genuine feeling, though bellicose, than he could muster when the victim of his antic disposition was still alive. The inward result of the two men's ranting against one another is registered by Hamlet's confession, in a quiet moment with Horatio, "That to Laertes I forgot myself, / For by the image of my cause, I see / The portraiture of his" (5.2.76–8). Again Shakespeare represents his hero as more thoughtful than Laertes, for the latter confesses only after he receives a dose of his own medicine. The family expression that he uses, rather touchingly, is one his father applied in speaking of Hamlet to Ophelia: "Why, as a woodcock to mine own springe, Osric" (5.2.286). Does the choice of that expression convey an awareness of his father's methods and entanglement with Hamlet's affairs, as well as regret

---

act 4 would come to see and believe? It is primarily in the construction of the action around this second family, rather than the characterization of the hero as such, that Shakespeare anticipates those nineteenth-century and later speculations, on the stage and page, that Hamlet was a woman, or man and woman both. For a recent sampling and further references, see Lawrence Danson, "Gazing at Hamlet, or the Danish Cabaret," *Shakespeare Survey* 45 (Cambridge: Cambridge University Press, 1993), 37–51.

for his own recourse to deceit? The subplot comes to a close with Laertes' death and the last words spoken of Polonius in the play: "Mine and my father's death come not upon thee, / Nor thine on me" (5.2.309–10).

If one is willing to make allowances for metempsychosis, Polonius still lives at the close of *Hamlet*. During four centuries Shakespeare has entertained audiences with two bravura pieces of theater in act 5, neither of which has any precedent in the old story: the gravediggers' performance and Osric's. Having brought on, in the first of these scenes, two clowns who are entirely new to the play, he brings on another new character, the courtier Osric. Yet Osric may seem vaguely familiar, a sort of infant reincarnation of Polonius.[28] For the audience, aware of the shuffling that Claudius has already rehearsed with Laertes, the appearance of this lightweight with an invitation to fencing is grotesque, like a shivery bad dream. In Hamlet it stirs some of the wonted resistance again. The hero's wit serves Osric as it formerly served Polonius, and he almost apologizes for the character to Horatio, who has no more heard of this strange courtier than we have. Thus the last lines of humor in *Hamlet* turn on a phenomenon newborn: Horatio compares Osric to a lapwing fallen from the nest; and Hamlet remarks, in a fresh dialect, "A did comply with his dug before a sucked it" (5.2.165). Earlier, he could refer to Polonius with similar contempt, in speaking to Guildenstern and Rosencrantz: "That great baby you see there is not yet out of his swaddling clouts" (2.2.351). The key to the mockery here is not the conventional reply of Rosencrantz about old men and second childhood but Hamlet's lasting irritation with the show of compliance in both courtiers. Osric "did comply with his dug" before he complied with Hamlet and Horatio; and Polonius has ever complied with the king, complied with the queen, complied with the prince even when bent on taking his own way.

The issues of whether, or when, or with whom to comply are no small matter in *Hamlet*, both in the represented action and in the acting of it. Compliance is a necessary social grace, a sine qua non of hierarchy, yet— because of the risk of contradiction it runs from one social occasion to the next and from moment to moment of polite discourse, as Hamlet demonstrates—potentially ridiculous, too. The openness of compliance to ridicule is behind some of the exchanges between Hamlet and Polonius that yield pleasure even though we do not, any more than the target figure, quite see why.

---

[28] Cf. Susan Snyder, *The Comic Matrix of Shakespeare's Tragedies* (Princeton: Princeton University Press, 1979), 110–12. "After Polonius becomes part of the tragedy, his comic function is carried on by Osric" (110).

HAMLET: Do you see yonder cloud that's almost in the shape of a camel?

POLONIUS: By th'mass, and 'tis like a camel indeed.

HAMLET: Methinks it is like a weasel.

POLONIUS: It is backed like a weasel.

HAMLET: Or like a whale?

POLONIUS: Very like a whale.

HAMLET: Then I will come to my mother by and by.

This bout of logic—the last between Hamlet and Polonius—retrospectively may strike one as somber rather than ridiculous. "They fool me to the top of my bent," Hamlet says of it (3.2.339–46), exultant at his own wit and fearful of what may pass between him and his mother in the scene to follow. His "they" fairly includes Rosencrantz and Guildenstern at this point, besides Polonius and his own mother and stepfather, or any who would use indirections to find him out. "Then I will come to my mother by and by": this apparent non sequitur sounds its anger in the peculiar conjunction of "I *will*" with the carelessness of "by and by."[29] But Hamlet, remember, is being asked to comply at this very moment, and much more profoundly so than the courtiers Polonius and Osric throughout, even though they make such a show of compliance. The sense is roughly this: you see how readily you comply with my suggestions about a cloud; just so will I comply with your message that my mother wishes to see me— when I am good and ready to. Hamlet has been asked to comply in every possible way since the commencement of the tragedy—by his mother, by his stepfather, and by the ghost of his father; so he may very well feel, now at the top of his bent and on the verge of his principal confrontation with any of those parents, that he is ready to comply with a vengeance—and Polonius, of course, will bear the brunt of his anger, as here.

Whether at the breast, like Osric with his dug, or by example from siblings and instruction from parents, children very quickly learn to comply. But Hamlet the Dane is the great antiparent of our mythologies—and misogynist par excellence, to be sure. "Farewell, dear mother" (4.3.45–6), he deliberately slurs his stepfather on departing from England.[30] And if the violent interview with Gertrude provides the critical turning of the play, as

---

[29] Granville-Barker, *Prefaces to Shakespeare*, 1:96, believes that Hamlet thinks he ought only to go to his mother after he has dealt with Claudius. As Granville-Barker's note attests, "by and by" could also mean at once. In that case, Hamlet's "I will" is more ominous than contemptuous.

[30] So I would construe the line. Philip Edwards does not set off "dear mother" with a comma, as if Hamlet were merely expressing the thought aloud that he would miss his mother.

I believe, it is plentifully reinforced by the nunnery scene with Ophelia at the commencement of act 3, as well as by such small inspirations as the man-child who complies with "his" nipple. Somehow the hero's fierce hatred of courting and contempt for courtiers, together with his intellectual resistance to compliance throughout, are prompted in the first place by that mind-bending parental demand, "List, list, oh list! / If thou didst ever thy dear father love—" (1.5.22–3). In his play Shakespeare represented a young man not just wronged by his uncle but surmounted by parents, teased by their busy surrogates and merely tormented by their love—their love of one another and of himself. These are aspects of *Hamlet* that the meddling of Polonius—ever "the father of good news," as Claudius remarks (2.2.42)—helps to bring out. Polonius's two good children are precisely those representatives of the younger generation who alert us to the troubles of compliance, from the third scene of the play onward: especially Ophelia, who well may be said to have "drowned herself in her own defence" (5.1.5–6).[31]

Before taking up the question of mourning within the family, I ought to say a word about the names in the play, since only the names of the hero and his mother seem to bear any relation to those in Saxo and Belleforest.[32] Most blatant, among characters' names that have been changed, the usurping Feng has become Claudius. Even though the name Claudius occurs but once in a stage direction (the entrance to 1.2) and is never spoken on stage, few can resist it when talking or thinking about *Hamlet*, because the emperor Claudius's reign is so richly associated with incest, parricide, and a political succession thoroughly confused with sensuality. The apparent allusion to the decadence of the Roman empire, in fact, makes Hamlet analogous to Nero, as the hero seems aware when about to confront his mother in a murderous state of mind ("let not ever / The soul of Nero enter this firm bosom"[3.2.354–5]).

The folio's Gertrude, a perfectly good Teutonic name in itself, may combine the names of Amleth's mother Geruthe and that of his second wife Hermetrude (to give the French spellings that Shakespeare presumably would have encountered). Hermetrude, after all, appears to have been the more sensual of the two wives in the old story, who makes much of her

---

Claudius, obviously, does not read it that way when he replies, "Thy loving father, Hamlet" (4.3.47).

[31] Cf. Everett, *Young Hamlet*, 31.

[32] For summaries of the basic changes, see Bullough's introduction, 7:34–36; and *Hamlet*, ed. Jenkins, 163–64, 421–23.

rank, her body, and her real estate in wooing Amleth.[33] This false but telling etymology of Ger-trude breathes with incest by itself, collapsing Amleth's mother's relation to Feng and his second wife's to Wiglek upon a figure who doubles as mother and wife to the same young man. This may be a case of Shakespeare outdoing Freud. If the choice of the name has this significance, it would seem to anticipate the nearly obsessive concern that Hamlet exhibits for his mother's sexuality in the closet scene and more broadly the bafflement he experiences in relation to her after the loss of his father.

Another change amplifies the son's responsibility to take the place of the father, simply by giving them the same name. Gone is Horwendil, Amleth's father, and instead there are two Hamlets: one recently dead of supposed natural causes but still prowling about at night in Denmark, the other "young Hamlet" (1.1.170), to whom Horatio proposes to tell of the first and who appears in black in the following scene. More than any other game played with the dramatis personae, bestowing on the father the same name as the son establishes a theme of inheritance that, in the inward-looking world of the younger, is still more personal than political. When the hero compares his uncle so disadvantageously to his father, he can hardly avoid comparing himself with his father too. As if immediately to reinforce this theme, Shakespeare gives the French-sounding name Fortinbras to the king of Norway defeated by Hamlet senior and has Horatio utter it three times before referring also to "young Fortinbras" (1.1.82,86,92,95).

That the last person in the play to pronounce Fortinbras's name is young Hamlet has given many people unease, especially since the hero dies before the other comes on stage.

> Oh I die, Horatio,
> The potent poison quite o'ercrows my spirit.
> I cannot live to hear the news from England.
> But I do prophesy th'election lights
> On Fortinbras; he has my dying voice.
> So tell him, with th'occurrents more and less
> Which have solicited—the rest is silence.   (5.2.331–7)

[33] "And I am not only a queene, but such a one as that, receiving whom I will for my companion in bed, can make him beare the title of a king, and with my body give him posses-sion of a great kingdome, and goodly province" ("Et ne suis seulement Royne, mais telle que recevant qui bon me semblera pour compaignon de ma couche, je peux luy faire porter tiltre de Roy et luy donner, avec mes embrassemens, la jouissance d'un beau Royaume et grand' Province") (Gollancz, 292–93; Bullough omits about 30 lines of this speech).

Hamlet displays as much political consciousness here as in any other juncture in the play, and the effacement of himself is troubling, if nonetheless in character. That the poison overcrows his spirit—the metaphor is from cockfighting—suggests that his sense of irony is still intact. But the most curious thing about the exchange of political fortunes is the gloss already put on it by the clown in the graveyard scene. That venerable sexton, when pressed, has claimed that the "day that our last King Hamlet o'ercame Fortinbras . . . was the very day that young Hamlet was born, he that is mad and sent into England" (5.1.120–1, 123–5). Interrogating the clown, Hamlet shows no surprise at this coincidence, but the point there is to exercise the man's wits rather than probe for facts. Very likely the clown has recognized the prince, or he wouldn't answer so pointedly; and no doubt they understand one another. A few lines later, without prompting, he offers that "I have been sexton here man and boy thirty years" (5.1.137–8). While this may be taken as a useful round number, approximating Hamlet's age and consistent with the claim that he can remember the jester Yorick, it is not necessarily accepted by the hero, and need not be accepted by the audience, that he was born precisely on Victory Day for the Danes. Rather, that is the conceit that will inform Hamlet's dying voice, the nod he gives to young Fortinbras before the latter arrives.

Hamlet's Mourning and Revenge Tragedy

BECAUSE DEATH imposes itself so heavily on the action—and because there is a much lamenting ghost—it seems odd that more interpretations of *Hamlet* are not directly concerned with grief and mourning. In 1930 Lily Bess Campbell contributed a chapter on the play as "a tragedy of grief." Hers was a level-headed assessment of "three young men—Hamlet, Fortinbras, and Laertes—each called upon to mourn the death of a father," which assumed that Shakespeare was concerned to show how men of different temperaments "accept sorrow when it comes to them." Campbell was not entirely consistent in her moralizing, for while she seemed to think that Fortinbras was the most rational of these young men—in truth *Hamlet* offers little evidence of his grief at all—she also believed the play demonstrated "the essential humanness of grief in its passionate refusal of the consolations of philosophy." Patently Shakespeare was less interested in Fortinbras's reasonableness than in Hamlet's excesses, but Campbell at least took the measure of the multiple plot: "Laertes, too, was the victim of excessive grief, but his grief was that which moved to rage. . . . Ophelia is also the victim of excessive grief, her own and Hamlet's." Campbell's reading was restorative, for "in our own day we are sentimental about grief and those who grieve." Her book set out to document instead a Renaissance theory of the passions.[1]

Today both the observation that we are sentimental about grief and the prospect of canceling sentiment by applying reason and morality seem rather Victorian—and indeed Campbell was born in that era. Awkwardly, her position is roughly that of Claudius also, in the first court scene. It is only in the twentieth century that the literature of consolation is less often at hand, as life expectancy has vastly increased in the developed world and death has become a more impersonal business, often relegated to an institution remote from home.[2] In such a remoteness, it is perhaps to be expected

[1] Lily B. Campbell, *Shakespeare's Tragic Heroes: Slaves of Passion* (1930; rpt. New York: Barnes and Noble, 1968), 109–10, 144–45. In the same year, G. Wilson Knight published his more free-wheeling "Embassy of Death," in *The Wheel of Fire* (1930; rpt. New York: Meridian, 1957), 17–46. His argument that *Hamlet* is essentially about death does not hold up as well as Campbell's, but again "Hamlet's pain is a complex of different themes of grief" (22).

[2] For the bearing of the classical literature of *consolatio* on Shakespeare, see Brian Vickers, "Shakespearean Consolations," *Proceedings of the British Academy* 82 (1993), 219–84. Geoffrey

that grief and mourning have not attracted many *Hamlet* critics. Romantic theories of the prince as a very special but flawed character also may discourage reading his experience as representative—this despite Hamlet's great popularity and the tendency of persons of both sexes to identify with him. An exception has been a book by Theodore Lidz, a practicing and teaching psychiatrist rather than a literary historian. Lidz treats the hero as representative and reads the play for its insights into the reaction of a grown son to the death of his father. Unlike orthodox psychoanalysts, Lidz stresses the importance of present rather than past causes, the conjugal family rather than the nursery.[3]

Recently Robert N. Watson has taxed the dramatic poetry of Kyd and Shakespeare, and the lyrics of Donne and Herbert, to support a thesis that the English Renaissance was extraordinarily concerned with death, because beset with doubts of immortality. Watson contends that a whole range of beliefs and institutions, from Christian rites to unholy revenge, and not excluding love lyrics, are energized by a wholesale or particular denial of death, in which we are all more or less caught up. So here also Hamlet will prove representative, but it is as if his grief were entirely subsumed by a single vector of mourning, the awareness of one's own death. The difficulty with this thesis is that grief is not reducible to metaphysics; the loss of another person is not strictly commensurate with death, which primarily renders the loss irreversible rather than terrifying. Grief actually distinguishes between loss and death as such, every time—as in Hamlet's case—it makes one feel like dying. But Watson nevertheless suggests how the fictions of revenge tragedy—ghosts, graves, murder, and revenge itself—may answer to the grief associated with death.[4] Meanwhile Michael Neill has argued more narrowly for a Protestant crisis in the capacity to cope with death in Shakespeare's time, since the removal of Purgatory and the forbidding of prayers of intercession for the dead turned the rites of mourning inward and placed a greater burden on personal memory. Eliza-

---

Gorer, *Death, Grief, and Mourning in Contemporary Britain* (London: Cresset, 1965), gives a contrasting account of twentieth-century attitudes.

[3] Theodore Lidz, *Hamlet's Enemy: Madness and Myth in "Hamlet"* (New York: Basic, 1975), 47–115. Within a few years a spate of articles along similar lines appeared: Alexander Welsh, "The Task of Hamlet," *Yale Review* 59 (1980), 481–502; Arthur Kirsch, "Hamlet's Grief," *English Literary History* 48 (1981), 17–36; Peter M. Sacks, "Where Words Prevail Not: Grief, Revenge, and Language in Kyd and Shakespeare," *English Literary History* 49 (1982), 576–601. Of these, only my own essay—which I have drawn upon in the present chapter—was consciously indebted to Lidz.

[4] Robert N. Watson, *The Rest Is Silence: Death as Annihilation in the English Renaissance* (Berkeley: University of California Press, 1994), 55–102, treats *The Spanish Tragedy* and *Hamlet* in detail. In some ways this book, conducted with Melvillean passion, follows in the steps of Theodore Spencer's *Death and Elizabethan Tragedy* (1936).

bethan revenge tragedy may seem violent and bloody enough, but in it vengeance has become "memory continued by other means," and *Hamlet* differs mainly in the "degree of conscious engagement" with these developments.[5] Above all, John Kerrigan's wide-ranging study of revenge tragedy, from classical times to the present, has made it possible to ask more forthrightly about the precise nature of revenge in a given play or story. He, too, singles out the importance of memory in the Elizabethan case and attributes to it the privacy of the heroes' thoughts, especially Hamlet's. Kerrigan's Aristotelianism provides some healthful correctives to character criticism, for "the story of Prince Hamlet would be tragic even if he had no character."[6]

The Utility of Most Unnatural Murder

To think of *Hamlet* as a play about the loss of a father and grieving for the same at once generalizes its significance and seems to jettison its most distinctive features. The characters of Shakespeare, as Johnson thought, "act and speak by the influence of those general passions and principles by which all minds are agitated, and the whole system of life is continued in motion"[7]—but how many young men have uncles who pour poison into fathers' ears, marry the mothers, and take over kingdoms? Every interpretation of the play needs to take into account just these unusual actions and more, including the imperative to revenge and the hero's response to it. But though Shakespeare adopted a family ethos that displays his hero's plight as modern and understandable to this day, he also adopted conventions of Elizabethan revenge tragedy that now seem more dated than the sparely told action of Amleth in Saxo's twelfth-century narrative.

The ghost, the ghost's to blame. "But why in the world did not Hamlet obey the ghost at once, and so save seven of those eight lives?" That question has loomed so large that virtually every argument about *Hamlet* depends from it. A. C. Bradley surrounded the question with his own quotation marks, perhaps because he was sensible that scarcely anyone bothered to ask it before the end of the eighteenth century; still his lectures assume that the "main fact" in need of interpretation is "Hamlet's inaction."[8] The

[5] Michael Neill, *Issues of Death: Mortality and Identity in English Renaissance Tragedy* (Oxford: Clarendon, 1997), 217–61; quotation from 246–47.
[6] John Kerrigan, *Revenge Tragedy: Aeschylus to Armageddon* (Oxford: Clarendon, 1996), 12.
[7] Samuel Johnson, Preface (1765), in *Selections from Johnson on Shakespeare*, ed. Bertrand H. Bronson (New Haven: Yale University Press, 1986), 11.
[8] A. C. Bradley, *Shakespearean Tragedy* (1904; rpt. New York: Meridian, 1955), 79–80, 104.

problem of Hamlet's infamous delay stems from the quaintness, the archaism of revenge tragedy rather than the ruses of the old story. Our enlightened historicism is at fault: instead of sympathetically examining the motive of revenge and the feelings accompanying it, we take the archaic imperative for granted and wonder why Hamlet delayed. "What is it, then, that inhibits him in fulfilling the task set him by his father's ghost?" Deferring any interest in the motive of revenge to past times, Freud thus seeks the motive of delay.[9] The best new criticism of *Hamlet* takes the same tack as the psychological. Turning from his expert reconstruction of the imagined world of the play to its action, Maynard Mack writes, "Hamlet's problem, in its crudest form, is simply the problem of the avenger."[10] But as Mack's qualification suggests, it is not clear that revenge is ever simple, or that Shakespeare's use of revenge can fully be assimilated to the religious, moral, legal, or honor codes of the sixteenth century.

At least Shakespeareans have become less fixated on the matter of Hamlet's delay.[11] In addressing the prayer scene, in which Hamlet most deliberately and expressly refrains from killing his uncle, Kerrigan pays new respect to the stated reason: that the man who is praying killed "my father grossly, full of bread, / With all his crimes broad blown, as flush as May" (3.3.80–1). Hamlet need not have been trying to shock Dr. Johnson by willing Claudius's damnation in this scene; it suffices that revenge calls for reciprocity, and that reciprocity is not finally possible. According to Kerrigan, Shakespeare's hero realizes "that revenge is incoherent unless it possesses that recapitulative power which ... the passage of experience makes impossible. If the prince found Claudius gaming or swearing, he would want him asleep in an orchard, and not *now* but *then*."[12] From a different perspective, Graham Bradshaw's comments on the play are also to the point. Bradshaw seizes on the universality of *Hamlet*'s appeal to refute complaints that the hero for some unfathomable reason puts off his revenge: "the death of Hamlet's father and his mother's remarriage provide a sufficient *occasion* for the mental disturbance which Shakespeare renders

[9] *The Interpretation of Dreams*, in *The Standard Edition of the Complete Psychological Works of Sigmund Freud*, ed. and trans. James Strachey et al., 24 vols. (London: Hogarth, 1953–74), 4:265.

[10] Maynard Mack, "The World of Hamlet," *Yale Review* 41 (1952), 520.

[11] See the conclusion of Paul N. Siegel, " 'Hamlet, Revenge!': The Uses and Abuses of Historical Criticism," *Shakespeare Survey* 45, ed. Stanley Wells (Cambridge: Cambridge University Press, 1993), 15–26.

[12] John Kerrigan, *Revenge Tragedy*, 187. See also Ramie Targoff, "The Performance of Prayer: Sincerity and Theatricality in Early Modern England," *Representations* 60 (1997), 49–69.

with unprecedented profundity—but then Hamlet's most profoundly representative problems could never be resolved by killing the King." Hamlet's situation at the beginning of the play and Shakespeare's understanding of it are what count for us. "Hamlet's problems cannot be resolved by killing a man whom his mother plainly loves, or by seeing that love as a perverse and obscene lust, or by hysterical outbursts of sex-nausea." In effect, Bradshaw conceives the task of revenge in this play as a fiction about "a developmental crisis," common enough when one generation of a family replaces another.[13]

Markedly different from Amleth's experience of his father's violent end, however, Hamlet's begins with a natural death and a ghost. Just as the alternation of scenes between those devoted to Hamlet and those devoted to Ophelia and Laertes in acts 1 and 2 introduces the audience to a subplot in which the emphasis is also on family, the sequencing of scenes presenting the hero's condition gives precedence to mourning rather than murder and revenge. Though the audience has become acquainted with a wordless ghost in the first scene, and Horatio has proposed to report the same to young Hamlet, the eponymous prince of Denmark is not cognizant of this episode; rather, as his costume, dialogue with the king and queen, and direct speech to the audience in scene 2 demonstrate, he is a person in mourning for his father and still more distressed by his mother's remarriage.[14] It is a fair inference that the marriage has exacerbated his grief, and his prolonged mourning is now the cause of complaint from mother and stepfather. The exposition in *Hamlet* thus presents a family and already privileges the inward feelings of the hero. Young Hamlet speaks his mind, and the ghost is thus far silent. The secret extent of the uncle's involvement, in contrast to Feng's coup, then fosters a more inward drama of thought and feeling, a drama still more suited for soliloquy.

A ghost in itself poses a mental question like nothing in Saxo or Belleforest. Thus Bernardo demands of Horatio, "Is not this something more than fantasy?" (1.1.54). His very use of the word "fantasy" presumes that each of the men on watch acknowledges the difference between a figure of the imagination and something whose presence before them is independent of their will or perception. That the audience sees and later hears from this ghost confirms the positive implied by Bernardo's rhetorical question, but

[13] Graham Bradshaw, *Shakespeare's Scepticism* (1987; rpt. Ithaca: Cornell University Press, 1990), 120–21.

[14] Roland Mushat Frye, *The Renaissance Hamlet: Issues and Responses in 1600* (Princeton: Princeton University Press, 1984), 76, remarks that "this is the only play in which Shakespeare tells us exactly how the protagonist was costumed."

a full answer to the question involves still other considerations. First, until now Horatio has withheld belief in those eyewitness reports of a ghost. Second, all the actors on stage behave as if they, as well as the audience, are seeing the ghost with their own eyes at this moment. Third, the actor impersonating Horatio should "tremble and look pale" if possible, since that is the demeanor indicated by Bernardo's previous line. Fourth, another actor—legend has it that it was Shakespeare himself—dressed in armor is more or less successfully representing a ghost. Fifth, in two subsequent scenes the same actor will speak and be heard by the actor playing Hamlet, and the latter will strive to convey by gesture and speech—"Angels and ministers of grace defend us!" (1.4.39)—that the ghost is like none of the other beings present.

One could go on unpacking the theatrical moment, as invited by Bernardo's I-told-you-so, but this much is sure: no amount of scholarship about what Elizabethan audiences believed about ghosts in other contexts, accordingly as they were Protestant or Catholic, can change the persuasion that a theatrical ghost is a more doubtful and doubted representation of reality than a theatrical live person such as Horatio, Bernardo, or Hamlet.[15] Shakespeare, dressed in armor and beckoning, represents a state of things such as the audience has never seen *except* on the stage or in fantasy, in the mind's eye alerted by hearsay or some book. For the best opportunity of encountering other sorts of being such as ghosts, go to a theater every time. The question of applied scholarship is finally whether Shakespeare's early audiences could distinguish represented ghosts from represented live people, and patently they could, as we can. The common assumption that, in the play of imagination, every personage and scene is representational upon the same level of possibility and experience is simply not valid—though the desired-for consistency is the ground of innumerable quarrels over the interpretation of texts both dramatic and narrative.[16]

The marshaling of the early scenes in *Hamlet* and the exclusive address of Hamlet père, himself secretly murdered, produce a second-level representation of the hero's situation that is fantastic yet all the more satisfying because it grows out of the commonplace fact of loss. As far as the hero is

---

[15] Cf. Eleanor Prosser, *Hamlet and Revenge*, 2nd ed. (Stanford: Stanford University Press, 1971), 97–143; and 11–29.

[16] Supernatural agents are hardly the only test of an audience's capacity to take in more than one level of representation in the same play: what is the audience supposed to think, for example, of the news brought by Rosencrantz and Guildenstern of child-actors "in the city" (2.2.304–33)? Similarly, readers of Dickens will one day have to adjust to some business about a mad writer named Mr. Dick—to say nothing about a good many ghosts still hovering about in Victorian times and later.

concerned the play commences with mourning for the death of his father and disgust with his mother. When Gertrude reminds him that he knows " 'tis common, all that lives must die," there is a temptation, though Hamlet answers only "Ay madam, it is common" (1.2.72,74), to exclaim that death is more like a crime when it touches one this nearly. The death of one's own father is a crime, and Hamlet feels this already and exclaims in our hearing, when the ghost accuses the man who now wears the crown, "O my prophetic soul!" (1.5.40). He was killed, and if anyone killed him, it was that uncle, now unbelievably become my stepfather. In experiencing *Hamlet*—and less sophisticated revenge plays as well—we enter not just one representation of imagined facts but a thicket of fictions, in which certain facts like the appearance of the ghost and his story of murder answer to the emotional needs of the hero just as surely as the play within the play answers to his intention to catch the conscience of the king.[17]

The first soliloquy in *Hamlet* expresses grief and disaffection, and there is little untoward in sorrowing for a father and hating the sexual bond accepted by the mother in exchange. Even if Hamlet were a princess instead of a prince, he might carry on so; the reaction is more nearly a comment on his filial relations. Young Hamlet suffers lectures on the propriety of mourning from the very two persons who have offended him: words of characteristic matter-of-factness from his mother and more studied advice on "mourning duties" (1.2.88) from his uncle. The most troubling aspect of this advice is its undeniable appropriateness. Mourning is the means of overcoming a loss. It is a process that pulls two ways, toward remembrance and forgetting, and is a remembering in order to forget—a process that has some unknown optimum time for completion. Hamlet is not yet ready to forgo mourning, as he makes plain; and the man urging him to put an end to it will turn out to be a murderer. But think of Hamlet's present state of mind and imagine how useful the case of murder might appear. There is nothing one can do about the death of a loved person, after death, unless—unless the person was actually murdered, in which case there would be an opportunity of doing something, of killing someone in fact, which is exactly what one feels like doing. No wonder a Senecan ghost can be a satisfying apparition. He is a godsend, we may feel, from the underworld

---

[17] Cf. Bradshaw, *Shakespeare's Scepticism*, 120–21: "The death of the idealized father and the remarriage of a mother whose sexuality Hamlet cannot accept provide a sufficient explanation for Hamlet's fatal inclination to believe the worst of Claudius before he has 'grounds,' and for the foul imaginings which distort his impressions not only of the loathed Claudius, but of his mother, Polonius, and even Ophelia."

to Denmark's prison. Death suffices for mourning, but crime calls for punishment as well.[18]

A clever instance of such a second-level representation of feeling, and one that is more relevant than it might seem, is provided by those earliest of commentators on *Hamlet*, the two gravediggers, within the hearing of Hamlet and Horatio. The riddling of the "Clown" and "Other," as the speech headings name them, like the riddling of the hero earlier in the play, is well within the ambit of medieval Amleth. The first, who is clearly senior, asks, "What is he that builds stronger than either the mason, the shipwright, or the carpenter?" and subsequently, like many proposers of riddles, supplies his own answer: "a grave-maker." But the other, like so many straight men set up in this fashion, manages to get in his own answer first: "The gallows-maker, for that frame outlives a thousand tenants." The first clown concedes the attractiveness of that answer, but it is not, he insists, as indisputable, as complete, as universal, and as lasting an answer as the one he had in mind, for the grave-maker's houses—the sexton of the parish of Elsinore is speaking—endure "till doomsday" (5.1.35–49). This clown has all the knowingness of the older generation—a bit like Polonius—yet doomsday is also a long time to wait. The intervening fiction of the other clown is youthful and satisfying because it substitutes for the generality of death something more dramatic, the thought of crime and punishment, or murder perhaps and the death penalty. There is a difference in short between death and murder, in respect to both agency and motive; also a motive for telling stories of murder. Death is the hardest thing to take; murder is at least easier to grasp; and stories of murder can actually make one feel good.[19]

The ghost in the first act is like an answer to a prayer and to the riddle of mourning and revenge. Hamlet accepts unhesitatingly the prospect of revenge as something he would like to do just now. "Haste me to know't, that I with wings as swift / As meditation or the thoughts of love / May

---

[18] Cf. Watson, *The Rest Is Silence*, 75: "Ghosts are the standard-equipment starters of Senecan revenge-tragedies; my point is that this convention reflects a deep motive for stories of blood-revenge, which sustain two precious beliefs: first, that our rights and even our desires exert some forces beyond our deaths; and second, that revenge can symbolically restore us to life by defeating the agency of our death, conveniently localized in a villain." Note "our deaths," however: Watson's theme is mortality itself rather than mourning.

[19] It is worth asking why murder is so much more common in novels of purposeful realism than it is in the experience of the readers of such novels. Again, unnatural murder is more manageable than ordinary death: or so I have argued in a *Hamlet*-haunted book, *Strong Representations: Narrative and Circumstantial Evidence in England* (Baltimore: Johns Hopkins University Press, 1992), esp. 163–76.

sweep to my revenge" (1.5.29–31). In this response Hamlet links revenge to love because that is how the ghost of his father has put the case: "If thou didst ever thy dear father love"—"O God!" Hamlet exclaims—"Revenge his foul and most unnatural murder" (1.5.23–5). The ghost himself has been so surprised by death that he longs to tell his story. The action that he demands, with his haunting fear of "the fat weed / That rots itself in ease on Lethe wharf"(1.5.32–3), is first and foremost proof of remembrance, and from this remarkable encounter with his father Hamlet summarizes only two points in his notebook: one has to do with the world in which he finds himself—Claudius and others are not what they seem—and the other is a reminder of remembrance:

> Remember thee?
> Yea, from the table of my memory
> I'll wipe away all trivial fond records,
> All saws of books, all forms, all pressures past,
> That youth and observation copied there,
> And thy commandment all alone shall live
> Within the book and volume of my brain,
> Unmixed with baser matter: yes, by heaven!
> O most pernicious woman!
> O villain, villain, smiling damned villain!
> My tables—meet it is I set it down
> That one may smile, and smile, and be a villain;
> At least I'm sure it may be so in Denmark.
> So uncle, there you are. Now to my word:
> It is "Adieu, adieu, remember me."
> I have sworn't.   (1.5.97–112)

Here Hamlet seems more youthful than at any other juncture in the play. He wants to give up something, give up his intellectual life and his youth, all but the memory of his father and what it portends. He does not set down as his word the ghost's imperative "Revenge" but the more pacific and general instruction, "Adieu, adieu, remember me." This subordination of revenge to mourning markedly differs from the medieval story.[20] Even when Hamlet speaks angrily of killing in his turn, the purpose is not to get his own back but painfully to remember, to bring his father back in that

---

[20] According to Neill, "The great discovery" of *Hamlet* can be put this way: "that revenge tragedy, at the deepest level, is less about the ethics of vendetta than it is about murderous legacies of the past and the terrible power of memory" (*Issues of Death*, 244).

unremarkable way. Before he has heard of the ghost, he has protested aloud, "heaven and earth, / Must I remember?" (1.2.142–3). He both does not wish to think of his father's death and mother's remarriage and cannot help doing so. By a startling coincidence, the same night he finds that there is more to think about.

Psychologically oriented interpretations of *Hamlet* have not thought it important to explain away the ghost. On the contrary, multiple-level representations in imaginative literature have probably inspired modern depth psychology. Campbell, for example, might have availed herself of a careful argument by W.W. Greg that the ghost essentially obeyed the dictates of Hamlet's imagination, but she did not. Greg began with some familiar puzzles of the play scene and worked back to the words of the ghost in act 1. Conceivably, Claudius misses the point of the dumb show and possibly the play of Gonzago's murder itself. He would hardly have turned to his nephew with the words "Is there no offence in't?" (3.2.213), according to Greg, if he had murdered his brother by the same means a couple of months before. Nowhere in the play, even after this scene, does he seem to worry about being found out by anyone but God. Moreover, Hamlet becomes so overwrought that he himself may be the cause of the breakup of the play scene. Yet Hamlet, obviously, is familiar with the means of poisoning represented in *The Murder of Gonzago*, since he has asked the players to perform it. At this point, Greg pauses dramatically in his argument with a disclaimer worthy of Freud himself: "But the ingenious reader will already have made the obvious inference. *The Ghost described this particular method of poisoning because it was already present in Hamlet's mind.*" In brief, Hamlet drew on his memory of the Gonzago play in hallucinating the ghost's revelation in act 1. And Greg does not fail to cite corroborative evidence, such as Horatio's observation that the hero at that point "waxes desperate with imagination" (1.4.87) or Hamlet's own awareness that the devil, at any rate, could stir such imaginings "Out of my weakness and my melancholy" (2.2.554). As for the other witnesses to the ghost's first visitation, they might be subject to "collective suggestion," though Greg does not press the point.[21] I recall this ingenious reading of the play first because it is largely successful, and thus testifies to Shakespeare's realization of Hamlet's situation and feelings, and second because, careful as the reading is, it is unnecessary. Typically, Greg seeks to interpret the givens of *Hamlet*—the dialogue and stage directions of the texts we possess—as if everything were on a consistent level of representation, a level commensu-

---

[21] W. W. Greg, "Hamlet's Hallucination," *Modern Language Review* 12 (1917), 416, 410.

rate in this case with a scientific idea of what can be experienced. He forgets that even people who, unlike himself, believe in ghosts do not insist that ghosts exist as live persons do. In a play or a fiction, ghosts are among the easiest characters to put to use because they are not bound to be plausible in ways that other characters may be. Yet nothing prevents Shakespeare from creating also an Ophelia or a Laertes, or a mere Osric, to suit the needs of the hero and the hero's situation, as well as some wider requisites of interest or plausibility. Fictional representations need never, even in the strictest piece of so-called naturalism, be confined to a single aim.

More important than the formal question of representation, to my mind, is the represented action before and after the ghost appears in *Hamlet*. The fencing is mainly with words, and the hero contemplative to the end. Mourning continues to fuel the revelation of the inward hero throughout the first half of the play, and the revelation is by no means confined to soliloquy: "Denmark's a prison" (2.2.234); "yet to me, what is this quintessence of dust?" (2.2.290); "use every man after his desert, and who shall scape whipping?" (2.2.485–6); "what should such fellows as I do crawling between earth and heaven?" (3.1.124–5); and a dozen more. Shakespeare then surrounds Hamlet with reflectors that further dramatize his mood, characters who are penetrated by his despair, wounded by it, without comprehending. The Polonius family are often alarming in their innocence of what is going on. Rosencrantz and gentle Guildenstern, or Guildenstern and gentle Rosencrantz, are examples of kindness by rote that seems treacherous to suffering. As for the indifferent mother and completely untrustworthy stepfather, they are precisely what youthful and lonely sorrow would invent; and though the latter may be steeped in crime, he goes on behaving as if he were the father who knows best. The entire cast of *Hamlet*, including the ghost and a friend "that is not passion's slave" (3.2.62), answer to the needs of a hero who mourns, and the one certain change we perceive in him by the end is that he has ceased to mourn before he ceases to be.

No other play by Shakespeare appears to be this egocentric in design, and one explanation of the marked attention to acting and rival theaters—amplified in the folio text—is that the ego was in some degree Shakespeare's. Certainly it is neither foolish nor improper to judge that *Hamlet* was in part a response to the death or impending death of his own father. That John Shakespeare was buried on 8 September 1601 is one of the few facts we possess about the playwright's family, and that date may be months or more after the first production of the play. But one may become aware, from apparent illness or the concern of others in the family, that a parent is dying. The death of his only son Hamnet five years earlier would have intensified Shakespeare's feelings about his father's death and made him still more mindful of his own death to come.[22] To take cognizance of these matters does not license us to believe that Shakespeare suffered a severe depression at the time, or that his mother or his wife—as Stephen Dedalus contends in *Ulysses*—was unfaithful. He was undeniably active in the theater and with his writing at the time. Very likely he took his father's death in stride and invented the melancholic Hamlet as great artists do, creating ambitious designs from slight experience or even anticipation: like Horatio, he lived to tell Hamlet's story. But a profound change in the weight and emphasis of Shakespeare's output coincides with the death of his father; with *Hamlet* he inaugurates the series of major tragedies and problem comedies that are relieved only by the magic of the late romances.[23]

The accommodation of Amleth's story to tragedy marks a vast difference from the spirit of Saxo or Belleforest, but Shakespeare still more pointedly refuses to indulge in the triumphant ritual ending that characterizes the revenge tragedies of his contemporaries. In *Antonio's Revenge*, the closest to Shakespeare's tragedy in time, the villain's tongue is torn out, he is bound, shown the limbs of his son in a banquet dish, made to think he is to die in a rush of masquers that proves to be merely a rehearsal, and then killed in this same fashion. John Marston's play shares many features with *Hamlet* yet is wildly different in atmosphere. "Tomb," Antonio apostrophizes, "I'll not be long / E'er I creep in thee, and with bloodless lips / Kiss my cold father's cheek."[24] Shakespeare, one imagines, did not feel this way about his father, and Hamlet most certainly did not.

The effects of tragedy are not directly translatable back into life: the finality with which revenge plays end would in life merely multiply mourning to come. That the contemplation of revenge may finally suffice for mourning, however, is suggested in *Hamlet* by the way the action devolves upon chance. Through it we have learned

---

[22] Hamnet died at age eleven and was buried 11 August 1596, when Shakespeare was thirty-two. One of the puzzles of the second quarto and folio texts is the apparent disparity between Hamlet's seeming youth in act 1 especially and the thirty years assigned to him in 5.1. He was about nineteen throughout, if the first quarto should be consulted: see Adolphus Alfred Jack, *Young Hamlet* (Aberdeen: Aberdeen University Press, 1950), esp. 143–55.

[23] The best comparison is not with Freud, whose career virtually awaited his father's death, but with Dickens. The novelist was as prolific as the dramatist and perhaps more precocious; but after John Dickens's death in 1851, he wrote the novels that contemporaries thought were too dark and today are respected as his greatest. The titles of the first two, *Bleak House* and *Hard Times*, suggest the difference in atmosphere.

[24] John Marston, *Antonio's Revenge: The Second Part of Antonio and Mellida*, ed. G. K. Hunter (Lincoln: University of Nebraska Press, 1965), 3.1.13–15.

Of carnal, bloody, and unnatural acts,
Of accidental judgements, casual slaughters,
Of deaths put on by cunning and forced cause,
And in this upshot, purposes mistook
Fallen on th'inventors' heads.   (5.2.360–4)

The emphasis in act 5 is increasingly on the hero's own readiness to die, and the need to deal with Claudius is canceled by Claudius's own plotting, which this time unravels before the audience without any mystery. "In *Hamlet*," Neill points out, "the catastrophe occurs when (and we are almost made to feel, because) the hero abandons all attempts to script it for himself."[25]

REVENGE AS A RECOURSE OF MOURNING

E. E. Stoll was among the first critics to react against a hundred years or more of Romantic assessments of Hamlet as a character peculiarly unsuited to action. There is something still refreshing in Stoll's dogged insistence that "the audience were accustomed to the revenger beating about the bush but reproaching himself for it."[26] But critics like Stoll who saw the play as belonging to a specific Elizabethan genre, distinctly influenced by Senecan drama, did not usually ask what human purposes were served by the conventions they described. Fredson Bowers, in his still useful survey of revenge tragedy, seemed content to assume that revenge plots afforded plenty of conflict and that "strong revengeful emotions" made exciting theater, even for audiences who did not harbor such emotions.[27] In sifting the contemporary literature, Bowers came up with some few homilies supporting revenge, but he largely failed to distinguish motives or to make the basic distinction between injury to oneself and the death of a loved one. Eleanor Prosser's study suggested that Elizabethan audiences were overwhelmingly opposed to revenge, but of course if the Christian preachments against such practice were as frequent and as strenuous as she reports, there must have been feelings that the idea of revenge appealed to.[28] Such feelings need

[25] Neill, *Issues of Death*, 238.

[26] Elmer Edgar Stoll, *Art and Artifice in Shakespeare: A Study in Dramatic Contrast and Illusion* (1933; rpt. New York: Barnes and Noble, 1968), 94. Stoll began this protest in *Hamlet: An Historical and Comparative Study* (1919).

[27] Fredson Thayer Bowers, *Elizabethan Revenge Tragedy, 1587–1642* (1940; rpt. Gloucester, MA: Smith, 1959), 264.

[28] Prosser, *Hamlet and Revenge* (note 15 above). Similarly, Arthur McGee, *The Elizabethan Hamlet* (New Haven: Yale University Press, 1987), gathers much valuable lore about ghosts

not originally manifest themselves as violence. Rather, grief finds relief in anger, and anger in violence. Thus Malcolm in Shakespeare's *Macbeth* describes the psychological work that revenge can do for Macduff, devastated by the loss of wife and children: "let grief / Convert to anger; blunt not the heart, enrage it."[29] It is my contention that the revenge tragedies closest to *Hamlet* in kind invoke revenge as a partial solution to mourning, as a means to mourn. These few plays feature grief more than they do justice; the justice sought for is their answer to grief.

The identification of the ghost with Senecan tragedy goes back at least as far as Thomas Nashe's sidelong crack at the *Ur-Hamlet* in 1589, and without question the convention of the dead crying out for revenge at the beginning of a play owes its existence to the ghost of Tantalus in Seneca's *Thyestes* and the ghost of Thyestes in his *Agamemnon*. The cruelty and rhetoric of these classical plays gave a certain license to Renaissance playwrights, and their numerous one-liners—certain axioms of crime and vengeance—supplied much quoted wisdom for plays performed in England's private theaters especially. But the curse of the house of Atreus, with its dark mood of fatality, remains foreign to Elizabethan drama, and the rather condescending assumption that Seneca taught native dramatists their business has been contested by G. K. Hunter and others.[30] Gordon Braden has since rejoined with a quiet argument for Kyd's and Shakespeare's refinement not of revenge but of "the inner resources of Senecan selfhood." *Hamlet* especially expands both psychologically and philosophically on this model.[31] Similarly, Robert Miola contends that Shakespeare both challenges and builds constructively on Senecan precedent: in sum, "Hamlet finally replaces the ethics of excess with the heroism of moral anguish and meditation."[32]

Seneca's two tragedies with ghosts, in fact, do not openly display grief and mourning to anything like the extent that *Hamlet* does. His *Troades* is another matter: the play is filled with keening voices, from the opening

and damnation but leaves the impression that the play could hardly be enjoyed, since the audience would be in terror for the fate of Hamlet's soul from beginning to end.
[29] *Macbeth*, 4.3.228–29.
[30] G. K. Hunter, "Seneca and the Elizabethans: a case study in 'influence' " and "Seneca and English Tragedy," in *Dramatic Identities and Cultural Tradition: Studies in Shakespeare and His Contemporaries* (New York: Barnes and Noble, 1978), 159–213.
[31] Gordon Braden, *Renaissance Tragedy and the Senecan Tradition: Anger's Privilege* (New Haven: Yale University Press, 1985), 214.
[32] Robert S. Miola, *Shakespeare and Classical Tragedy: The Influence of Seneca* (Oxford: Clarendon, 1992), 67.

speeches of Hecuba and the chorus onward. The losers in the Trojan war—most notably Hecuba, as *Hamlet* itself recalls—had become emblematic of grief before Seneca's time. The action of the *Troades* may be thought of as a perverse exercise in mourning, since still more pain is inflicted upon sufferers from the war; as a spectacle, the play works on suffering by initially making it worse—a process more bearable to the audience, of course, than to the fictive personages on stage. As a philosopher Seneca labored in roughly the opposite direction, instilling calm in his readers as persistently as he evoked horror from his audiences. Braden points up the complementarity of these impulses, though interestingly in a reflection on the denouement of *Hamlet*: "Stoicism is the natural alternative to revenge because it is a twin endeavor, a complementary strategy for establishing the self's belief in its own dignity and power."[33] So attuned to the acceptance of death and so opposed to anger was the philosopher Seneca, that he could only have conceived of the antagonists in his revenge plays as deserving to be drenched in blood. He does not seem to have had a problem with revenge as such, so long as it can be conducted without anger. Quite specifically, it is a son's duty to avenge a murdered father, but his revenge should not be undertaken because of grief.[34] That sort of advice virtually cedes the point that revenge satisfies because it gives vent to anger, the anger arising from grief.

The plays and essays of Seneca were both well known to English writers in the sixteenth century, yet the linkage of grief, through anger, to revenge seems almost a native strain. In *Gorboduc* (1561)—often called the first English tragedy, though admittedly influenced by Seneca—grieving is prominently shown as prior to revenge. The themes of *Gorboduc* are mainly political, but even before any action has occurred the queen laments that the kingdom is to be divided between her sons Ferrex and Porrex. Act 3 begins with the king lamenting the civil war between the two princes, and upon the death of the older, Ferrex, the queen enters with a long speech in act 4 in which her determination on revenge follows expressly from her mourning state: "Why should I live and linger forth my time / In longer life to double my distress?" As in Hamlet's case, Videna first dwells on her own longing for death because of her loss.

[33] Braden, *Renaissance Tragedy and the Senecan Tradition*, 219.
[34] Seneca, "On Anger," 1.12.1, in *Moral Essays*, trans. John W. Basore, vol. 1 (1928; rpt. Cambridge: Harvard University Press, 1994). A still more chilling statist endorsement of *ratio* in revenge will be found at 1.19.2.

So had my bones possessed now in peace
Their happy grave within the closed ground,
And greedy worms had gnawn this pined heart
Without my feeling pain; so should not now
This living breast remain the ruthful tomb,
Wherein my heart yelden to death is graved;
Nor dreary thoughts, with pangs of pining grief,
My doleful mind had not afflicted thus.[35]

For twenty-seven lines the queen thus projects the loss of Ferrex inward; then for fifty-four lines she projects it outward, vowing revenge against her other son, Porrex. The tightly conceived no-win situation of the mourning parent is closer in manner to the soliloquies of Hieronimo in *The Spanish Tragedy* than to anything in *Hamlet*.[36] But I am not arguing that grief modulates to revenge in identical ways: the plays afford a commentary on one another. The queen Videna directs her anger against the son who has, at the head of an army, openly slain his brother. Hieronimo discovers his son hanged—a murder that the audience has witnessed—but knows not by whom. Hamlet grieves and protests the canon against self-slaughter without being aware that his father's death was other than accidental.

When first performed, Thomas Kyd's popular revenge play *The Spanish Tragedy* (1589) was roughly contemporaneous with the *Ur-Hamlet*, possibly also by Kyd. Its Senecan ghost, however, has less personal stake in the action than has Hieronimo, the Marshal of Spain. The ghost of Andrea seeks revenge for his death in battle at the hands of Balthazar's troops, but the murder of Hieronimo's son Horatio by Lorenzo and Balthazar impels the main action of grief and revenge. The hero states the case directly when he comes upon his son's body in the arbor: "To know the author were some ease of grief, / For in revenge my heart would find relief."[37] Hieronimo also dwells on suicide, feigns madness and is driven mad, but most of all brings home the connection between mourning and thoughts of revenge by engaging in both to the very end. His repeated soliloquies as he comes on stage convey a true sense of the contradictions of mourning, of plotting

[35] Thomas Sackville and Thomas Norton, *Gorboduc, or Ferrex and Porrex*, ed. Irby B. Cauthen, Jr. (Lincoln: University of Nebraska Press, 1970), 4.1.1–2,15–22.
[36] Videna's embittered violence against one child in frustration over the loss of the other—not a very happy move—anticipates *King Lear*; but so does Hieronimo's passion—his treatment of Bazulto, especially—resemble Lear's.
[37] Thomas Kyd, *The Spanish Tragedy* (in the same volume with *The First Part of Hieronimo*), ed. Andrew S. Cairncross (Lincoln: University of Nebraska Press, 1967), 2.5.40–41.

worse in order to feel better, remembering in order to come to terms with memory, concentrating in order to forget. Hieronimo therein both grieves and is conscious of the helplessness of grieving.

> Yet still tormented is my tortured soul
> With broken sighs and restless passions,
> That, winged, mount and, hovering in the air,
> Beat at the windows of the brightest heavens,
> Soliciting for justice and revenge.

This is not a hero procrastinating; his keening dominates *The Spanish Tragedy* even as his acting of revenge in the play within the play masters the Spanish court in the end. Helped by quotation from Seneca's *Troades* and *Agamemnon*, his grief contemplates life and death in the abstract—"For he that thinks with patience to contend / To quiet life, his life shall easily end."[38] Meanwhile his wife Isabella grieves first with him and then apart, as she takes the same gendered course that Ophelia will follow from evident insanity to suicide.

Kyd also anticipates Shakespeare's use of analogous actions of loss and grieving. In one particularly vivid scene, Hieronimo as marshal confronts a petitioner for justice whose case exactly parallels his own. Initially he received the old man Bazulto sanely enough.

> But wherefore stands yon silly man so mute,
> With mournful eyes and hands to heaven uprear'd?
> Come hither, father, let me know thy cause.

But this sympathy rapidly dissolves in confusion with his own cause—"No, sir; it was my murder'd son! / Oh my son, my son, oh my son Horatio!"—before gathering again in Hamlet-like comparisons and chidings of himself:

> See, see, oh, see thy shame, Hieronimo!
> See here a loving father to his son!
> Behold the sorrows and the sad laments,
> That he delivereth for his son's decease!
> If love's effects so strives in lesser things,
> If love enforce such moods in meaner wits,
> If love express such power in poor estates:
> Hieronimo, when as a raging sea,

[38] Ibid., 3.7.10–14, 3.13.10–11.

Toss'd with the wind and tide, o'erturneth then
The upper billows, course of waves to keep,
Whilst lesser waters labor in the deep,
Then shamest thou not, Hieronimo, to neglect
The sweet revenge of thy Horatio?[39]

The deep impression made by Bazulto is again that of grief, which Hiero-nimo repeatedly and profoundly attributes to the old man's love for his son. For in the desire for "sweet revenge" love achieves, or seeks to achieve, continuity after death. Upon that line, as so often in this play, the speech as a whole turns from grief to vengeance. Typically, the turn is also from heaven to hell, a direction underlined in this instance by successive allusions to Juno, Hercules, and Orpheus.

Far more originally, even brilliantly, Kyd has Hieronimo in his passion tear to pieces the legal papers of poor Bazulto, as if he were tearing his enemies. Still more grotesquely, with a visible pathos, the hero exits running, re-enters, and imagines the old man to be his son Horatio returned from the grave.

And art thou come, Horatio, from the depth,
To ask for justice in this upper earth,
To tell thy father thou art unreveng'd,
To wring more tears from Isabella's eyes,
Whose lights are dimm'd with over-long laments?

It is this ghost in *The Spanish Tragedy*, not Andrea's, which most closely resembles that of *Hamlet*, and more especially the latter's revisitation in the closet scene. And this ghost is plainly and unmistakably the pitiful coinage of Hieronimo's brain, which begins to waver even as he studies more closely the features of Bazulto:

But let me look on my Horatio.
Sweet boy, how art thou chang'd in death's black shade!
Had Proserpine no pity on thy youth,
But suffered thy fair crimson-color'd spring
With withered winter to be blasted thus?
Horatio, thou art older than thy father.

The pathos of Hieronimo's delusion, despite the aggression and rending of the law papers, touches Bazulto, who plays opposite the mad Hieronimo

---

[39] Ibid., 3.13.67–69,80–81,95–107.

43

somewhat the way Gloucester will to Lear on the beach near Dover. The suffering father who is still sane—"I am a grieved man, and not a ghost, / That came for justice for my murdered son"—attempts and succeeds in restoring a measure of sanity to the other, who replies:

> Ay, now I know thee, now thou namest thy son:
> Thou art the lively image of my grief;
> Within thy face my sorrows I may see.
> Thy eyes are gumm'd with tears, thy cheeks are wan,
> Thy forehead troubled, and thy mutt'ring lips
> Murmur sad words abruptly broken off.

And the long moving speech ends on a turn even more Lear-like, and a sad pun that recalls that Horatio, like Cordelia, was hanged.

> Come in, old man, thou shalt to Isabel.
> Lean on my arm; I thee, thou me shalt stay;
> And thou, and I, and she, will sing a song,
> Three parts in one, but all of discords fram'd.—
> Talk not of cords, but let us now be gone;
> For with a cord Horatio was slain.[40]

No play could make clearer that, where mourning is concerned, the contemplation of revenge is as efficacious as revenge itself. The aim is justice, to be sure, but more than justice, too. The hero seeks to make his adversaries feel as bad or worse than he does, but also to impress them with how bad he feels—something the audience must understand as well.

Francis Bacon disparaged the idea that revenge was "a kind of wild justice"; yet in arguing against private revenge, Bacon came close to appreciating its significance for mourning: "This is certain, that a man that studieth revenge keeps his own wounds green, which otherwise would heal and do well."[41] By plotting revenge Hieronimo keeps his own wound open until such time as he is willing his grief should pass. The final scene of *The Spanish Tragedy* treats revenge as both fact and fiction, for during the Turkish play in which he has cast his enemies, Hieronimo's allies thrust home with real knives and swords. As he says with fine ambiguity in his exit line from the previous scene, now "nothing wants but acting of revenge." In the aftermath of the acting, which claims the lives of Lorenzo and Balthazar along with that of Bel-imperia—a second female suicide, though far more

---

[40] Ibid., 3.13.133–37,145–50,159–60,161–66,170–75.
[41] Francis Bacon, "Of Revenge," in *Essays, Advancement of Learning, New Atlantis, and Other Pieces*, ed. Richard Foster Jones (New York: Odyssey, 1937), 13–14.

tellingly defiant than Isabella's—Hieronimo abruptly displays the corpse of his murdered son. The object of this gruesome show, again, is not merely to justify his actions, or to terrify the court, but to persuade the others of his pain—to make his loss somehow unforgettable even though every loss is bound someday to be forgotten.

> See here my show; look upon this spectacle!
> Here lay my hope, and here my hope hath end!
> Here lay my heart, and here my heart was slain!
> Here lay my treasure, here my treasure lost!
> Here lay my bliss, and here my bliss bereft!
> But hope, heart, treasure, joy, and bliss,
> All fled, fail'd, died, yea, all decay'd, with this.

From this moment Hieronimo's only further object is to take his own life. To those who try to stop him, whether because they sympathize or because they would condemn him to worse torture and death, he offers reasons for dying that apply to other heroes of revenge. "Viceroy, I will not trust thee with my life, / Which this day I have offered to my son." Having put off suicide so that he might also project his despair outward—his offering to the one he loved—he will now please himself. At the same time he implicitly accepts the penalty of violating the tenets of law and religion. In a passage added to the play by 1602, he further expresses the sense that he is prepared for death: "Methinks, since I grew inward with revenge, / I cannot look with scorn enough on death."[42] If the object were merely justice, he would not have to turn inward to such a degree. Identification with his son in mourning, discovering the murderers and contemplating their deaths, have left him feeling little else. The play has in common with *Hamlet* a tendency to exclude any perspective other than that of the hero's self-enclosed grief.[43]

Shakespeare's early revenge tragedy *Titus Andronicus* (1594?) is his most Senecan play, no doubt, while many of its most distinctive features and part of the action are drawn from Ovid. But the play owes much to *The Spanish Tragedy*, too, and similarly tells of grief's recourse to revenge. Though associated by theme and year of publication with Shakespeare's poem *The Rape of Lucrece* rather than his later plays from Plutarch, *Titus Andronicus* is also very much a Roman play. Thus the hero's first line is "Hail, Rome, victorious in thy mourning weeds!" That initial funeral rite is strictly statist, em-

---

[42] Kyd, *The Spanish Tragedy*, 4.4.89–95,159–60,(195–96).
[43] See C. L. Barber and Richard P. Wheeler, *The Whole Journey: Shakespeare's Power of Development* (Berkeley: University of California Press, 1986), 267, 272.

bodying the old republican ideal that ties to Rome are always to be placed above ties to family. With pride and without flinching, Titus the distinguished general has lost twenty-one sons in combat before the commencement of the action. In a profound sense, the play's turning in act 3 is about those losses too, as well as the rape of Lavinia and execution of two sons who have been framed for the murder of Bassianus: at that point, soldier though he is, Titus experiences grief at last. "For two and twenty sons I never wept, / Because they died in honor's lofty bed"—a statistic that now includes a son he himself has executed in act 1 for insubordination. Now, for the two sons falsely accused of murder and rape, "in the dust I write / My heart's deep languor, and my soul's sad tears." For all its cruel mutilations and enforced cannibalism, in act 3 the play becomes suffused with mourning on the part of Titus and his remaining family. One small sign of this reformulation of grief is the remark of a nameless messenger bearing the sons' two heads and Titus's uselessly severed hand: "woe is me to think upon thy woes, / More than remembrance of my father's death."[44] In the midst of horrors and treachery, the messenger recalls a commonplace, the death of fathers; yet for him and his family that death was not commonplace.

Other exchanges in *Titus Andronicus* touch on revenge as a function of mourning. Both indurate villains of the play, Aaron the Moor and Tamora the queen of the Goths, also practice revenge, while the flawed hero has at least feelings with which the audience can sympathize. When Aaron is captured by Titus's remaining son Lucius near the end, he boasts unrepentantly, first, of what he has accomplished during the play and second, of the kinds of evil deeds to which he has dedicated a lifetime. The rhetoric of the second list is intriguing, for he devotes one line each to five crimes and, by way of suitable climax or personal preference, no fewer than six lines to a grisly practice upon innocent mourning:

> Oft have I digg'd up dead men from their graves,
> And set them upright at their dear friends' door,
> Even when their sorrows almost was forgot,
> And on their skins, as on the bark of trees,
> Have with my knife carved in Roman letters,
> "Let not your sorrow die, though I am dead."[45]

---

[44] *Titus Andronicus*, 3.1.10–13,239–40.

[45] *Titus Andronicus*, 5.1.135–40. When Aaron boasts that he has done such things "As willingly as one would kill a fly" (5.1.142), he may have triggered the contrasting dialogue, in the folio text, between Titus and his brother also about killing a fly, which begins in sorrow—

46

As for Tamora, now empress in Rome, she in the end pretends to be the spirit of Revenge, as if in a play by Seneca or Kyd, "to ease the gnawing vulture" of Titus's grief. The hero sees through her ruse and, notoriously, serves up her sons in the pie. The last lines of the play, spoken by Lucius, declare that Tamora's body shall be treated like those Aaron has dug from their graves:

> No funeral rite, nor man in mourning weed,
> No mournful bell shall ring her burial,
> But throw her forth to beasts and birds to prey:
> Her life was beastly and devoid of pity,
> And being dead, let birds on her take pity.

And here the word "pity," rhyming only with itself, is meant to cancel out. The play concludes more satisfactorily than *Hamlet*, one might suppose, since Titus is survived by one last son who is named emperor, as well as a grandson and a noble brother. The hero is also aware that he should not have refused the emperorship himself: "Ah, Rome! . . . I made thee miserable / What time I threw the people's suffrages / On him that thus doth tyrannize o'er me."[46] Hamlet experiences no such anagnorisis, for he is caught up in tragedy without any choice in the matter. As Martin Dodsworth has particularly argued, Hamlet's commitment to set things right is a bind of honor that demands nothing less than his life.[47]

In *Antonio's Revenge*, the play by John Marston performed as nearly as we can tell in the same season as *Hamlet* (1600–1601?), the two avengers Antonio and Pandulpho do not die in the end but, ironically, plan on joining a religious order. The ghost of Andrugio, Antonio's father, is still very much present in the last scene, applauding the elaborate stabbing of his enemy Piero. Marston's play affords the double spectacle of Antonio avenging his father's death and Pandulpho, his son's. It superficially shares so many motifs with *Hamlet* that it is hardly surprising that Shakespeare should have added, in the folio version, the dialogue of Hamlet with Rosen-

---

"How if that fly had a father and mother?"—and ends with revenge—"it was a black ill-favor'd fly, / Like to the Empress' Moor" (3.2.60,66–67). Reuben Brower, *Hero and Saint: Shakespeare and the Graeco-Roman Tradition* (New York: Oxford University Press, 1971), 180–94, calls on these lines among others to argue that the play anticipates *King Lear* as well as *Hamlet*.

[46] *Titus Andronicus*, 5.2.31, 5.3.196–200, 4.3.18–20.

[47] Martin Dodsworth, *Hamlet Closely Observed* (London: Athlone, 1985), esp. 9–68. The title of Edwin Honig's *Calderon and the Seizures of Honor* (Cambridge: Harvard University Press, 1972) is expressive of the way honor abruptly makes its demands, irrespective of a hero's wishes.

crantz and Guildenstern on the "eyrie of Children" who have supposedly—the dialogue is with tongue in cheek—driven the adult players out on the road (2.2.313–33). It would seem that *Hamlet* and *Antonio's Revenge* were rival productions, both exploiting the long success of *The Spanish Tragedy* and the materials of the *Ur-Hamlet* but differing radically according to the moral and aesthetic criteria of the public and private theaters in London.[48] Still, for all his fondness for gothic self-indulgence, Marston does not fail to bring out the connection of grief to revenge.

There are two Antonio plays by Marston, the first of which ostensibly ends happily. Yet *Antonio and Mellida* begins with the hero grieving from a misapprehension of Andrugio's death:

Heart, wilt not break? And thou, abhorred life,
Wilt thou still breathe in my enraged blood?
Veins, sinews, arteries, why crack ye not,
Burst and divuls'd with anguish of my grief?
Can man by no means creep out of himself
And leave the slough of viperous grief behind?[49]

As if to recall the mood of that opening scene of the first play, the prologue to *Antonio's Revenge* expressly welcomes among the audience those who may be mourning at this time. Some there are who may be frightened of the show—

But if a breast
Nail'd to the earth with grief, if any heart
Pierc'd through with anguish, pant within this ring,
If there be any blood whose heat is chok'd
And stifled with true sense of misery,
If ought of these strains fill this consort up,
Th' arrive most welcome.

Should there be such stricken persons in the audience, the rule once more seems to be that feeling worse can lead to feeling better. Antonio dreams of the ghost of his father crying for revenge before he receives news of his death or the bloodied corpse of Pandulpho's son is displayed on stage.

---

[48] See Alfred Harbage, *Shakespeare and the Rival Traditions* (1952; rpt. Bloomington: Indiana University Press, 1970), esp. 29–57, 166–68.

[49] John Marston, *Antonio and Mellida: The First Part*, ed. G. K. Hunter (Lincoln: University of Nebraska Press, 1965), 1.1.1–6.

From there on the play is full of mourning and revengers living "Only to numb some others' cursed blood / With the dead palsy of like misery." Very evidently it is the idea of vengeance that Antonio covets. He charges himself to "Invent some stratagem of vengeance / Which, but to think on, may like lightning glide / With horror through thy breast."[50] Compare Hamlet's "wings as swift / As meditation or the thoughts of love" (1.5.29–30). And as in *Hamlet* and *The Spanish Tragedy*, revenge is fully predicated on love, having to do with the loss of a person and not with just any wrong.

From *Gorboduc* on, revenge plays of the English theater invoke the fall of Troy, and specifically the death of Priam, as the classic occasion for mourning. *Titus Andronicus* alludes five or six times to Troy, and even Titus's grandson has "read that Hecuba of Troy / Ran mad for sorrow." About the same year, Shakespeare's Lucrece at length compared her "Troy" of grief to a painting of the scene, much as it was described by Virgil in the second book of the *Aeneid*.[51] These precedents help place in perspective the player's speech in *Hamlet* and remind one that that too is a sign, a set piece, of mourning. Explicitly an adaptation of "Aeneas' tale to Dido . . . where he speaks of Priam's slaughter" (2.2.404–6), the heavily stylized speech recalls not only *The Rape of Lucrece* but another adaptation of the story in Christopher Marlowe's *The Tragedy of Dido*. The player's Hecuba, running "barefoot up and down" in tears, a cloth upon her head instead of a crown, "and, for a robe, / About her lank and all o'er-teemed loins / A blanket" (2.2.463–7), is both pathetic and perhaps more homely than any in this literature. The patriarchal theme remains the death of Priam, father of fifty heroes, at the hand of Pyrrhus, the son of Achilles. Both Virgil and Marlowe include the cruel symmetry by which Pyrrhus first kills Priam's youngest son. Hamlet's personal contribution is to throw the narrative into question, to cast the emblematic case as a fiction and the performance he has called for as a charade compared with his own cause of grief. Significantly, too, he fixes attention on the grieving person, the player's Hecuba rather than his Pyrrhus:

[50] Marston, *Antonio's Revenge* (note 17 above), Prologue 21–27, 4.2.19–20, 3.1.48–50. As Hunter observes in his introduction, the hero is not concerned with any delay but with expressing his feelings: "The plot (like that of *Antonio and Mellida*) is primarily designed to exhibit a series of states of mind rather than any linear movement by which desired actions are achieved" (xv).

[51] *Titus Andronicus*, 4.1.20–21; *The Rape of Lucrece*, 1366–568. Emrys Jones, *The Origins of Shakespeare* (Oxford: Clarendon, 1977), 90–107, offers evidence that Shakespeare was acquainted with a translation of Euripides' *Hecuba*.

Is it not monstrous that this player here,
But in a fiction, in a dream of passion,
Could force his soul so to his own conceit
That from her working all his visage wanned,
Tears in his eyes, distraction in's aspect,
A broken voice, and his whole function suiting
With forms to his conceit? And all for nothing?
For Hecuba! (2.2.503–10)

In its egotism, the gesture of going one better than any famous or imaginable grief might be called quixotic, if it were not bracketed by the self-recrimination of "O what a rogue and peasant slave am I" (2.2.502) and the rest of the soliloquy. No other revenge tragedy pursues an antiliterary strategy in quite this way. The repudiation of fiction is the path of Cervantine realism rather than quixotism itself: in *Hamlet* Shakespeare frequently seems to be engaged in a Cervantine exercise with the genre to which the play adheres, by saying that this is what a real revenge tragedy must be like.[52]

Hamlet, Hieronimo, Antonio all contemplate suicide—which is a strange idea of justice, since it amounts to taking revenge upon oneself. Such a severe turning against the self is common, however, in mourning. A momentary instance occurs at the end of Shakespeare's play when Horatio offers to take his own life. His gesture is hardly that of "an antique Roman" (5.2.320)—for whom Seneca indeed prescribed suicide under certain circumstances and which Shakespeare carefully represented in his plays from Plutarch—but simply of grief so new and sharply felt that Horatio identifies with his dying friend or is unwilling at that moment to survive him. Suicidal feelings are a familiar aspect of mourning for reasons both conscious and unconscious. Chiefly, the death of a loved or loving person deprives life of purpose in the first instance or comfort and safety in the second. But grief may also be colored with self-reproach when it is too late to make amends for real or imagined slights, and because it is possible to have sometimes willed the absence or death of those who were close to one: the actual death brings such failings and resentments home. The death of a member of the immediate family confers the inescapable knowledge of the survivor's own death, and identification is especially strong with persons of the same sex in the direct generational line—fathers and sons, mothers and daughters. When the death is that of a parent, the son or

[52] Hamlet and Don Quixote have been seen as two opposite types, notably by Ivan Turgenev: "Hamlet and Don Quixote—The Two Eternal Human Types," in *Shakespeare in Europe*, ed. Oswald LeWinter (New York: Meridian, 1963), 171–89.

daughter may undergo the loss of an ideal that may never have been consciously thought much about, or the loss of a sense of command. When the death is that of a child, the parent loses its chief hope of continuance through the family. In general considerations such as these are found the pathos of *Hamlet* as a sequel to *The Spanish Tragedy*—the loss of fathers complementing the loss of sons—or the tactical inclusion of both losses in *Antonio's Revenge*. In *Hamlet* itself the two conversions of loss to suicide are Ophelia's act and Hamlet's meditations. It is not necessary to argue, as in a Freudian analysis, that suicide originates in murderous impulses turned back on the self—it may be the other way around. In either event, the contemplation of revenge can relieve feelings against the self by redirecting them outward.

Freud's superior contribution to the study of *Hamlet* is not the classic Oedipal theory—though that theory did arise from a footnote to the section in *The Interpretation of Dreams* devoted to dreams of the deaths of persons close to one. The Oedipal interpretation as elaborated by Ernest Jones and others is one of many that take revenge as unanalyzable and regard Hamlet's delay as the problem; and even on those grounds it fails to explain very much.[53] Far more useful is Freud's "Mourning and Melancholia," in which he drew upon the accepted and recognizable behavior of mourning to help explain the nature of melancholia, or what is usually called depression today. The original difference in the two states, he thought, is that in mourning the object-loss is conscious but in melancholia it is not. Furthermore, "in mourning it is the world which has become poor and empty; in melancholia it is the ego itself." On this definition of the two, only melancholia poses "a problem which is hard to solve"—namely, the process by which reproaches against the object become reproaches against the self.[54] But Freud's paper reveals as much about mourning as the condition he sets out to investigate. If the argument has a weakness, it is that the two states are not as distinguishable as he seemed to think.[55]

In mourning the identity of the deceased may be known, for example, without a full consciousness of the extent of the loss. In mourning the ego does not always escape reproach, for reasons that I have just enumerated— or as one might gather from Hieronimo:

[53] See above, note 9, and Ernest Jones, *Hamlet and Oedipus* (1949; rpt. New York: Norton, 1976). Avi Erlich, *Hamlet's Absent Father* (Princeton: Princeton University Press, 1977), 20–25, states succinctly what is wrong with the Freud-Jones reading, though some of Erlich's readings of *Hamlet* seem just as indefensible.
[54] Freud, "Mourning and Melancholia" (1917), *Standard Edition* 14:246, 247.
[55] See Lidz, *Hamlet's Enemy*, 195–209; and Kirsch, "Hamlet's Grief," 22–24 (note 3 above).

> Oh eyes! no eyes, but fountains fraught with tears;
> Oh life! no life, but lively form of death;
> Oh world! no world, but mass of public wrongs,
> Confus'd and fill'd with murder and misdeeds.[56]

The opening quatrain of Hieronimo's soliloquy is thus precisely divided between the ego and the world, and he and other revengers are much given to self-reproach—the melancholic Hamlet only more so, perhaps. According to Freud, the question of how long mourning should last corresponds to the uncertainty of melancholia; both conditions, as it happens, pass "after a certain time has elapsed without leaving traces of gross changes," though we do not understand the economics of the lifting of depression any more than we do the cessation of grief. "Mourning and Melancholia" is important for the subsequent development of Freud's thought because of its postulation of a "critical agency" that judges the rest of the ego. "What we are here becoming acquainted with is the agency commonly called 'conscience,'" he writes. Though Freud refers to Hamlet only parenthetically in his paper, many sentences read as if he were deeply impressed by Shakespeare's play. The melancholic patient merely "has a keener eye for the truth than other people"![57]

If Freudian theory is an epitome of modernism, as some historians believe, *Hamlet* is a very modern play. Shakespeare's revenge tragedy differs from others not only in the more meditative cast of its hero's mind but in its psychology. Hamlet's grief is to a certain extent pathological. It has passed beyond what Freud conceives as normal mourning to leave him stricken with melancholy, then as now regarded as an illness of the mind. Apparently Shakespeare was interested enough in the condition to have read at least one contemporary medical work, Timothy Bright's *A Treatise of Melancholie* of 1586.[58] The audience's first idea of this complication stems

[56] Kyd, *The Spanish Tragedy*, 3.2.1–4.

[57] Freud, "Mourning and Melancholia," 252, 247, 246. In his headnote to the paper, 240, James Strachey quotes at length from draft N of the Fliess papers, dated 31 May 1897, where Freud first writes of something like the Oedipus complex; about half the ideas broached in that passage—hostility to parents, "distrust of rulers and monarchs," mourning and self-reproach upon the death of a parent, hysterical behavior, and even "the idea of retribution"—recall *Hamlet*.

[58] John Dover Wilson summed up the case for Shakespeare's knowledge of Bright's *Treatise* in an appendix to *What Happens in "Hamlet,"* 3rd ed. (1951; rpt. Cambridge: Cambridge University Press, 1961), 309–20. In the same year, Lawrence Babb, in *The Elizabethan Malady: A Study of Melancholia in English Literature from 1580 to 1642* (East Lansing: Michigan State University Press, 1951), 106–10, dismissed the need for any such specific knowledge. "To Elizabethan playgoers Hamlet's melancholy would seem quite sufficient explanation for his

from the concern of Hamlet's mother and stepfather and subsequently Ophelia's report of his behavior (if he was not putting her on); but Hamlet is himself conscious of it: "I have of late, but wherefore I know not, lost all my mirth, foregone all custom of exercises," and he remarks how "it goes so heavily with my disposition" that the world seems changed to him (2.2.280–91). The word "melancholy" is used twice in the play, by Hamlet and by the king. At the close of his Hecuba speech—in soliloquy, lest we should think he is just making this up—he wonders whether the devil has taken advantage of "my weakness and my melancholy" by appearing in the shape of his father's ghost (2.2.551–6). In the following scene, Claudius worries that "there's something in his soul / O'er which his melancholy sits on brood" (3.1.158–9). What makes these speculations still seem current today is the clinical atmosphere of much of the action. Rosencrantz and Guildenstern are spies, of course, but they are also health workers, employed to "glean / Whether aught to us unknown afflicts him thus, / That opened lies within our remedy" (2.2.16–8). The play's most determined investigator, Polonius, is not pursuing crime or conspiracy, after all, but a psychological explanation. Mistakenly—though the false positions he has forced on his daughter may have had their effect—Polonius diagnoses love melancholy, a different cause for the patient's symptoms. But indications are, as Gertrude recognizes, that Hamlet's melancholy has been brought on by his father's death and her remarriage.

Most Seeming Virtue and Grief's Insincerity

Two ambivalences pose grave difficulties for the interpretation of *Hamlet* and at the same time teach certain hard truths about loss and mourning. The first is the question of Gertrude's infidelity to her first husband, which so wretchedly moves her son and provokes—the more so if it prompts his behavior to Ophelia—the hero's worst moral showing. The bitter irony of

---

procrastination" (109). Paul A. Jorgensen, in "Hamlet's Therapy," *Huntington Library Quarterly* 27 (1964), 239–58, may have been the first Shakespearean to place Freud alongside the sixteenth-century authorities on the disease. Bridget Gellert Lyons, *Voices of Melancholy: Studies in literary treatments of melancholy in Renaissance England* (London: Routledge, 1971), 77–112, makes so thorough an application to *Hamlet* that one comes to believe the play is about melancholy. As for Hamlet's thoughts of suicide, the propensity of some persons suffering from depression to commit suicide has been recognized from ancient and medieval times: see Stanley W. Jackson, *Melancholia and Depression: From Hippocratic Times to Modern Times* (New Haven: Yale University Press, 1986), 32, 72, 92. Jackson, 78–115, provides summaries of treatises on melancholy in Shakespeare's time, including Bright, from a perspective of late twentieth-century psychiatry.

the ghost sets the tone. The ghost's words simply do not make clear whether he is accusing his wife of adultery during his lifetime or after. He both condemns her entire sex outright and wishes not to disturb her peace of mind, unless conscience should "prick and sting her." Whether or not beastly adultery and incest awaited his death, it may be that his queen could not be seduced but for his brother's "witchcraft." When he refers to her as his "most seeming virtuous queen," it is hard to know which word he stresses (1.5.88,43,46). Hamlet's confusion on the same score is certainly not less than that of his late father's. The second ambivalence, however, is that of the hero's own heart: the question raised by the play whether the son's mourning for his father is wholly sincere. This ambivalence cannot be attributed altogether to character, since it is also a matter of Hamlet's feelings and situation.

We have noted the tendency of revengers to think of suicide, but what about their propensity—and the tendency of revenge plays themselves—to dwell on women's sexual infidelity? Indeed, given the standard folklore about widows, it would hardly require a ghost or a psychoanalyst to start a young man worrying about his deprived mother's sexual life. At least since Bradley, students of *Hamlet* have generally acknowledged that the hero is more disturbed by his mother's remarriage than by his father's death.[59] Even after the ghost claims that the death was unnatural, Hamlet is arguably more concerned with sexuality than with fratricide. But the pattern of Elizabethan revenge tragedy should serve as a check on character criticism here, including psychoanalytic criticism. *The Spanish Tragedy*, though the main action is mourning and revenge for the death of a son, still introduces doubts of sexual choice and fidelity. *Titus Andronicus* introduces more doubt, in the rivalry of two brothers for Lavinia and in the fatal weakness of Saturninus for the adulteress Tamora. In *Antonio's Revenge*, Piero falsely impugns the honor of his daughter Mellida to prevent Antonio's marriage and also expects to marry the hero's mother, whose widowhood he has brought about by murdering Andrugio. The subject is a large one, since adultery plays such a prominent part in the Greek tragedy of Agamemnon, for example, in the Spanish honor plays of the period, and notoriously in the (male) honor code of all periods, including our own. The aim of interpretation might be to understand *Hamlet* as a fiction that discovers adultery in the context of mourning and revenge, or to ask ourselves whether, if Gertrude had not hastily married her brother-in-law, she still might be suspected of infidelity.

[59] A. C. Bradley, *Shakespearean Tragedy* (1904; rpt. New York: Meridian, 1955), 100–103.

In terms of the modern conjugal family, Theodore Lidz outlines why Hamlet's disillusionment with his mother is so shattering for him. A son expects to take his father's place in this family, and whatever the son's feelings about his mother's sexuality may be, the father until his death makes it possible for the son not to dwell on the subject. In the patriarchal scheme of things, except for the father, no one has a greater stake in monogamy than a woman's son (or so he must believe). Then it is not hard to see why the occasion of the father's death should be a time for heightened demands and even suspicions of the mother.[60] The son may blame his mother for some disloyalty felt by himself at the same time that he officiously attempts to take charge of her affairs. In the first quarto of *Hamlet*, the hero chides his mother—"O mother, if ever you did my dear father love"—in virtually the same words with which the ghost has chided him—"Hamlet, if ever thou didst thy dear father love."[61] Though the echo might be scribal rather than Shakespearean, it is fully in harmony with Shakespeare's psychology. The influence of that psychology is such that it seems only natural to us that Hamlet would repeat the words he hears, or imagines he hears, his father speaking.

For a blunt statement of putative sexual infidelity in the context of death and mourning and revenge, and ultimately of inheritance, Shakespeare employs Laertes, who reappears on stage after the death of his father with a mob behind him, threatening revenge. "Where is this king?" he shouts, as if suddenly he had Hamlet's reasons to question the legitimacy of Claudius's rule, Hamlet's motive to stir a revolution. The queen, wary of violence, urges the young man to be calm, and he wildly replies:

> That drop of blood that's calm proclaims me bastard,
> Cries cuckold to my father, brands the harlot
> Even here, between the chaste unsmirched brow
> Of my true mother. (4.5.112,118–21)

Never mind that this is the sole admission in the play that Laertes and Ophelia had a mother. The parallel of the imagined infidelity to Hamlet's

---

[60] Lidz, *Hamlet's Enemy*, 50–54, 82–83. Cf. Jacqueline Rose, "Sexuality in the Reading of Shakespeare: *Hamlet* and *Measure for Measure*," in *Alternative Shakespeares*, ed. John Drakakis (London: Routledge, 1985), 102: "So what happens indeed to the sexuality of the woman when the husband dies, who is there to hold its potentially dangerous excess within the bounds of a fully social constraint?"

[61] Lines 1538 and 482 of Q1, as printed in the New Variorum *Hamlet*, ed. Horace Howard Furness, 2 vols. (1877; rpt. New York: Dover, 1963). I have modernized the spelling.

accusations of his mother is unmistakable, even to the recall of the latter's angry allusion to branding of her forehead:

> Such an act
> That blurs the grace and blush of modesty,
> Calls virtue hypocrite, takes off the rose
> From the fair forehead of an innocent love
> And sets a blister there, makes marriage vows
> As false as dicers' oaths.
>
> (3.4.40–5)

Freud takes note in "Mourning and Melancholia" of the surprising arrogance of some sufferers from depression, who "make the greatest nuisance of themselves, and always seem as though they felt slighted and had been treated with great injustice." According to Freud, "the reactions expressed in their behaviour still proceed from a constellation of revolt."[62] While Hamlet displays more than enough arrogance to his mother in act 3, Laertes' public outburst in act 4 is closer to this description. Angry over the death of his father, he reproduces one aspect of Hamlet's state of mind without Hamlet's melancholia—which will have lifted in any case when the latter returns in act 5. Meanwhile the compassionate king begins to counsel Laertes on mourning, much as he counseled Hamlet on the subject in act 1. "Laertes, was your father dear to you? / Or are you like the painting of a sorrow, / A face without a heart?" (4.7.106–8). The mere difference is that Claudius, who previously advised the early and peaceable cessation of mourning, now urges the satisfaction of carefully pondered revenge.

One does not need the extraordinarily sensitive characterizations in the play, or the dreamlike aspect of making one character speak for another at times, to be struck by the argument of those four lines on a drop of blood that are given to Laertes. And when Shakespeare deliberately condenses the argument and renders it vulgar, he invites us to reconsider the entire fiction that is *Hamlet*. Laertes is saying that if he were able to be calm about the death of his father (a death that is, like the death of Hamlet's father, ambiguously accident or murder), he would not be his father's son. He states this convoluted argument (so much as a drop of calmness adulterating the blood imputes the adultery of his mother) with the extremity of the code of honor that Hamlet, in the second quarto text, has likened to the "eggshell" or "straw" for which entire armies struggle and die (4.4.47–56). And what it all comes down to is that the death of a father, merely his

---

[62] Freud, "Mourning and Melancholia," *Standard Edition*, 14:248.

death, raises the doubt of the mother's fidelity, since the son is born of woman and has only his mother's chaste marriage to guarantee his patrimony. People of Shakespeare's time may have been more sharply aware of this aspect of inheritance than we are, yet the basic assumptions about the family are the same as those appealed to by Lidz. With the words "even here," the actor playing Laertes pathetically clutches or points to his own forehead. Still more pathetically, Laertes is talked out of his passion by Claudius. In this doubling of the action, Shakespeare is surely defending the deeper intellectual grasp of Hamlet, which Coleridge and others have thought to be the defect of his character.

The concern with sexual infidelity receives greater play in *Hamlet* than in the revenge tragedies most nearly resembling it. The plot inherited from Saxo and Belleforest promises that Gertrude's remarriage will remain an integral part of the action, and this interest is sustained in the working out of Hamlet's relation to Ophelia and then fulfilled by the emotional closet scene, the turning point of the action. Granted that by naming the turning point one fits the play to a certain interpretation; but in the previous chapter I have already given some grounds for attending more closely to the closet scene. Notoriously, insisting on the play scene raises even more questions about Hamlet's and Claudius's subsequent behavior.[63] One claim of the play scene to be the center of the action is simply the ritual that unfolds there: as in 1.2 and 5.2, virtually the full cast is present. The opposing claim of the closet scene is its terrible intimacy: the parallel here is to the shorter interview with the ghost in 1.5. In the earlier one-on-one confrontation of the play, the father towers over the son. In the agonizing recapitulation, the son taunts the mother, but is still young Hamlet in the presence of his parent.

In a recent book on *Hamlet*, William Kerrigan calls this scene the "greatest" in the play, and presumptively the greatest in Shakespeare. What is particularly impressive, in Kerrigan's view, is the way Hamlet's anger and passionate entreaty are deeply, almost simply, based in family experience. It is nighttime, and the scene between mother and child is freighted with the very cares and blessings ordinarily exchanged before sleep, then and now. Kerrigan adds that "when someone was bade good night in the English Renaissance, he was wished protection against ghosts and demons, sleeplessness and bad dreams, attacks of guilty conscience and fits of

---

[63] For an argument that the play and closet scenes constitute a double center, see Alastair Fowler, "The Plays within the Play of *Hamlet*," in *"Fanned and Winnowed Opinions": Shakespearean Essays Presented to Harold Jenkins*, ed. John W. Mahon and Thomas A. Pendleton (London: Methuen, 1987), 166–83.

mourning, his criminality and that of others, death and damnation." The "good night" we exchange with others today, particularly those charged with our love or protection, still expresses warning as well as blessing. The phrase for parting at night is repeated by Hamlet five times before he is done: "Good night—but go not to my uncle's bed"; "Once more good night, / And when you are desirous to be blessed, / I'll blessing beg of you"; "So again, good night"; "Mother, good night"; and finally, "Good night mother" (3.4.160,171–3,178,214,218). Kerrigan does not insist that the practice, learned by all from childhood, now marks a turning point in *Hamlet*; but he observes that "the reconstitution of a family dispersed by villainy, misrecognition, and ill fortune is always the end-point in Shakespearean romance," and that after this scene "the ghost never appears again, as if it were in some manner already satisfied." And he is mindful also of Horatio's "Good night sweet prince" (5.2.338), in parting from Hamlet at the end.[64]

It is never clear what the assembled court of Denmark makes of *The Murder of Gonzago* and the ensuing commotion. The queen herself never refers to what has happened there after her line, "Hamlet, thou hast thy father much offended." In rejoining, "Mother, you have my father much offended" (3.4.9–10), Hamlet wrenches from her the appelation "father," reverses its denotation, and their quarrel commences—"with an almost childish lack of dignity," as Granville-Barker remarks.[65] The quarrel is that of a very bad moment in family life. Suddenly one person is blurting out how he actually feels, and the deep reticences of this particular family become terrible innuendos. Since only one of the participants *is* a child—the grown child of the other—thrilling and all too cruel rebellion is in the air. Hamlet's innuendos about murder and direct assault on his mother's choice, his insinuations of lust coupled with scorn for her age, his very appeal to her judgment while insulting her intelligence, are not easily to be forgotten, and they strike home: "Oh speak to me no more. / These words like daggers enter in my ears. / No more sweet Hamlet" (3.4.94–6). But there is more—in this the only frank confrontation with either his mother or stepfather until Hamlet finds himself mortally wounded and stabs back at the end.

The closet scene can be thought of as the skewed outcome of the play about Gonzago, Baptista, and Lucianus: skewed, that is, because while Hamlet is still at large and Claudius is left praying undisturbed, Gertrude

[64] William Kerrigan, *Hamlet's Perfection* (Baltimore: Johns Hopkins University Press, 1994), 34–62, 114–15.

[65] Harley Granville-Barker, *Prefaces to Shakespeare*, 2 vols. (1930; rpt. London: Batsford, 1958), 1:102.

bears the brunt of her son's anger, grief, and imagination. When he physically frightens her, and she, motherlike, scolds him for striking through the arras, Hamlet accuses *her* of killing her first husband and marrying with his brother. The sudden equivalence of a wife's unfaithfulness with murder, the unfair equation of Gertrude with the murderer Claudius, is neither what the ghost has told Hamlet nor what Claudius has revealed by crying "Give me some light. Away!" (3.2.244). Rather, this is the lesson learned from the player queen's righteousness about second marriages—the lesson authorized for the stage by Hamlet, from the character who his mother believes protests too much. "In second husband let me be accurst: / None wed the second but who killed the first"; and "A second time I kill my husband dead / When second husband kisses me in bed" (3.2.160–1, 165–6). Since kissing in bed is exactly the kind of thing Hamlet is about to discuss with his mother, it is worth remembering that the murder talked about by his player queen is figurative only: she and the player king are discussing at the time the prospect of his natural death. The issue arises in a conversation about a husband who, whether because of age or illness, after thirty years of marriage (3.2.136–41), warns his wife that he is likely to predecease her. As in the play of *Hamlet*, first natural death is the issue and then unaccountably the king becomes the victim of murder, the queen of seduction: first we are treated to the commonplace, then—as if experimentally—to a violent dramatization. Baptista only speaks of killing first husbands, just as Hamlet subsequently intends to speak rather than use daggers upon his mother. Murder is metaphor—but in the event, in both plays, it is metonymy, and the extreme case.

Hamlet may be summoned by Gertrude in furtherance of Polonius's scheme, but the closet scene unfolds as an interrogation of his elders. The occasion in a deep sense turns out to be his opportunity to ask his mother just what she had in mind by marrying Claudius. In truth, the ghost of his father seems to have prompted the entire discomforting scene by counter-suggestion, with his "Taint not thy mind, nor let thy soul contrive / Against thy mother aught" (1.5.85–6). What could be more inviting, when she is the one person who might have a clue to this family business? Hamlet's mind is already tainted with melancholy and disgust with his mother's behavior when the ghost issues this warning, so it is perhaps not surprising that he takes it upon himself to prick and sting her when the time comes. The confrontation, however, displays Hamlet's consciousness rather than hers. The queen's angry "What have I done" and "what act" (3.4.39,51) give no measure of her actual feeling; even the innocence that her demands imply is purely reactive. Shakespeare chooses not to give her point of view, desirable as that might be for her son to know. Belleforest, it is worth noting, at this juncture does narrate some of the queen's thought, even if it is mostly pious moralizing.[66] In the first quarto's closet scene, the queen explicitly denies knowledge of the murder and promises to assist her son's revenge, but the audience is still not privileged to know what she is thinking: that version just seems very perfunctory, poor theater.[67] In the folio and second quarto texts, however, only a subtle pantomime makes Gertrude's position known. Until now in the play she has entered the stage at the side of her second husband, but later she will be linked with Ophelia and even, familiarly, with Hamlet in the end.[68]

Gertrude's close-mouthedness, in truth, is her character. It becomes a sort of trademark, permitting us to infer sensuality if we wish but hardly to deny her capacity for sense. On the cause of Hamlet's distemper, she is firm: "I doubt it is no other but the main: / His father's death, and our o'erhasty marriage." Dwelling among men of many words, she calls for "More matter with less art," without feeling the compunction to complete a sentence (2.2.56–7,95). At Ophelia's funeral she speaks belatedly, "I hoped thou shouldst have been my Hamlet's wife" (5.1.211). Such a woman as this does not see ghosts, and when her son claims to see one she can assure him that "This bodiless creation ecstasy / Is very cunning in" (3.4.139–40). But with Hamlet it is the very opposite: he does the talking in the closet scene and cringes before the ghost, which here more than ever appears to be the coinage of his brain. Hamlet the father walks on, as many have noted, just when Hamlet his son is countering his expressed wish that he should leave his mother to heaven.[69]

Some large ironies of body and spirit pervade this scene. Polonius has been the persistent instigator of the interview of mother and son—this is

[66] See Gollancz, 206–9, 218–19; also Bullough, 7:94–95, 98. Saxo makes no such attempt to tell Gerutha's thoughts. (See chapter 1, notes 4 and 2.)

[67] See lines 1532–33, 1544–47 of Q1, in Furness (note 54 above).

[68] Ellen J. O'Brien, "Revision by Excision: Rewriting Gertrude," *Shakespeare Survey* 45, ed. Stanley Wells (Cambridge: Cambridge University Press, 1993), 27–35.

[69] The behavior of Hamlet himself in 3.4 is consistent, when it comes to that, with his mere imagining of the ghost's words in 1.5. Apart from his own premonitions, Hamlet has two reasons to believe that Claudius killed his father: the word of the ghost and Claudius's behavior in the play scene. But instead of conveying these reasons to his mother, he speaks as indirectly and ironically as ever. To her shocked question at his killing of Polonius, he replies, "Almost as bad, good mother, / As kill a king and marry with his brother" (3.4.28–29). To her question "What have I done," he replies with such extravagant indirection that she can only repeat, "what act." At which point he launches into a less than spontaneous comparison of her two husbands. Marry that uncle is what she has done; at least, all he finally accuses her of is going from Hamlet senior to his brother as bed partner.

the scene he has been preparing at least since the twelfth century. And unlike the schemes Shakespeare has added to the part, this one—after Polonius's removal for good—eventuates in a profound revelation of Hamlet's state of mind: his anger and bewilderment, hurt and resentment, love and frustration, impertinence and command, to say nothing of his foolishness or madness. So thoroughly engaged are mother and son in the quarrel they have both picked, that the killing of Polonius scarce gives them pause. After his unexpected cry for reinforcements, "What ho! Help, help, help!" (3.4.23), it takes no more than ten lines to be rid of him and get back to business. But neither Hamlet nor the stage is yet rid of Polonius's body, and there is also the problem of how to play, or interpret, Hamlet senior's ghost. Neither father, Ophelia and Laertes' or Hamlet's, has a long part to speak in the closet scene. The ghost has only six lines to Polonius's seven; after both interruptions the dialogue conducted by Hamlet with his mother reknits itself and carries right along without them. The two dead fathers, in their different ways, are finished by 3.4.

But the fathers are not easy to play for all that. Physically, the actor playing Polonius has the harder part, since he is on stage from the opening line of the scene, "A will come straight. Look you lay home to him" (3.4.1), until the close, and the folio's stage direction, "Exit Hamlet tugging in Polonius" (3.4.218f). Once Hamlet has thrust through the arras and killed him, every production must decide what to do with the body in the meantime. I have already intimated what a difference that body makes for the alteration in dramatic irony and Hamlet's attitude in the graveyard and duel scenes. The disposal problem was addressed by Saxo and Belleforest too—as it must be addressed in life, if usually in less lurid ways. For the space of thirty-six lines between two other stage directions, "Enter Ghost" and "Exit Ghost" (3.4.101f,137f), there are two dead fathers on stage. Though the ghost pronounces "Do not forget," and "This visitation / Is but to whet thy almost blunted purpose," Hamlet anticipates him by speaking first; the son begins, "Do you not come," and the father echoes, "Do not forget."[70] The ghost's remaining four lines are strictly impromptu and conclude helplessly, "Speak to her, Hamlet" (3.4.106–14)—as if recalling a line he once overheard, "Thou art a scholar, speak to it Horatio" (1.1.42). The only concern Hamlet senior shows is for Gertrude. He then falls silent until, in his son's words, he "steals away" (3.4.135).[71]

[70] Cf. William Kerrigan, *Hamlet's Perfection*, 54.

[71] Cf. Barbara Everett, *Young Hamlet: Essays on Shakespeare's Tragedies* (Oxford: Clarendon, 1989), 126: "The Ghost is a presence that fades. And this fading of the Ghost is a part of the narrative of *Hamlet*, a play which offers such temporal changes and transformations as simply

All this while, Polonius has not stolen away but remains where he is, to be tugged in at the scene's close. While the family quarrel of Hamlet with his mother rages in the foreground, in the background is a sort of tableau: a crossing between the vertical and the horizontal of the play's two dead fathers. *Hamlet* contrasts two ways of imagining the dead: the difference between the ways we choose to see, or cannot help seeing, some deaths and not others. Hamlet senior lives in his son's memory, his grief, his anger, his cynicism, and thoughts of revenge, but Polonius has become pure dead weight—a body for the rotting, as mentioned or recurred to relentlessly in the rest of the play. Neither the hero aware of the ghost nor the mother incredulous can do much about that old familiar, but with this other deceased person they can do very much as they like—poke him with their feet, check his pulse, cover him with a blanket if necessary. The presence of this second father and sometime husband is positively liberating for the young man who killed him—a freedom that is nicely symbolized by the vertical father's stealing away forever. Hamlet's father's ghost may have put in this last appearance not to spur Hamlet on (as both seem to think), or to halt the tongue-lashing (as his concern for his wife betrays), but from awe at what Hamlet has just done. If anything has changed the hero and prepared him to accept death, it is not just having it out with his mother but taking a life with his own hand.[72]

Though handing out death clears a space around Hamlet, it destroys Ophelia, swiftly overtakes Rosencrantz and Guildenstern, and culminates in the overkill at the end of the play. None of the four corpses strewn about the stage after the fencing match threatens to walk again, except as the actors make their ways homeward; they are dead as Polonius is dead—or almost, since Shakespeare perhaps makes an exception for the soul of young Hamlet.[73] The final tableau of the final scene of *Hamlet* has become some-

---

an aspect of the real that we know. The Ghost is first a royal presence coming to the waiting sentries; and then he is a great shadow of a loved father burdening the son with dread; and then a devil in the cellarage, friendly and bad; and finally a man in a dressing-gown whose wife cannot even see him. In the Closet Scene the Ghost stays just long enough to make us realize that we had almost forgotten him. After it, Hamlet Senior is neither present nor missed, and there is no word of him at the end of the play."

[72] This is not a happy thought, but Hamlet has his defense ready and he enjoys the privilege of a prince. William Empson, "Hamlet When New," *Sewanee Review* 61 (1953), 15–42, 185–205, notes several times that Hamlet never loses class. "This emphasis on style rather than on one's incidental murders seems now madly egotistical, but it would then appear as consistently princely behavior" (40).

[73] Cf. Braden, *Renaissance Tragedy and the Senecan Tradition*, 222: "No other English avenger, indeed no other Shakespearean character, dies with such a sense of attained grace." Braden cites Horatio's "Good night sweet prince, / And flights of angels sing thee to thy rest"

thing of a popular joke about the theater, just because the play is so famous and so finalizing. Besides the ethical and political recuperation called for by tragedy, the long play has generated some reasons of its own for requiring an emphatic conclusion. One is that which Harry Levin handily summarized as its rhetoric of interrogation, doubt, and irony.[74] Another is the indefinite duration of mourning, fueled by that within which passes show. And still another is the troublesome and troubling insincerity of mourning, more especially the mourning of the young for the old. The ghost of a father has intruded upon Hamlet with crushing weight, or the son would not be melancholic. Yet the ghost has asked to be remembered and revenged in the name of love, and will not be dismissed as merely intrusive, like Polonius. It is not that the various extremes of grief represented in the play have to be admonished by the tragedy, as Campbell suggested, but that the uncertainties of grief—Hamlet's, Laertes', and Ophelia's—must come to an end.

"Heaven and earth, / Must I remember?" (1.2.142–3). As Granville-Barker noted, in Hamlet's first soliloquy "there is already something of that flogging of the will which is to be so manifest later."[75] It may be shocking but is hardly unlikely that mourning should be partly insincere, if only in the consciousness of the mourner that he or she is still alive. Grief, it might be said, can never be truly sincere except if its Horatio-like gestures toward suicide are completed. The trick of mourning is to remember in order to forget, and to learn to live with the contradiction between living and the other's dying. Particularly, therefore, when it is the task of the younger generation to mourn, this contradiction must be felt, since in the normal course of things sons and daughters expect to outlive parents. The bias of Shakespeare's *Hamlet* on the side of youth entails such insincerity in much greater degree than *The Spanish Tragedy*; Hieronimo and Isabella's loss is of their hope in part, for the family that should live after them. Thinking about revenge does not resolve the seeming contradiction. Swearing revenge, as is customary in this genre, may be another symptom of flogging the will, since it should not be necessary to swear to a straightforward intention. "Am I a coward?" (2.2.523): Hamlet comes to ask this of himself, yet he has sworn.

On the stages of revenge tragedy, actors represent avengers who are themselves actors—dissemblers and experimenters with roles. A number

---

(5.2.338–39). On the play's apparent contradictions when it comes to unshriven deaths, see Bradshaw, *Shakespeare's Scepticism*, 121–23.

[74] Harry Levin, *The Question of Hamlet* (1959; rpt. New York: Viking, 1961).

[75] Granville-Barker, *Prefaces to Shakespeare*, 1:154.

of students of the genre, from very different points of view, have sensitively approached this doubleness. Bridget Gellert Lyons places her emphasis on an affinity of melancholia for theater: "Hamlet's playing of a great variety of stereotyped melancholy parts, for example, is itself symptomatic of a character who refuses to be identified entirely with any of the roles that he plays, and whose real melancholy is made evident through the evasiveness and aggressive wit with which he manipulates such roles."[76] Gordon Braden attributes the capacity of the character to stand aloof from the role more positively to stoicism: in Hieronimo, for example, "Kyd presents the drama of a selfhood separated from the world by the passion of its involvement in it, of a selfhood conscious that all such involvement is in some important dimension distant and incomplete: like an actor playing a role."[77] Peter Mercer takes note of the acting of revenge in plays by Seneca, Kyd, Marston, and Tourneur, then relies on Shakespeare to show how "in acting—the performance of a fiction—revenge loses indeed the name of action."[78] And John Kerrigan invokes a host of authorities, from Aristotle to Roland Barthes, to suggest why revenge tragedy imposes the role of actor on the hero. Basically, the hero is forced to adopt a role because the task—to redress the wrong done to someone else, "a raped mistress or murdered father"—comes upon him uninvited. Yet the peculiar mechanism of revenge itself demands a show: "The avenger reflects upon what has been done in order to reflect what has been done. His killings are distinguished from common murder by the sign, the evidence of their fittingness. Hence the impulse to display, where the murderer's urge is to conceal."[79] Each of these scholars would probably agree with Harold Bloom that Hamlet is the finest—and the strangest—actor of them all. Bloom is "struck by the varied and perpetual ways in which Hamlet keeps *overhearing himself speak*" and keeps changing as a consequence. "Hamlet is something radically new, even for and in Shakespeare: his theatricality is dangerously nihilistic because it is so paradoxically *natural* to him."[80]

The author of the *Ur-Hamlet* presumably altered the narrative of Amleth's revenge to make the uncle's murder a secret crime of poisoning. The alteration enhanced the capacity of *Hamlet* to explore thoughts of revenge

[76] Lyons, *Voices of Melancholy*, 78.

[77] Braden, *Renaissance Tragedy and the Senecan Tradition*, 214–15; see also 26–27.

[78] Peter Mercer, *"Hamlet" and the Acting of Revenge* (Iowa City: University of Iowa Press, 1987), 7.

[79] John Kerrigan, *Revenge Tragedy*, 12–20.

[80] Harold Bloom, *Shakespeare: The Invention of the Human* (New York: Riverhead, 1998), 423–24.

rather than the politics of succession, say, while it preserved various practical motives for the hero's acting of a part. But more importantly, Shakespeare could dramatize the private and necessarily hidden nature of mourning. In the words of Antonio, in Marston's revenge tragedy, "grief's invisible / And lurks in secret angles of the heart."[81] Not all grief is invisible, perhaps, but very often those tendencies of grief that are in one way or another outwardly unacceptable. And these include—especially in the loss of a parent—feelings of vulnerability, the knowledge of one's own death, as well as relief or gladness, self-blame for past behavior and present feelings, the comparison of the living and the dead, and conceivably thoughts of murder. Revenge then replicates rather than resolves the secret contradictions of mourning. It is not only that revenge demands a life, thus undercutting the principal value for which it is undertaken (two deaths do not make a life), but that the demand for revenge is made in the name of love. The revenge in question in these murderous plays is not for a direct injury to oneself, but for the fatal injury to a friend or member of the family, and its expressed motive is love. *The Spanish Tragedy* makes the point repeatedly in the keening of Hieronimo, who chides himself for not loving his son enough, and in the demands of the ghost and Bel-imperia for revenge. "Awake, Revenge! If love—as love hath had— / Have yet the power or prevalence in hell!" cries the ghost of Andrea, and the following scene opens with Bel-imperia's scolding, "Is this the love thou bear'st Horatio? / Is this the kindness that thou counterfeits?"[82] The supernatural agent thus relishes the opposed emotions, while the heroine unhelpfully insists that the hero prove his sincerity. The ghost in *Hamlet* puts the case in similar terms: "If thou didst ever thy dear father love"—and his conditional "if . . . ever" is so understated as to give the son no space for denial. As Harold Goddard protests, the ghost contends against the hero's dedication to life and "pronounces 'most foul' even the act he is urging on his son."[83]

Yet that ghost is effectively exorcised from the play once he has stolen away in the closet scene, especially so in the folio text of *Hamlet*, in which the hero's soliloquy on his "dull revenge" (4.4.33) is dropped along with his encounter with Fortinbras's army. Pointedly Hamlet's father does not materialize again like Andrugio in the last scene of *Antonio's Revenge*, to applaud the carefully choreographed stabbing of Piero: " 'Tis done; and now my soul shall sleep in rest. / Sons that revenge their father's blood

[81] Marston, *Antonio's Revenge*, 2.2.71–72.

[82] Kyd, *The Spanish Tragedy*, 3.15.12–13, 4.1.1–2.

[83] Harold C. Goddard, *The Meaning of Shakespeare*, 2 vols. (1951; rpt. Chicago: University of Chicago Press, 1967), 1:349.

are blest."[84] Shakespeare has not only rid his play of its ghost but mainly illuminated the ways in which sons and daughters mourning their fathers are not blest. In act 4 he concentrates on Ophelia and Laertes. Claudius, the brother who has shrink-wrapped his own grief in a single concessive clause and wisely mixed it with "remembrance of ourselves" (1.2.7), patiently explains to Laertes that love and mourning are subject to time.

> Not that I think you did not love your father,
> But that I know love is begun by time,
> And that I see, in passages of proof,
> Time qualifies the spark and fire of it.   (4.7.109–12)

Love in *Hamlet* is the given that governs mourning—as it governs revenge, Claudius's next topic.

The king makes assiduous use of the argument that the player king urged upon the player queen, to encourage her to remarry after his death. That argument is also about love over time, and how "Purpose is but the slave to memory," for "What to ourselves in passion we propose, / The passion ending, doth the purpose lose" (3.2.169,175–6). Gonzago, of course, is raising the possibility of new love after mourning, whereas Claudius employs a similar argument to hurry on Laertes to kill before his thoughts turn to life once more. Critics of *Hamlet* usually claim that both dialogues— admittedly preachy, a bit long-winded—glance indirectly at Hamlet's problem of purpose and action, as they undoubtedly do: he is another mourner, after all. But just as remarkably the dialogues are about what must happen to love when death comes. In the second quarto, Claudius continues:

> There lives within the very flame of love
> A kind of wick or snuff that will abate it,
> And nothing is at a like goodness still,
> For goodness, growing to a plurisy,
> Dies in his own too much. That we would do,
> We should do when we would, for this "would" changes,
> And hath abatements and delays as many
> As there are tongues, are hands, are accidents;
> And then this "should" is like a spendthrift sigh,
> That hurts by easing.

[84] Marston, *Antonio's Revenge*, 5.3.114–15.

Possibly the lines were cut in the folio version just because of the references to delay when this is no longer an issue in the play. The folio picks up the earlier text of the speech again with:

> Hamlet comes back; what would you undertake
> To show yourself in deed your father's son
> More than in words? (4.7.113–25)

At which point Laertes offers to cut Hamlet's throat in the church. Clearly Shakespeare finds love that requires a death—and soon, before love dies— a more troubling proposition than Claudius's apt pupil finds it. Instead of composing more soliloquies for his own pupil Hamlet, however, he puts before the audience an alternative from which Hamlet's unease can be inferred. By means of this contrast, the dramatist suggests the virtues of a spendthrift sigh.

Before the end of the scene in which Laertes burst in with his "Where is this king" and "Give me my father," Claudius has decided the track he must take: "Laertes, I must commune with your grief" (4.5.112,117,197)— with the result we have noted. That scene is still more memorable for the two entrances of Ophelia, first to Gertrude alone, joined by the king, then to her brother as well. The mere fact of her singing at court, apart from how she behaves and sings, marks Ophelia as having lost control of herself; and throughout the shifting interpretations of her madness over four centuries most audiences have grieved for her as well as with her.[85] Characteristically, it is Claudius who makes the diagnosis, treating her like a child but instantly understanding her speech as "Conceit upon her father." As she goes out again, with unintended irony he explains that grief is a kind of poison (it is the one metaphorical use of the word in *Hamlet*): "Oh this is the poison of deep grief, it springs / All from her father's death." And as Claudius counts the battalions of sorrows that have come down upon him and Gertrude, he makes the sort of gendered discrimination about Ophelia's loss that the play itself does in registering her reactions. According to him, in missing her father Ophelia has become "Divided from herself and her fair judgement" (4.5.45,74–5,84).

Ophelia sings a medley of sadly bawdy folk ballad and lament, with the latter clearly predominating in her second appearance:

---

[85] F. W. Sternfeld, *Music in Shakespearean Tragedy* (London: Routledge, 1963), 54–57; Elaine Showalter, "Representing Ophelia," in *Shakespeare and the Question of Theory*, ed. Patricia Parker and Geoffrey Hartman (1985; rpt. New York: Routledge, 1991), 77–94.

They bore him bare-faced on the bier
Hey non nonny, nonny, hey nonny,
And in his grave rained many a tear

—which would seem to apply to Polonius. Then:

And will a not come again?
And will a not come again?
No, no, he is dead,
Go to thy death-bed,
He will never come again

—which might apply to Hamlet as well. But the second and last stanza fixes the sense on death of fathers:

His beard was as white as snow,
All flaxen was his poll,
He is gone, he is gone,
And we cast away moan,
God-a-mercy on his soul.   (4.5.164–6,185–94)

The surrounding action of *Hamlet* must count for something in Ophelia's eroticized grieving, which has seemed more analyzable to some students of the play than to others. "Go to thy death-bed," she sings, "He will never come again": the young woman whom Hamlet has proleptically compared to Jephtha's daughter (2.2.368–76) laments her father's death and her own, and her virginity as well.[86] No psychoanalysis of the patient is necessary to make the basic observation that her grieving is for lost love. Her brother Laertes, though he is not especially sensitive in the advice tendered to his sister in 1.3, and though he professes surprise that the loss of a father could entail the loss of "a young maid's wits," nonetheless speaks simply of the role of love: "Nature is fine in love, and where 'tis fine, / It sends some precious instance of itself / After the thing it loves" (4.5.159,161–3).

It is a pity that Laertes is not a woman, since for all the condescension implicit in the sister's weakness and her fate, hers is the more attractive response to their father's death—attractive, that is, so long as Ophelia is a fiction, not one of our own sisters. And Hamlet, traditionally, has been thought to have more of the woman in him than Laertes has. An angry determination on revenge promises to rid the aggrieved one of pain by an

[86] Cf. Judges, 11:30–40. Jephtha's daughter asks, "Let this thing be done for me: let me alone two months, that I may go up and down upon the mountains, and bewail my virginity, I and my fellows" (37).

act of surprise, and of insincerity by excessive demonstration. Marston's ghost cites Seneca's Atreus on the general principle: "Scelera non ulciscere, nisi vincis"—crimes are not avenged unless they are exceeded.[87] By that definition revenge is not justice but something emotionally more demanding, and when revenge nevertheless pretends to justice it merely betrays a fresh insincerity. Profoundly entered into, the process of remembering a loved person teaches that justice cannot be realized. There is no other father but the one who has died, and no course of action that will return him to life—truths that may be generalized as a law of history, or the passing of time.

Death, more than birth, is sadly the human measure of time, since birth is never conscious to the individual being born and death is so much more certain. Death and killing hold greater sway in history also. I tend to agree with Hamlet that the killing of Polonius may be justified under the circumstances, and as the prince of Denmark he could get away with it more easily than he might today, or as a private person in Shakespeare's time. I have argued also that killing alters his perspective on death. If one also believes—and Hamlet states this, in the folio text, as a rhetorical question rather than a promise—that a hero would "be damned" who "let this canker of our nature come / In further evil" (5.2.68–70), then the killing of Claudius is justified. Even later times accept that death and its justification, which Hamlet expresses as a concern for his soul. *Hamlet* is a fiction, but one which reminds us of how often history witnesses to killing. History tells of whole armies that "fight for a plot . . . Which is not tomb enough and continent / To hold the slain" (4.4.62–5). Yet history offers many arguments that it may be a duty on the part of the living sometimes to kill.

The actions of very many tragedies, including *The Spanish Tragedy*, *Titus Andronicus*, *Antonio's Revenge*, and *Hamlet*, are framed by warfare yet unfold in peacetime, as if to examine the role—if any—of accepted forms of violence in the ordinary and accustomed days of life. In peacetime, acts that would be exalted in war are probably indivisible from a sense of guilt—though it has to be said that the story of Hamlet's guilt has changed radically over time. Wonderfully, by the nineteenth century, Hamlet rather than Claudius becomes the guilty party, as he is in the standard Freudian analysis of the play. Evidently *Hamlet* also led Freud, via his thoughts on mourning and melancholia and the conception of the superego, to a much wider view of psychological guilt associated with aggression.[88] A general

[87] Marston, *Antonio's Revenge*, 3.1.51. The axiom is from Seneca's *Thyestes*, 195–96.

[88] When Freud writes in *Civilization and Its Discontents* (1930) of his "intention to represent the sense of guilt as the most important problem in the development of civilization and to

sense of guilt has earlier religious foundations, an awareness of which is expressed—quite properly—by Claudius in the prayer scene. Hamlet's grief and melancholy, his meditations and bitter speeches, are caught up in the first three acts in the close atmosphere of revenge, but his personal tragedy is not finally separable from the great, and comparatively healthful epics that are representative of our civilization and yet portray heroes who are, in their fashion, as reluctant to act as is the prince of Denmark. I have in mind the careers not only of such famed killers as Achilles and Gunnar Hamundarson, but of pious Aeneas, and the way duty always seems fraught with death.[89] Mourning, if not melancholy, approaches something like a universal experience, in which members of a family realize their ties to one another, and individuals to history. It is now to history, as represented in the novel rather than epic, that I wish to turn. It seems that Shakespeare prepared Hamlet well for an unexpected role in modern history.

---

show that the price we pay for our advance in civilization is a loss of happiness through the heightening of the sense of guilt," he drops a footnote to the line, "Thus conscience does make cowards of us all" (3.1.83), which he can count on his readers recognizing without attribution. *Standard Edition*, 21:134.

[89] Brower, *Hero and Saint* (note 45 above), 315–16, makes the comparison to Achilles. Ronald Levao, *Renaissance Minds and Their Fictions: Cusanus, Sidney, Shakespeare* (Berkeley: University of California Press, 1985), 341–45, writes of Hamlet and Aeneas.

History, as between Goethe's
Hamlet and Scott's

R EVENGE AS THE REAL or imagined recourse of mourning has its human appeal, and the popularity of Shakespeare's *Hamlet* both attests to this appeal and very likely enhanced it. The conventions of revenge tragedy were not put to an end by the closing of the English theaters; some were reinvented for the Restoration stage, and *Hamlet* made its own way with, or was taken over by, European enterprises of widely different sorts. No composite work of the Enlightenment, for example, could be more imposing than Mozart and da Ponte's *Don Giovanni*, which owed its existence to another legendary hero altogether.[1] Yet the slaying of the commendatore in the first scene, which provides an impetus and gives a shape to the plot, produces a situation resembling that of the young Hamlet. The principal dramatic source, Tirso de Molina's *Burlador de Seville* of 1630, stages the murder halfway through the action, with little regard to mourning; the opera, however, has Dona Anna grieving for her father's death from the start, and throughout her determination on revenge is the means of fighting back her grief. The statue or ghost of the commendatore, armed cap-a-pie, then fuels Senecan expectations, the conflagration of which is supplied by Christian eschatology when Don Giovanni refuses to repent. The Hamlet role strictly falls to Dona Anna's betrothed, Don Ottavio, the avenging tenor who sings beautifully but awaits the intervention of Providence; while for her part, in this serio-comic development, Dona Anna continues to put off marriage out of respectful remembrance of her father.

In a novel of the same era, no better known than *Don Giovanni* but far more famously connected with *Hamlet*, the deceased father is scarcely given the time of day. Instead, when the characters in *Wilhelm Meisters Lehrjahre* come to perform Shakespeare's play, the part of the ghost is left to a mysterious person who is unknown to the hero and not a member of the cast, after Wilhelm's own father passes away, and out of the novel, with little

---

[1] According to Flaubert, "The three finest things God ever made are the sea, *Hamlet*, and Mozart's *Don Giovanni*": to Louise Colet, 3 Oct. 1846, in *The Letters of Gustave Flaubert, 1830–1857*, ed. and trans. Francis Steegmuller (Cambridge: Harvard University Press, 1980), 83.

other notice. Goethe's long bildungsroman, composed and refashioned with Hamlet-like deliberation from about 1776 to 1796, is at once a product of the Enlightenment and—implicitly in the life of its hero, explicitly in the hero's interpretation of Hamlet—a Romantic redaction of Shakespeare. By the novel's Enlightenment quality I mean its cool concurrence in the bias of Shakespeare's play toward youth, including the need to be free of parents, and its frank investigation of psychological and social assumptions. The Romantic contribution is more familiar—a warm acceptance of the same bias, an eagerness for development, and a quest for a self; and Goethe's novel also instigates the particular Romantic tradition that conceives of Hamlet as the poet or artist—it is both bildungsroman and *Künstlerroman*.

Born in 1770, Walter Scott was another celebrated poet old enough to have strong roots in the eighteenth century, and he set about inventing a different Enlightenment hero. Because of the profound influence of his Waverley Novels on nineteenth-century fiction and historiography, it might be argued that his rehabilitation of Shakespeare outweighed even Goethe's. Specifically, *Redgauntlet*, though autobiographical, deploys a political and historical interpretation of Hamlet's predicament rather than an emphasis on a Hamlet-like artist. The bias toward the younger generation is again marked, but the resistance to fathers significantly coincides with resistance to the ancien régime and quite literally to patriarchy. The young heroes (there are two) are not finally devoted to self-development but are representative of a present and future political order. They will not be initiated into a secret Society, as in Goethe, but stay steadfastly attached to civil society. They are in truth, as Hamlet remained for the theater, prototypical heroes of the nineteenth-century novel. And so I might argue, close thy Goethe, and open thy Scott.[2]

Wilhelm Meisters Lehrjahre may be thought of as a project without an end, a novel with a hero but without any fully conceived plot. The early draft known as *Wilhelm Meisters theatricalische Sendung* had a more definite purpose: to explore in fiction what a young bourgeois writer like Goethe himself might accomplish by joining the theater, directly and indirectly critiquing the current state of German theater and doubtlessly reforming its relation to the people.[3] Thus from the start Wilhelm possesses one sa-

---

[2] Cf. Thomas Carlyle, *Sartor Resartus*, ed. Charles Frederick Harrold (New York: Odyssey, 1937), 192: "Close thy *Byron*; open thy *Goethe*." Carlyle's translation, *Wilhelm Meister's Apprenticeship*, appeared in 1824. His severely constrained estimate of Scott was set forth after the latter's death in the *Westminster Review* 28 (1838), 293–345.

[3] See Eric A. Blackall, *Goethe and the Novel* (Ithaca: Cornell University Press, 1976), 56–77. The manuscript that came to light in 1910 has recently been retranslated by John R. Russell as *Wilhelm Meister's Theatrical Calling* (Columbia, SC: Camden House, 1995).

lient interest of Shakespeare's Hamlet: a thrilled but slightly condescending engrossment with professional, itinerant theater. His initial approach is nothing less than erotic—witness the affair with Mariane—but determinedly theoretical as well; he subsequently writes for the theater, advises the players, bankrolls them, and tries to become one of them. Some petty realities of vanity, greed, and timorousness are more often than not what Wilhelm discovers in their company. For all the intrinsic interest of this material, Goethe worked at the novel very slowly, almost against the grain—forcing himself during one period to complete a modest portion each year while he applied himself to new duties in the ducal court of Weimar.[4] Apparently he used the writing as an exercise in self-development; at least that became his novel's theme. In the published version, for which the first six books of the *Sendung* were compressed to four and more books added, Wilhelm's theatrical mission is no longer in question but distinctly repudiated. He becomes loosely attached to a handful of gentry; after patronizing he is now one of the patronized, one might say, though all very kindly. The *Lehrjahre*, or apprenticeship, of the title is given meaning in book 7 by the presentation to the hero of a *Lehrbrief*, his articles of induction into the mysterious Society comprising Lothario, Jarno, the Abbé, and presumably others.

From this gradually evolving fiction, in both versions known to us, emerges the estimate of Hamlet's character that can still be felt in the criticism of Bradley or the theory of Freud, and in theatrical productions to this day. Eighteenth-century British commentary on Shakespeare's play had already swung toward character, Hamlet's sensibility and procrastination, and even the suggestion of a hero who fails to be one.[5] But Wilhelm Meister's articulation of the character had the most powerful impact on literary history. Citing but two lines from the play, "The time is out of joint: O cursed spite, / That ever I was born to set it right" (1.5.189–90), the young hero instructs Serlo the director and Serlo's sister Aurelie as follows:

> In these words, so I believe, lies the key to Hamlet's whole behavior; and it is clear to me what Shakespeare set out to portray: a heavy deed placed on a soul which is not adequate to cope with it. And it is in this sense that I find the whole play constructed. An oak tree planted in a

[4] Nicholas Boyle, *Goethe: The Poet and the Age*, vol. 1 (Oxford: Oxford University Press, 1991), 343.

[5] For a summary, see Paul S. Conklin, *A History of "Hamlet" Criticism, 1602–1821* (1957; rpt. New York: Humanities Press, 1968), 63–81.

precious pot which should only have held delicate flowers. The roots spread out, the vessel is shattered.

A fine, pure, noble and highly moral person, but devoid of that emotional strength that characterizes a hero, goes to pieces beneath a burden that it can neither support nor cast off. Every obligation is sacred to him, but this one is too heavy. The impossible is demanded of him—not the impossible in any absolute sense, but what is impossible for him. How he twists and turns, trembles, advances and retreats, always being reminded, always reminding himself, and finally almost losing sight of his goal, yet without ever regaining happiness.[6]

Although earlier in book 4 Wilhelm has described to his friends a Hamlet with whom he shares many characteristics, he has never shouldered so heavy a burden as Shakespeare's hero; like the young Goethe, in truth, he has not always followed his living father's wishes. The sweeping imputations on Hamlet's character seem overblown, a hazardous extrapolation from that hero's chidings of himself later in the play. The slowly growing oak tree is a strained metaphor for an action in which, from Hamlet's point of view, marriage has followed all too rapidly upon the funeral rites. Shakespeare's tragic hero has been feminized as a vessel too fragile to hold anything but delicate flowers; and since even in fragile vessels roots spread only over time, some idea of character or response to experience is at stake rather than the exigencies of a dramatic situation. The play *Hamlet*, we may feel, is being absorbed by a bildungsroman rather than inspiring one. The completed *Wilhelm Meisters Lehrjahre* of 1796 contains a new motif, the painting of "a sick prince consumed by passion for his father's bride," and Goethe's deliberation in the introduction of this motif may be judged from his repeating it twice near the end of the extended novel.[7] Very likely

---

[6] Goethe, *Wilhelm Meister's Apprenticeship*, trans. Eric A. Blackall (1989; rpt. Princeton: Princeton University Press, 1995), 4.13.146. I cite book, chapter, and page number of the translation and—for key passages such as this—the original from Johann Wolfgang Goethe, *Sämtliche Werke*, vol. 9 (Frankfurt: Deutscher Klassiker, 1992).

"In diesen Worten, dünkt mich, liegt der Schlüssel zu Hamlets ganzen Betragen, und mir ist deutlich, daß Shakespear habe schildern wollen: eine große Tat auf eine Seele gelegt, die der Tat nicht gewachsen ist. Und in diesem Sinne find' ich das Stück durchgängig gearbeitet. Hier wird ein Eichbaum in ein köstliches Gefäß gepflanzt, das nur liebliche Blumen in seinen Schoß hätte aufnehmen sollen; die Wurzeln dehnen sich aus, das Gefäß wird zernichtet.

"Ein schönes, reines, edles, höchst moralisches Wesen, ohne die sinnliche Stärke, die den Helden macht, geht unter einer Last zu Grunde, die es weder tragen noch abwerfen kann; jede Pflicht ist ihm heilig, diese zu schwer. Das Unmögliche wird von ihm gefordert, nicht das Unmögliche an sich, sondern das was ihm unmöglich ist. Wie er sich windet, dreht, ängstigt, vor und zurück tritt; immer erinnert wird, sich immer erinnert, und zuletzt fast seinen Zweck aus dem Sinne verliert, ohne doch jemals wieder froh zu werden" (9:609).

[7] Ibid., 1.17.37, 8.2.314, and 8.10.371.

he was reflecting further on his own childhood, or picking up on the action of Schiller's *Don Carlos* of 1787. The painting of the sick prince clearly anticipates the Freudian explanation of Hamlet's abulia. A shrewd observation by Wilhelm, on Hamlet's loss through his mother's remarriage of "the image of reliability, which every loving child likes to attach to its parents," anticipates the reading of the play by Theodore Lidz.[8]

The potential of Goethe's own hero for failure is a function of the openness of his career: Wilhelm might do anything or might do nothing with his life. There is already in *Hamlet* the aspect of a hero who is only acting revenge, adopting different roles, and unable for the present to be himself.[9] Goethe's hero is more narcissistic than Shakespeare's, however, and therefore has both less and more at stake. Wilhelm even looks to *Hamlet*, in part, for a resolution of his own dilemma of choice and development, having accurately observed that the play's ending is not governed by the hero's wishes. "Historians and poets like to persuade us that . . . pride of purpose may be the lot of mankind," he contends; but in *Hamlet*, for once, "we are differently informed: the hero has no plan, but the play has." In sum, "How marvelously this is presented in the play before us! Purgatory sends a spirit to demand revenge, but in vain. Circumstances combine to hasten this, but in vain! Neither humans nor subterranean powers can achieve what is reserved for Fate alone."[10] Serlo receives this idea skeptically, yet Wilhelm's confident reading of Shakespeare seems to predict his own fate. Once he has left the theater, in the completed novel, he claims to understand "less than ever what I can do, or what I desire, or should do," but Jarno reassures him. "A person who has great potentiality for development will in due course acquire knowledge of himself and the world. Few people have the understanding and simultaneously the ability to act. Understanding extends, but also immobilizes; action mobilizes, but also restricts."[11] A little woundingly, Jarno adds that perhaps Wilhelm's mood and temperament suited him to play Hamlet in the theater but little else. The trouble is that

---

[8] Ibid., 4.13.145. See Theodore Lidz, *Hamlet's Enemy: Madness and Myth in "Hamlet"* (New York: Basic, 1975), esp. 47–115.

[9] See above, chapter 2, notes 76, 77, and 78.

[10] Goethe, *Wilhelm Meister's Apprenticeship*, 4.15.151. "Geschichtsschreiber und Dichter möchten uns gerne überreden, daß ein so stolzes Los dem Menschen fallen könne. Hier werden wir anders belehrt; der Held hat keinen Plan, aber das Stück ist planvoll. . . . Hier in unserm Stücke wie wunderbar! Das Fegefeuer sendet seinen Geist und fordert Rache, aber vergebens. Alle Umstände kommen zusammen, und treiben die Rache, aber vergebens! Weder Irdischen noch Unterirdischen kann gelingen, was dem Schicksal allein vorbehalten ist" (*Sämtliche Werke*, 9:618).

[11] Ibid., 8.5.337. "Derjenige, an dem viel zu entwickeln ist, wird später über sich und die Welt aufgeklärt. Es sind nur wenige, die den Sinn haben und zugleich zur Tat fähig sind. Der Sinn erweitert, aber lähmt, die Tat belebt, aber beschränkt" (*Sämtliche Werke*, 9:930).

his fate—after a careful revision of the earlier *Sendung* chapters—turns out to have been manipulated throughout by the leaders of the secret Society. It is hard to ascertain the degrees of irony with which the telling of *Wilhelm Meisters Lehrjahre* is invested. The Masonic goings-on may not be treated with irony enough. Deference to such all-too-human authorities ought to take human weakness more into account—to say nothing of the self-appointment of this particular male sect. One feels that Hamlet would never have trusted them.[12]

The novel treats the hero's father's death with notable detachment. In the concluding chapters of the *Sendung* Serlo hears that Wilhelm's father has died and that Werner, the son-in-law, has taken over the family business. He informs Wilhelm of the news, and in the upshot the hero casts his lot with the theatrical company. In the *Lehrjahre*, as published, the father's death is treated almost as casually, reported by letter at the beginning of book 5. There is no mention of a funeral; we are told that "this unexpected news affected Wilhelm deeply," but this assurance is followed by a general observation about the deaths of "friends and acquaintances." The narrator remarks that Wilhelm's "distress at the untimely departure of this good man was mitigated only by the feeling that his father had been little loved, and the conviction that he had gained little pleasure from life." Furthermore, "Wilhelm's thoughts soon turned to his own circumstances, and here he felt extremely uneasy"; he "suddenly found himself a free man, without as yet having achieved harmony within himself."[13]

The father thus passes out of Wilhelm's life very lightly—except for an unspoken but unmistakable connection to *Hamlet*. For suddenly we read that Wilhelm—who decides that he will no longer go by the name of Meister—makes it a condition of joining Serlo's company that they produce Shakespeare's play in full, with himself in the title role. This indeed has become a production with a purpose, the purpose of exorcising that ghost. No wonder—though unbelievably—the part of the ghost is not cast but left for the night of the performance: Wilhelm is persuaded by a mysterious letter that an actor will simply appear on cue. This improbable arrangement guarantees a first night on which the hero need not *act* Hamlet's

---

[12] Franco Moretti, *The Way of the World: The Bildungsroman in European Culture* (London: Verso, 1987), 29–32, takes a much more sanguine view of the secret Society than I. But the distance of Goethe from the Society, as from his hero, is hard to judge. On the irony of the novel, see Hans Reiss, *Goethe's Novels* (London: Macmillan, 1969), 97–103.

[13] Goethe, *Wilhelm Meister's Apprenticeship*, 5.1.170–71. Oddly, Boyle in his detailed biography is even more perfunctory about Goethe's father's death, which is conveyed by two unexpected sentences at the end of a long paragraph about other matters: see his *Goethe*, 1:342.

emotion and anxiety because, of course, he is thoroughly bewildered himself: "when the first sounds emerged from beneath the helmet, uttered in a pleasing but somewhat rough voice, out came the words: 'I am thy father's spirit,' Wilhelm stepped back shuddering, and the whole audience shuddered. The voice seemed familiar to everyone, and Wilhelm thought it sounded like that of his own father."[14] Yet in truth the elder Meister has been eliminated by the impersonation, for as the hero and readers discover in book 8, the ghost is played by the Abbé, who has watched over the younger man's fortunes all along and is one of the small band who comprise the Society. The entire production of *Hamlet* within this novel seems bent on supplanting parents. The casting of Claudius and Gertrude is barely mentioned: they end up being played by Madame Melina and the actor known as the Blusterer (*der Polterer*), whereas Polonius is played by Serlo, Ophelia by Aurelie, Laertes by the young man who is called by that name throughout—all distinctly more important characters in the novel. The production of the play thus both honors Wilhelm's parents and elides them. The action of the novel is henceforth directed onward to whatever harmony with himself Wilhelm can find in the company of the secret—and aristocratic—Society. In such a group some authority may be vested in a first among equals, but that is much different from the authority of a parent.

In *Dichtung und Wahrheit*, Goethe took the measure of his own father coolly but also more kindly, repeatedly stressing the good intentions of the methodical, possessive Johann Caspar Goethe and even noting how his contrary ways sometimes yielded lasting benefits to the son. "All fathers cherish the pious wish to see their sons achieve what they themselves have not managed to do; they want to live, as it were, a second time and now really profit from the experience of their first existence." But still more to the point, "at certain junctures children detach themselves from parents, servants from masters, and protégés from patrons; and such attempts to stand on one's own feet, to be independent, to live for one's own self, whether successful or not, are always in keeping with nature's will."[15] In some respects the hero of the autobiography is as Hamlet-like as he of the novel. The whole exercise is one of recovering the perspective of youth, not overlooking the ways in which the young are casually or deliberately kept in their place by their elders. Goethe might be said to have Hamlet's

---

[14] Goethe, *Wilhelm Meister's Apprenticeship*, 5.11.195.

[15] Goethe, *Poetry and Truth*, trans. Robert R. Heitner (1987; rpt. Princeton: Princeton University Press, 1994), 36, 186.

fondness for disguise and, appearances to the contrary, a stubborn determination not to defer or surrender to anyone. As in the novel, there is in the autobiography a less than fully acknowledged leaning to self-gratification where women are concerned, and perhaps a touch of Hamlet's misogyny.

Goethe's response to *Hamlet* in *Wilhelm Meisters Lehrjahre* is not confined to identification or bemused sympathy with its hero. Just as striking as the well known description of Hamlet's character is a theory for which Shakespeare's problematic play stands as the exception that proves the rule, of the generic difference between drama and the novel. Goethe himself, it may be noted, was at this time renowned in both genres. Again the pertinent conclusions arise from remarks among the actors of *Hamlet*, but this time the opinion is attributed to the group rather than to Wilhelm:

In the novel it is predominantly sentiments and events that are to be presented; in drama, characters and deeds. The novel must move slowly and the sentiments of the main personage must, in some way or another, hold up the progression of the whole toward its resolution. But drama must move quickly and the character of the main personage must press toward the end, not himself holding up this progression, but being held up by it. The hero of a novel must be passive, or at least not active to a high degree; from the hero of a play we demand effective action and deeds. . . .

They agreed that in the novel Chance might well be given free play, but that it must always be guided and controlled by the sentiments of the personages; whereas Fate, which, without any action by human beings on their part, drives them through circumstances unrelated to themselves toward an unforeseen catastrophe, can have its function only in drama. . . .

These reflections led them back again to the peculiarities of *Hamlet* as a play. The hero, it was said, really only has sentiments, and it is only external events that work upon him, so that this play has something of the breadth of a novel. But since Fate determines its plan, since it begins with a terrible deed and the hero is driven ever further toward another terrible deed, it is tragic in the highest sense of the term and cannot but end tragically.[16]

[16] Goethe, *Wilhelm Meister's Apprenticeship*, 5.7.185–86.
"Im Roman sollen vorzüglich *Gesinnungen* und *Begebenheiten* vorgestellt werden; im Drama *Charaktere* und *Taten*. Der Roman muß langsam gehen, und die Gesinnungen der Hauptfigur müssen, es sei auf welche Weise es wolle, das Vordringen des Ganzen zur Entwickelung aufhalten. Das Drama soll eilen, und der Charakter der Hauptfigur muß sich nach dem Ende drängen, und nur aufgehalten werden. Der Romanenheld muß leiden, wenigstens nicht im hohen Grade wirkend sein; von dem dramatischen verlangt man Wirkung und Tat. . . .

These far-reaching conclusions have immediate reference both to *Hamlet* and to the novel in hand. Just as they preclude a happy ending for the play (Serlo wistfully suggests such an ending, as a means to please the audience), they hint that since Wilhelm is the hero of a novel, fate will not determine his lot; and strictly speaking the action of the *Lehrjahre* is comedic, the novelistic outcome of those mysterious interventions in Wilhelm's life by the agents of the secret Society. Yet as theory, the conclusions arrived at by Serlo's company on the differences between drama and the novel will continue to be recalled as late as the writings of the Hungarian critic Georg Lukács.[17]

It so happens that Goethe's examples of novels in these reflections are exclusively English ones: all three of Samuel Richardson's novels, Henry Fielding's *Tom Jones*, and Oliver Goldsmith's *The Vicar of Wakefield*. But the distinctions drawn apply all the better to the novels that Scott would write from 1814 until 1832, the year in which both he and Goethe died. In Britain a so-called improvement in manners as well as political conservatism called for representation in the decades after the French Revolution and the Napoleonic wars, and Scott's heroes were in fact more rigorously passive than their eighteenth-century forebears.[18] Since the plot of the novels was fairly constant even as the historical settings varied, the passivity of these heroes did not go unnoticed. Scott himself thought of them as ob-

---

"So vereinigte man sich auch darüber, daß man dem Zufall im Roman gar wohl sein Spiel erlauben könne; daß er aber immer durch die Gesinnungen der Personen gelenkt und geleitet werden müsse; daß hingegen das Schicksal, das die Menschen, ohne ihr Zutun, durch unzusammenhängende äußere Umstände zu einer unvorgesehenen Katastrophe hindrängt, nur im Drama statt habe. . . .

"Diese Betrachtungen führten wieder auf den wunderlichen Hamlet, und auf die Eigenheiten dieses Stücks. Der Held, sagte man, hat eigentlich auch nur Gesinnungen; es sind nur Begebenheiten die zu ihm stoßen, und deswegen hat das Stück etwas von dem gedehnten des Romans: weil aber das Schicksal den Plan gezeichnet hat, weil das Stück von einer fürchterlichen Tat ausgeht, und der Held immer vorwarts zu einer fürchterlichen Tat gedrängt wird, so ist es im höchsten Sinne tragisch, und leidet keinen andern als einen tragischen Ausgang" (*Sämtliche Werke*, 9:675–76).

[17] See especially *The Historical Novel*, trans. Hannah and Stanley Mitchell (London: Merlin, 1962), 89–170. As will be clear, I do not find supportable Lukács's contention in *Goethe and His Age*, trans. Robert Anchor (1968; rpt. New York: Grosset and Dunlap, 1969), 50–68, that *Wilhelm Meisters Lehrjahre* reflects either an historical consciousness of the goals of the French Revolution or the capitalist division of labor.

[18] In *The Hero of the Waverley Novels* (1963; rpt. Princeton: Princeton University Press, 1992), 21–26, I featured this hero's fondness for soliloquy, a convention of Shakespeare's stage for which narrative should have little need. That these soliloquies are Hamlet-like in construction and recur often in later British novels has been shown by Carol Hanbury MacKay, *Soliloquy in Nineteenth-Century Fiction: Consciousness Creating Itself* (London: Macmillan, 1987).

servers of the action, and in an anonymous review of his own fictions to date, he remarked in 1817 that "Waverley, Brown, or Bertram in *Guy Mannering*, and Lovel in *The Antiquary*, are all brethren of a family; very amiable and very insipid sort of young men." These "chief characters are never actors, but always acted upon by the spur of circumstances, and have their fates uniformly determined by the agency of subordinate persons." The review described the "insipidity of this author's heroes" at some length: "The ease with which Waverley adopts, and afterwards forsakes the Jacobite party in 1745, is a good example of what we mean."[19] William Hazlitt presumably remembered this review, for ten years later in an essay entitled "Why the Heroes of Romance Are Insipid" he too pitched into the protagonists of the Author of Waverley. "Instead of acting, they are acted upon, and keep in the back-ground and in a neutral posture, till they are absolutely forced to come forward, and it is then with a very amiable reservation of modest scruples." Hazlitt's explanation, however, puts a somewhat different slant on the matter. He argues that such novel heroes must be broadly representative, so that they may "conciliate all suffrages and concentrate all interests" of the greatest number of readers. Author and readers collaborate in this passivity of heroes. "In fact, the hero of the work is not so properly the chief object in it, as a sort of blank left open to the imagination."[20]

The same critic brings us full circle to Goethe and Shakespeare again. For in his *Characters of Shakespeare's Plays* of 1817, Hazlitt proffered a theory of Hamlet's popularity similar to the one he held in store for Scott's heroes. Wide identification with Hamlet, then, explains why this particular play has, according to the players in *Wilhelm Meisters Lehrjahre*, "something of the breadth of a novel" about it. Here is Hazlitt:

> It is *we* who are Hamlet. This play has a prophetic truth, which is above that of history. Whoever has become thoughtful and melancholy . . . whoever has known "the pangs of despised love, the insolence of office, or the spurns which patient merit of the unworthy takes" . . . who cannot be well at ease, while he sees evil hovering near him like a spectre; whose powers of action have been eaten up by thought, he to whom the universe seems infinite, and himself nothing; whose bitterness of soul makes him careless of consequences, and who goes to a play as his best resource to shove off,

---

[19] *Quarterly Review* 16 (1817), reprinted in *Sir Walter Scott on Novelists and Fiction*, ed. Ioan Williams (London: Routledge, 1968), 240.

[20] *New Monthly Magazine*, Nov. 1827, reprinted in *The Collected Works of William Hazlitt*, ed. A. R. Waller and Arnold Glover, 12 vols. (London: Dent, 1902–4), 12:66.

to a second remove, the evils of life by a mock representation of them—this is the true Hamlet.

The true Hamlet is also a philosopher, according to Hazlitt, one whose "distresses . . . are transferred, by the turn of his mind, to the general account of humanity," and that philosopher melds with ourselves: "Whatever happens to him we apply to ourselves, because he applies it so himself as a means of general reasoning." Hazlitt cedes something to character—Hamlet's "ruling passion is to think, not to act"—but subordinates each character trait to the hero's wide appeal.[21] Thus his account of the matter not only assimilates Hamlet to the heroes of modern romance, or the novel, but helps to distinguish him from the now familiar Romantic Hamlet: the "soul which is not adequate to cope" in Wilhelm Meister's parlance, or Coleridge's man who is "continually resolving to do, yet doing nothing but resolve."[22] The Enlightenment Hamlet, also recognized by Goethe and invented many times over by Scott for the century to come, is both more representative and harder to characterize than that Romantic figure.

Relations between Scott and Goethe were distant but cordial. There was even a plan to meet in Weimar on Scott's return from Italy in 1832, but the news of Goethe's death turned the ailing Scott homeward. Goethe was senior by twenty-two years: so it happens that one of the younger man's first literary ventures was a translation of *Götz von Berlichingen* in 1799. Both were sons of lawyers, and both continued in worldly pursuits even as they gathered vast reputations as literary giants. Scott knew at least *Werther* and *Egmont*—and later *Faust*, of course—and very likely Goethe's bildungsroman influenced his own first novel, *Waverley*.[23] It is certain that Scott had read *Wilhelm Meisters Lehrjahre* by 1822, since he attempted something like Goethe's Mignon in the character Fenella, in *Peveril of the Peak* of that year.[24] But I contend that Goethe's novel left its strongest impress on *Redgauntlet*, another bildungsroman and perhaps the most autobiographical of Scott's novels. Carlyle's translation, *Wilhelm Meister's Apprenticeship*, became available around January 1824, and whether or not Scott reread the novel in English, he wrote *Redgauntlet* that spring. The British novelist

[21] Hazlitt, *Collected Works*, 1:232–35.

[22] Samuel Taylor Coleridge, *Lectures 1808–1819 on Literature*, ed. R. A. Foakes, 2 vols. (Princeton: Princeton University Press, 1987), 2:541.

[23] So G. H. Needler argued, unhesitatingly yet tenuously, in a little book called *Goethe and Scott* (Toronto: Oxford University Press, 1950), 39–43.

[24] As Scott confessed in the 1831 introduction to that novel, and as Goethe registered in conversation: see *Conversations of Goethe with Eckermann and Soret*, trans. John Oxenford (London: Bell, 1906), 108.

followed Goethe's precedent in exploiting *Hamlet*, but for his own quite different purposes: more than in any other novel he adopted significant features of the play to an historical myth that proved to be of great service to the nineteenth century.

This bildungsroman boasts two heroes, Darsie Latimer and Alan Fairford, who are bound by intense friendship and by the novelist's identification, it seems, with both. Instead of Wilhelm's brittle friendship with Werner—whose correspondence affords news from home, who marries the hero's sister but seems more and more the usurper and philistine—the narrative of *Redgauntlet* balances the interests of the two friends, first by recourse to an epistolary exchange and thereafter by attending the adventures of each in turn, until they rejoin one another at the end. Instead of the one autobiographical center of Goethe's novel, there are two: the roving Latimer, uncertain of who he really is, serves initially as the Romantic artist and dreamer in Scott, while the young advocate Fairford, based in Edinburgh, represents the business and domestic interest. If Werner is a closer replica of Wilhelm's father than is Wilhelm himself, Alan Fairford is bound a little too closely to Saunders Fairford, a Writer to the Signet fully and conventionally determined that his son will belong to the College of Advocates (the Scottish equivalents of solicitor and barrister respectively). Latimer, however, turns out to be no other than Sir Arthur Redgauntlet, romantically situated as the son of the Sir Henry who was publicly beheaded for his involvement in the Stewart rising of 1745. The manipulation of Wilhelm's "fate" by the brothers of the secret Society apparently translates into the equally mysterious—and more threatening—attempt to enlist Latimer in the lost Stewart cause. (A precedent for Scott's shifting of narrative modes in midnovel was provided by Goethe's abridging of the epistolary sequence in the second part of *Die Leiden des jungen Werthers*.) It may be said that *Wilhelm Meisters Lehrjahre* is as open-ended as Goethe's own life to the time of writing: even after the sorting out of relationships and the hero's betrothal to Lothario's sister, Nathalie, in the sequel to the novel—the *Wanderjahre*—he is still unmarried. *Redgauntlet*, however, closes with the same sharp definition, of marriage and of historical significance, as most of Scott's novels.

The two friends in *Redgauntlet* fall in love with the same woman. They describe her, the intriguing "Green Mantle," in their letters to one another. But Green Mantle turns out to be Lilias Redgauntlet, who is Darsie's sister and like him held in thrall by their manipulative uncle, Hugh Redgauntlet. So it happens that Darsie is left with a frisson of incestuous desire, perhaps, whereas Alan Fairford can and does marry the sister: the next best thing, we may suppose, to marrying Darsie himself. "Alan doated on his friend Darsie, even more than he loved his profession, and . . . threw everything aside when he thought Latimer in danger; forgetting fame and fortune, and hazarding even the serious displeasure of his father, to rescue him whom he loved with an elder brother's affection." In the earlier epistolary portion of the novel, Darsie has taken the same stance. In writing to Alan about Green Mantle, in fact, he cedes first place to a love like that of Jonathan and David in the Bible: "however the recollection of her may haunt my own mind, my love for Alan Fairford surpasses the love of woman." When Alan replies, he echoes the friendship of Hamlet for Horatio: "I give you my word I am heart-whole; and moreover, I assure you, that before I suffer a woman to sit near my heart's core, I must see her full face, without mask or mantle."[25] Or as one might say,

> Give me that man
> That is not passion's slave, and I will wear him
> In my heart's core, ay in my heart of heart,
> As I do thee.   (3.2.61–4)

Such is the literature of male friendship, which receives an erotic boost from an episode of cross-dressing at the end of Scott's novel. Hugh Redgauntlet, the bad uncle, orders Darsie to be clothed as a woman to inhibit his escape, and it is during this interval that (girl to girl, so to speak) Lilias reveals that she is his sister. The cross-dressing then affords a comic half-revelation when the two friends are reunited: his feet encumbered by his riding skirt, Darsie stumbles on dismounting and is caught by Alan, who fails to recognize him. But the reader is invited to share Darsie's surprise, "when the hurry of the moment, and of the accident, permitted him to see that it was his friend Alan Fairford in whose arms he found himself! A thousand apprehensions rushed on him, mingled with the full career of hope and joy, inspired by the unexpected appearance of his beloved friend at the very crisis, it seemed, of his fate."[26] Once acknowledged as Sir Arthur Redgauntlet and the heir to his mother's fortune—and in male dress once more—Darsie relinquishes his sister to his friend in marriage. The erotic substitutions, unusual for Scott, are thus in keeping with the games played

---

[25] Walter Scott, *Redgauntlet*, ed. G.A.M. Wood with David Hewitt (Edinburgh: Edinburgh University Press, 1997), 10.205, 12.113, 13.114. References are to chapter or letter number followed by the page.

[26] Ibid., 19.322.

among friends with sisters at the end of Goethe's novel. All of the women in whom Wilhelm is sexually interested are fully capable of representing themselves as men. The actresses Mariane and Philine, and the androgynous Mignon, are each adept at cross-dressing in their own way; Therese is distinguished by her strong vocation for estate management as well as her stunning huntsman's outfit; and Nathalie, of course, has first appeared, and reappeared in Wilhelm's daydreams, as "the Amazon." The only exception is the Countess, but she like Nathalie is sister to Lothario, as Therese is the sometime betrothed of Lothario. Thus in the *Lehrjahre* the noble Lothario would seem to be the true unskirted object of desire.[27]

Three or four verbal eches of *Hamlet* in *Redgauntlet* scarcely outnumber echoes of the same play in other Scott novels, all of which are mindful of Shakespeare. What distinguishes *Redgauntlet* is the autobiographical cast of the fiction together with an attack at once humorous and searing upon fathers, and a thoroughgoing repudiation of the hold of past generations on the present. The humorous attack is carried out by Alan Fairford's letters to Darsie protesting Saunders Fairford's largely successful attempt to run his life for him, not only to train him in a more prestigious practice of the law than his own—the Advocate's as opposed to the Writer's—but fussily to intervene at every step. Saunders in truth is a Polonius, offering more continuous advice than his son can readily follow and warning against the deleterious influence of his friend. "Think of your oath of office, Alan, and your duty to your father, my dear boy"; and "You may find wiser advisers, Alan, but none that can wish you better."[28] As if his own verbosity were not enough, he saddles his son with Peter Peebles, the notorious and impoverished suitor at law who is as practiced by now in pursuing his own pleaders as he is in avoiding paying them. Parallel to this humorous attack upon the previous generation is the treatment, in a Gothic mode, of Darsie Latimer's family. This dark and threatening action mounts an attack against Darsie's and Lilias's uncle, Hugh Redgauntlet. In a twisted version of *Hamlet*, strangely, the usurping uncle demands revenge for the ghost of his brother. (Does the title of the novel refer to the powerful uncle or to the son and heir?) Darsie, indeed, has no idea of his relation to this mysterious uncle, who passes under another name. To him he first appears on a black horse as something of a supernatural force, bearing "a longer spear" than the

[27] Xue-Qui Chiang has pointed out to me that, except for the initial letter, Lothario is an anagram of Horatio: if so, perhaps the play on names can be traced to Nicholas Rowe's *The Fair Penitent* (1703), in which Altamount's friend Horatio is pitted against his enemy Lothario.

[28] Scott, *Redgauntlet*, 13.118.

other salmon fishers and producing in Darsie "an involuntary shudder."[29] Shudder he well may, for the uncle's plan is to conceal the young man's very identity from himself until he can be coerced, if necessary, into avenging his father's death! The violent and secretive man kidnaps the nephew who has unknowingly inherited the executed brother's baronetcy, and he carries him across the border to England to help authenticate a hopeless revival of the Stewart rebellion. It is as if ghost and usurping uncle were rolled into one, and Hamlet's very fears of the ghost being the devil were coming true.

Once the young Sir Arthur is in his uncle's power, understands who he is, and learns that his father's head is still perched atop the gates to the city of Carlisle with those of others who rebelled in the forty-five, he speaks in the formal language of Scott's heroes and adopts their usual stance, while the strange obsession of the uncle and brother, who would pursue the Stewart cause forever, is apparent:

> "I will not pretend to misunderstand you, sir," said Darsie; "but an enterprize directed against a dynasty now established for three reigns requires strong arguments, both in point of justice and of expedience, to recommend it to men of conscience and prudence."
>
> "I will not," said Redgauntlet, while his eyes sparkled with anger,—"I will not hear you speak a word against the justice of that enterprize, for which your oppressed country calls with the voice of a parent, entreating her children for aid—or against that noble revenge which your father's blood demands from his dishonoured grave. His skull is yet standing over the Rikargate, and even its bleak and mouldered jaws command you to be a man. I ask you, in the name of God, and of your country, will you draw your sword, and go with me to Carlisle, were it but to lay your father's head, now the perch of the obscene owl and carrion crow, and the scoff of every ribald clown, in consecrated earth, as befits his long ancestry?"[30]

Thus if the older generation is oppressive to the young in *Hamlet*, it is even more so in *Redgauntlet*. With a kind of monomania the unpleasant uncle conveys the commands of a deceased father; the politics he would impose is patriarchal, both for royal families and every subject's family. The young man of "conscience and prudence"—the character of every Scott hero— resists, but in this novel he has been rendered so passive as to have been placed under house arrest and transported about in woman's clothing. His

---

[29] Ibid., 4.20,23.
[30] Ibid., 19.317.

alter-ego, young Fairford, by now in search of his friend in western Scotland, is soon captive also and shipped for England. Unlike Hamlet, Alan is too scrupulous to inspect the letter that he bears, which similarly calls for his own arrest, and he is more alarmed than pleased to discover that the skipper of the bark that plies the Solway Firth is a pirate.

Hugh Redgauntlet has a more limited repertoire of persuasion than Claudius; nor does he even perfunctorily appeal to love, as the ghost did in the play. Duty is to be enforced by threats. Therefore it is he himself who tells Darsie the mind-numbing story of the ancestral Redgauntlet, Alberick by name, and his son. In medieval times, Sir Alberick passionately opposed Edward de Baliol, the usurper in his view of the throne of Scotland. But this Redgauntlet's "only son, now a youth of eighteen, had shared so much the haughty spirit of his father, that he became impatient of domestic control, resisted paternal authority, and, finally, fled from his father's house"—to join the forces of Baliol. In an ensuing combat, the son tried to cut off Alberick's pursuit of Baliol, but was "unhorsed and overthrown" by his father. Alberick had just time to recognize his son and tried to leap his horse over the body on the ground. But the steed's hind foot fatally struck the boy "as he was in the act of rising." Ever since, male Redgauntlets have born "the miniature resemblance of a horseshoe" on their brow.[31] As if that were the only sign of trouble for the sons of fathers in *Redgauntlet*! Besides the officious parental interference endured by Alan Fairford and the bewildering threats to Darsie Latimer, the skipper Nanty Ewart—the pirate whose ambivalence favors the young heroes—has suffered his entire lifetime from the false charge of being his father's murderer, that being the coloring put on the matter by the father himself. The novel keeps ringing changes on the ghosts of fathers: even the Pretender, who holds Darsie prisoner for a while, travels under the name of "Father Buonaventure."[32]

Instead of the antic disposition adopted by Hamlet or the clever antics of young Amleth in the Danish story, the imputation of madness becomes one of the weapons of these older men in constraining the younger. Darsie realizes that their legal pretext for confining him, if necessary, will be a

---

[31] Ibid., 8.190–91.

[32] As Robert C. Gordon remarks of this novel, "one cannot help being amazed at the amount of sheer narrative energy and motivation that Scott finds in the impercipience of fathers." See his *Under Which King? A Study of the Scottish Waverley Novels* (Edinburgh: Oliver and Boyd, 1969), 149–66. More recently, Ian Duncan, in *Modern Romance and Transformations of the Novel: The Gothic, Scott, Dickens* (Cambridge: Cambridge University Press, 1992), 93–99, has meditated on this theme. See also Homer Obed Brown, *Institutions of the English Novel: From Defoe to Scott* (Philadelphia: University of Pennsylvania Press, 1997), 151–60.

commitment for madness. The ghost-uncle Redgauntlet, not a little crazy himself, obsessively pursues the heir to the family misfortunes and is not above threatening his victim—his adopted loved one, it now seems—with his own instability:

> "Peace," he said, "heir of my ancestors' fame—heir of all my hopes and wishes—Peace, son of my slaughtered brother! I have sought for thee, and mourned for thee, as a mother for an only child. Do not let me again lose you in the moment when you are restored to my hopes.— Believe me, I distrust so much my own impatient temper, that I entreat you, as the dearest boon, do nought to awaken it at this crisis."[33]

The mourning, one has to conclude, is finally for the slaughtered brother and the failure of the Stewart rebellion twenty years earlier; the uncle wants to shape the nephew into the image of that brother. The only decent father-figure available to the youth of *Redgauntlet*—no pretender, no fanatic, no lawyer—is Joshua Geddes, the honest Quaker whose faith is steadfast against both violence and litigation. Along with almost every other character in the novel, Geddes shows up again at the end "travelling, as he said, in the sorrow of his soul, and mourning for the fate of Darsie Latimer as he would for his first-born child."[34]

Putting aside the character assigned to Hamlet by Wilhelm Meister, then, we can grasp how both partially autobiographical novels confess to the possibility of a new Hamlet for the Enlightenment, by seizing on the bias toward youth in Shakespeare's play and elevating it to a principle: fathers may die, yet the mission of sons is to live. Goethe's bildungsroman and Scott's romance of personal identity eschew tragedy and the debt to fathers and turn resolutely toward the future, in which sons will live enhanced or fuller lives. Recall the ease with which the former novel elides the father's death: Meister senior, according to his son, had few friends and small happiness in life; the story affords him no funeral, unless it is the production of *Hamlet*; the part of the ghost is taken over by one of the leaders of the secret Society, which can play a more intriguing role than parents can in a hero's development. In Scott's novel, the one hero's curiosity about his father is overwhelmed by his uncle's readiness to play both ghost and Claudius; only this uncle claims that the father's "bleak and mouldered jaws command you to be a man." The ghoulishness, in effect, transports the ghost's command in *Hamlet* to the graveyard scene, whereas

---

[33] Scott, *Redgauntlet*, 19.318.
[34] Ibid., 20.326.

in the play Hamlet has by then come to some kind of terms with death by killing Polonius. Moreover, the voices of uncles or surrogate fathers can and should be resisted on principle; young Sir Arthur and Lilias concede nothing to the retrograde politics of Hugh Redgauntlet. As for Alan Fairford, that young man's officious parent literally disappears from the novel. In the dramatic concluding scene, in which most of the characters converge and Father Buonaventure is revealed to be Charles Edward Stewart (as fictitious here as the rest of the scene), Saunders Fairford is absent and unmentioned, as forgotten as Polonius in the last scene of *Hamlet*. The marriage of Arthur's sister Lilias to Alan is arranged and authorized solely by the three of them, even though Scott in his other works is as pleased as any British novelist to portray fathers giving their children in marriage. In the well orchestrated finale of *Redgauntlet*, only the death of Nanty Ewart sounds a tragic note.

Although Alan Fairford leaves his father and his law practice behind in Edinburgh to search for his friend in the west of Scotland, once there he is as passive an agent in the action as Darsie. Such are the heroes of novels, who according to the players in *Wilhelm Meisters Lehrjahre*, must be passive—and Goethe had in mind heroes such as his own or Tom Jones, not the far more constrained protagonists of Scott and nineteenth-century British novels. As for the unreal politics of a Stewart rebellion, Darsie "began to believe that the conspiracy would dissolve of itself, without the necessity of his placing himself in direct opposition to so violent a character as his uncle, and incurring the hazard with which such opposition must needs be attended."[35] Is it cowardice for Darsie to await the outcome and avoid the hazard? The novelist's privilege of narrating the hero's thoughts here spells out for the reader the same sort of interpretation that a member of an audience for *Hamlet* is free to make of its hero. Who calls him coward? Hamlet may entertain the same unspoken thought that Darsie is said to. In *Redgauntlet*, the eventuality that Darsie foresees is precisely what comes to pass: the conspiracy dissolves of itself. If *Hamlet* is the most novel-like of tragedies, *Redgauntlet* may claim to be an enlightened telling of the same tale, with a happy conclusion put to the quandary of revenge. Again, it is only the bad uncle, not even Sir Henry from his uncomfortable perch on the gates of Carlisle, who is calling for revenge; and famously, at the novel's end the uncle and Prince Charles and his followers are utterly vanquished by the forgiveness of the Hanoverian government, instead of receiving the expected punishment for their contemplated crime against a

[35] Ibid., 22.346.

United Kingdom. By forgiveness and refusal of revenge on the winning side, the Stewart conspiracy is dissolved forever.

The defeat of the terrible uncle (himself destined for a monastery at this point, as the only conceivable resting place for his peculiar temperament) is anticipated halfway through the novel by a devastating encounter with Peter Peebles, one of Scott's famed eccentrics, in a scene that perhaps owes more to the mixture of high and low styles in Shakespeare's histories than to *Hamlet*. Peebles recognizes Hugh Redgauntlet as Herries of Birrens-work, his other name, and addresses him as such. Redgauntlet and his brother both dwelt with Peebles briefly during the rebellion twenty years ago. Redgauntlet—or Herries—denies this "sternly": that is, threateningly, as always. But Peebles persists, as always, and this wonderfully boring litigant thereby cuts the political conspirator down to size:

> "The de'il a bit," answered the undaunted Peter Peebles; "I mind ye weel when ye lodged in my house the great year of the forty-five, for a great year it was; the Grand Rebellion broke out, and my cause—the Great Cause—Peebles against Plainstanes, *et per contra*—was called in the beginning of the winter Session, and would have been heard, but that there was a surcease of justice, with your plaids, and your piping, and your nonsense."
>
> "I tell you, fellow," said Herries, yet more fiercely, "you have confused me with some of the other furniture of your crazy pate."
>
> "Speak like a gentleman, sir," answered Peebles; "these are not legal phrases, Mr Herries of Birrenswork, speak in form of law, or I sall bid ye gude day, sir. I have nae pleasure in speaking to proud folks, though I am willing to answer anything in a legal way. . . . And where is Captain Redgimlet now? he was a wild chap, like yoursell, Birrenswork."[36]

And so on: it would be hard to count the number of hits Peebles scores on the novel's dark satanic adversary, by measuring the rebellion against the cause of Peebles vs. Plainstanes, prating of the law to this dangerous outlaw, and worst of all misremembering the family name as Redgimlet. Gimlets are used by cobblers and sailmakers, not by bloodied baronets and their younger brothers.[37]

Redgauntlet is a fiction. Except for the autobiographical aspect—the web of analogies to the author's own situation and feelings similar to that of

[36] Ibid., 7.180.
[37] The *gauntlet* of the novel's title is no accident. Much is made of a bit of Jacobite folklore about a woman—imagined by Scott to be Lilias—taking up the glove thrown down by the

Wilhelm Meisters Lehrjahre—it contains less matter of fact than most Scott novels. The Redgauntlets and the whole business about an abortive Stewart rising around the year 1765 Scott simply made up, including the grand final scene in which General Campbell extends the free pardon and forgiveness of the government, and Redgauntlet, the Pretender, and their few remaining followers cave in—" 'Then, gentlemen,' said Redgauntlet, clasping his hands together as the words burst from him, 'the cause is lost for ever!' "[38] Yet for all that, *Redgauntlet* is a historical fiction, like the other productions of the Author of Waverley; it is the last of the historical novels on his favorite theme, the Stewart rebellion of the previous century. The interpretation of the past in relation to the present that the novel centers on that lost cause distinguishes it from Goethe's bildungsroman and from *Hamlet* itself. According to Hazlitt, remember, Shakespeare's play is somehow "above" history; but the role conceived by Scott for Hamlet-like heroes makes sense only in terms of history. An idea of history informs all of Scott's novels, and the novels themselves undoubtedly made their mark on nineteenth-century historiography as well as literature. Just as Goethe's novel became the model bildungsroman for the next century, Scott's novels collectively gave a powerful impetus to the dominant literary form of realism, which, in Lukács's words, "transforms the social novel into a genuine history of the present."[39]

Goethe certainly had a lively idea of social relations, and in Weimar in the 1780s he had ample experience in political administration. In the *Lehrjahre* he treats in a realistic vein the relations of actors and writers to their audience and patrons and among themselves. Yet even though the French Revolution commenced well before the novel was completed, Goethe neither assumes nor speculates upon historical change, whether change in the past or to come. In his novel he simply does not attach political significance to recent events or national history the way Scott was about to do. Jürgen Habermas cites a passage from the novel in which Wilhelm writes at length to his self-announced brother-in-law, Werner, on the constrictions placed upon the burgher class.[40] According to Wilhelm's letter, only the nobleman

---

ceremonial challenger to any and all who would oppose the new king at the coronation of George III in 1761 (*Redgauntlet*, 18.303–8).

[38] Scott, *Redgauntlet*, 23.373.

[39] Lukács, *The Historical Novel*, 169. For a closer view of this achievement, see Harry E. Shaw, *The Forms of Historical Fiction: Sir Walter Scott and His Successors* (Ithaca: Cornell University Press, 1983); and Ina Ferris, *The Achievement of Literary Authority: Gender, History, and the Waverley Novels* (Ithaca: Cornell University Press, 1991).

[40] Jürgen Habermas, *The Structural Transformation of the Public Sphere*, trans. Thomas Burger (1989; rpt. Cambridge: MIT Press, 1995), 12–14.

is "a public person," "someone who represents by his appearance" and may "act and achieve," whereas the burgher may only "labor and create, developing some of his capabilities in order to be useful." This social difference provides the rationale of Wilhelm's decision to go on the stage, where "a cultured human being can appear in the full splendor of his person, just as in the upper classes of society." It is, as Habermas is aware, a striking categorization of Goethe's time and experience of life. Yet the momentary recognition in the letter that these conditions may be historical in the modern sense—that is, subject to change—is quickly squashed:

> The differences are not due to any pretentiousness on the part of the aristocracy or the submissiveness of the bourgeoisie, but to the whole organization of society. Whether this will ever change, or what will change, does not really concern me. Given the present state of things, what I have to do is think about myself, maintain what I know to be the basic need of myself, and achieve its fulfillment.[41]

In short, though Habermas can cite this letter for its very historicity, as evidence of the status quo before the transformation of the public sphere, Wilhelm refuses to think of historical change, and this refusal is the closest he ever comes to contemplating it. Even his adherence to the theater is short-lived, whereas the fulfillment of his self will occupy a lifetime. Goethe no more than Wilhelm conceives, in his novels, of a present that has evolved from the past or of a polity other than the feudal one of his time.[42]

Possibly Goethe, like his hero, made a conscious decision in this matter. He had ample acquaintance with the intellectual roots of modern historicism, in which German thinkers were in the forefront. He had access to the successive parts of Herder's work on the philosophy of history as they were written.[43] He became more and more interested in the study of geology, the science more responsible than any other before the triumph of evolutionary biology for the awareness that the conditions and forms of life on earth are still changing. He also wrote outstanding historical dramas. The publication in 1773 of *Götz von Berlichingen* had attracted considerable attention, before *Die Leiden des jungen Werthers* brought him fame a year later. The merits of the play, obviously, were recognized as far away as Edinburgh, and translating it taught Scott a great deal, both of technique

---

[41] Goethe, *Wilhelm Meister's Apprenticeship*, 5.3.174–75.
[42] Cf. Blackall, *Goethe and the Novel*, 14–15.
[43] Boyle, *Goethe*, 1:345–53.

and of congenial themes. An action spread out over time is represented in short swift scenes, full of motion; the play celebrates the courage and independence of the sixteenth-century Götz, but also his fealty to the emperor. The same is true of *Egmont*, the better known play that Goethe worked on during the years he was occupied with *Wilhelm Meisters Lehrjahre*.[44] Yet there is no progressive idea of history behind these works, no sense of the achievement of the time or of a different polity in the future. The tragedies introduce good and bad adherents of a feudal world, not persons who can be thought of as coming before or after their time, as in Scott's novels.

Without question Shakespeare's history plays made a deep impression on both Goethe and Scott. But *Hamlet* is not a history play, or a study of politics of the kind afforded by tragedies like *Richard II* and *Richard III*, or *Julius Caesar* and *Coriolanus*, which are also history plays. That is not to say that *Hamlet* makes no topical allusions to events of Shakespeare's time, for such allusions are not the exclusive property of any genre. But the possible allusions afford no key to the play such as would fix, or even aid the task of interpretation. Even if it were true, as one scholar argued point-blank, that Hamlet was modeled on the putative inner life of the Earl of Essex, or as another has urged more subtly, that the play responds to "a *fin de siècle* malaise" of the 1590s, the main burden of interpreting *Hamlet* is scarcely alleviated.[45] A more coherent pattern of possibly allusive design was discerned in the time of Scott and Goethe by James Plumptre: he pointed out the resemblance of murdering a king in his orchard and marrying his queen within a few months to the murder of Lord Darnley by the Earl of Bothwell, who thereupon married Queen Mary of Scotland, in 1567. There were enough similarities here to warrant speculation as to the source of the circumstances surrounding the death of Hamlet's father, yet they hardly support Plumptre's notion that Shakespeare composed the play in 1596 to flatter Queen Elizabeth.[46] Shakespeare, let us grant, worked with what he knew—just as one may argue that he knew by the time of writing the play

---

[44] For Scott's borrowing in *Kenilworth* of a scene from *Egmont*, and Goethe's borrowing from *Kenilworth* in act 3 of the second part of *Faust*, see Needler, *Goethe and Scott*, 50–74.

[45] See John Dover Wilson, *The Essential Shakespeare: A Biographical Approach* (Cambridge: Cambridge University Press, 1932), 104–7, and Annabel Patterson, *Shakespeare and the Popular Voice* (Oxford: Blackwell, 1989), 93–106.

[46] James Plumptre, *Observations on "Hamlet"* (Cambridge: Burges, 1796). A briefer and more persuasive handling of this material is that of Roland Mushat Frye, *The Renaissance Hamlet: Issues and Responses in 1600* (Princeton: Princeton University Press, 1984), 29–37, 102–10.

of his own father's impending death. But the politics of *Hamlet* and the history are neither those of England nor of Scotland, nor even of the elective monarchy distantly limned as that of Denmark.

There is indeed a political study in *Hamlet*, of an action basically independent of specific institutions or even personalities. This is roughly the politics adumbrated by Francis Fergusson in his classic study of western drama.[47] In characterizing the action of Shakespeare's play, Fergusson passed over in silence the obvious parallels that might be drawn to the *Oresteia* of Aeschylus and directed attention to a basic similarity to Sophocles' *Oedipus Rex*. Both Shakespeare and Sophocles appeal to "ancient and publicly accepted values and modes of understanding, rather than preaching, inventing, and arguing in the mode of modern drama," and in the two plays in question "a royal sufferer is associated with pollution, in its very sources, of an entire social order." As in *Wilhelm Meister's* reading of Hamlet's character, Fergusson could be said to begin with the proposition that "the time is out of joint," but he insists on coming to terms with the play as a whole rather than the capacity or will and purpose or personality of the hero. Like Freud, but from a very different standpoint, he sees Hamlet's situation as similar to that of Claudius. In fact the two adversaries' intentions converge as the play proceeds, since just as Hamlet regards Claudius as the source of pollution, Claudius is increasingly determined to be rid of Hamlet. The play is far more intricate and drawn out than *Oedipus Rex* because of what Fergusson calls "improvisations" and "improvisational entertainments," which hold off and ironically comment upon the ancient ritual of ridding the community of pollution yet never wholly reject or turn aside from this purpose; the hidden crime, as in Sophocles, must be disclosed. The climax, peripety, and recognition—or Aristotelian centers of *Hamlet*—come in the play scene, which functions as "both ritual and entertainment, and shows the Prince as at once clown and ritual head of state." In sum, "the main action of *Hamlet* may be described as the attempt to find and destroy the hidden 'imposthume' which is poisoning the life of Claudius's Denmark."[48] Obviously neither Fergusson's account nor any other will catch all the ironies of the play. The metaphor he singles out is not directed at Claudius but at young Fortinbras's campaign in Poland:

[47] Francis Fergusson, *The Idea of a Theater* (1949; rpt. New York: Anchor, n.d.), 109–54.
[48] Fergusson, *Idea of a Theater*, 130, 126, 117. To distinguish the meaning of the play from the character of its hero, Fergusson makes use of the disease imagery noted by Caroline Spurgeon, *Shakespeare's Imagery and What It Tells Us* (1935; rpt. Cambridge: Cambridge University Press, 1968), 133–34, 316–19.

Two thousand souls and twenty thousand ducats
Will not debate the question of this straw.
This is th'impostume of much wealth and peace,
That inward breaks, and shows no cause without
Why the man dies.   (4.4.25–9)

Hamlet, the chief ironist and improviser as well as actor in the drama, bases his comparison on the experience of war and peace throughout history, not excepting the potential destructiveness of his late father's campaign against Norway, while Fergusson's own language—"poisoning the life of Claudius's Denmark"—both as metaphor and as metonymy seems redundant.

The traditional action that *Hamlet* shares with *Oedipus Rex* is certainly political, but neither specifically historical nor a representation of politics as usual. It is not even particularly rational: the desire to rid the community of a scapegoat has usually more to do with redefining the sense of the group than getting at the cause of the trouble. But unlike supposed representations of Essex or the murder of Darnley, a recurring collective need to rid the state of that which is rotten, of secret crime or disease within, helps to explain the tragedy of *Hamlet* in broad terms. Something other than politics as usual has been going on, something all the more worrisome because Claudius appears to be competent at government and—for a murderer—strives to be a good stepparent. Hamlet in his grief is deeply conscious of the theme, but without much faith in action against the inherent evil. He does not fancy himself Hercules and perhaps would not welcome, as he does not deserve, the compliment paid to Antonio at the end of Marston's revenge play: "Thou art another Hercules to us / In ridding huge pollution from our state."[49] In *Hamlet*, Fergusson would say, this action has to be understood as represented by the tragedy as a whole; but then the action must be conceived as recurrent, not historical in a modern sense. The timelessness sometimes attributed to Shakespeare is not altogether bardolatry, for it may measure the distance between his representations and those of historicism. Hazlitt seems to touch on this difference, again, when he compares Hamlet to characters in Scott's novels. "We have, I think, a stronger fellow-feeling with [Hamlet] than we have with Bertram or Waverley. All men feel and think, more or less: but we are not all foundlings, Jacobites, or astrologers. We might have been overturned with these gentlemen in a stage-coach: we seem to have been school-fellows with Hamlet at Witten-

---

[49] John Marston, *Antonio's Revenge*, ed. G. K. Hunter (Lincoln: University of Nebraska Press, 1965), 5.3.129–30.

berg."[50] This is not just a put-down of Scott, but a commentary on nine-teenth-century realism.

In *Redgauntlet* Scott does copy some features of the generalized politics sketched by Shakespeare in *Hamlet*. If Claudius is constrained from acting against Hamlet because of "the great love the general gender bear him" (4.7.18), for example, Redgauntlet is constrained from acting without the concurrence of his nephew, and for similar reasons. Lilias spells out this motive to Darsie: their uncle's followers "are no longer willing to obey his summons," and "they allege your absence as their natural head and leader." But observe the difference in the situation imagined by Scott, when Darsie repudiates the attempt to obtain his authority for an uprising by kidnap-ping him:

> "That he shall never obtain," answered Darsie; "my principles and my prudence alike forbid such a step. Besides, it would be totally unavailing to his purpose. Whatever these people may pretend, to evade your uncle's importunities, they cannot, at this time of day, think of subjecting their necks again to the feudal yoke, which was effectually broken by the Act of 1748, abolishing vassalage and hereditary jurisdictions."[51]

No doubt speeches like this, insisting in the high style on principles and prudence, make Scott's heroes unreal to today's readers, but "this time of day" is, precisely, the time of history. The novel comes down to the position that one cannot turn the clock back. There is indeed a new set of rules governing present social relations—broadly speaking, a social contract—that is explicitly not of the feudal past. The present has come into being in too many ways to account for simply, but in the matters at issue a new polity has been ratified by the defeat of the forty-five, by the altered sentiments of Redgauntlet's followers, by the rule of law that the young heir of the family accepts, and by the legislation he cites as an historical marker.

When, during the same conversation, Darsie asks Lilias how she could discover Whig principles while her education was in the charge of such a backward uncle, she surprisingly replies that she learned something of po-litical freedom "in the nunnery where my uncle placed me." But Scott does not imagine this to be just any nunnery, such as one to which Ophelia might be sent, but a Parisian nunnery in which one of the older nuns who took Lilias in charge "had adopted the tenets of the Jansenists, with perhaps a still further tendency towards the reformed doctrines, than those of

---

[50] Hazlitt, "Sir Walter Scott, Racine, and Shakespeare" (1826), *Collected Works*, 7:344.
[51] Scott, *Redgauntlet*, 18.309; see also 22.347–48.

Porte-Royale." From this historically specific—if unlikely—source, she came in touch with "freedom of religious opinion," which proved contagious with "freedom of political creed"; and "I had no sooner renounced the Pope's infallibility, then I began to question the doctrine of hereditary and indefeasible right." Thus Lilias shares her brother's principles as well as his prudence, is quite aware that their uncle is a "political enthusiast of the most dangerous character," and will be an eminently suitable wife for the advocate Alan Fairford.[52]

In *Redgauntlet* Scott adopts the youthful bias, the process of mourning, and the treatment of revenge from *Hamlet* and maps them onto the recent history of England and Scotland. The younger generation in the novel are the adherents of the present, of present institutions and present laws, which are emphatically not the laws and institutions of the past. The retrograde uncle, now almost alone, claims that the past "calls with a voice of a parent"; but the youths who have inherited the past adhere to the social contract. They can do so because in their view, and in the decided view of this and the other novels devoted to British history, the contract is already in place and has been since the settlement of 1688. It is the uncle, and as recently as 1745 the uncle and the father, and Charles Edward Stewart with his other followers, who are hopelessly archaic and think of revenge for that defeat.[53]

For one traditional reading of the novels, including *Waverley* and *Rob Roy*, Scott's sympathies are said to be with the Stewarts, the deposed kings of another era; and to be sure, Latimer is as pleased to shake hands with the living representative of that royal dynasty as Waverley was only a few years earlier. But that complicated sympathy, a nostalgia vicariously experienced by means of these popular fictions, may be compared to an act of mourning, with all its ambivalence for the lives of the young.[54] The rise of historicism gives this mourning its value, for the past has become as irretrievable as a dead parent. Mourning is the way to treat it, and of course the mourning is not for the benefit of the dead but for the living. Thus Scott's novels of the Stewart rising, or *Old Mortality* with its devotion to the Revolution of 1688, make present times more comfortable for the nov-

---

[52] Ibid., 18.302–3.

[53] Duncan, *Modern Romance*, 138, observes the parallel to *Hamlet* not only of *Redgauntlet* but of *The Bride of Lammermoor*, which—atypically for Scott—ends tragically.

[54] Rohan Maitzen notes the aspect of mourning in *Redgauntlet*: see his " 'By No Means an Improbable Fiction': *Redgauntlet*'s Novel Historicism," *Studies in the Novel* 25 (1993), reprinted in *Critical Essays on Sir Walter Scott: The Waverley Novels*, ed. Harry E. Shaw (New York: Hall, 1996), 129–30.

elist and his readers. *Redgauntlet*, especially, can be thought of as an act of mourning; the events in it are gratuitous, invented for the purpose of visiting one more time the Stewart cause and rejecting revenge.

In none of these novels is conspiracy against the present government and rule of law contemplated as a source of pollution: such a conspiracy might be dangerous in the present, but Scott insists that this bit of history is over with. The arrow of time points in one direction and one direction only. This is quite different from the view of time implicit in the political action of *Hamlet* as described by Fergusson. Still, it would be rash to say that the mapping of some kind of history upon the death of parents was strange to Shakespeare. His overlay of familiar, family relations of father and son with the end of the reign in *Henry IV* is enough to confute that supposition. *Hamlet* itself has recently been read by R. A. Foakes as a play in which the father stands for the past:

> The Ghost is a central image from the past, a past that exerts a constant pressure on characters and events in the play. Hamlet's idea of his father, our sense of what he was like, his war with Norway, his marriage to Gertrude, his death, his appearances as a ghost, are matters that bear upon almost all the play's action. *Hamlet* is a play in which the past is recalled again and again, in memories of what was, in changes that have taken place, or in dealing with the consequences of past actions or events.

These are the very features that make the play an inspiration for *Redgauntlet*, and less specifically for many other novels. Though Foakes elaborates this reading of *Hamlet* in some detail, however, there is nothing to suggest that such a fixation on the past will not recur again and again from generation to generation. He is really spelling out what Hazlitt calls the "prophetic truth" of the play, as when he subsequently suggests, taking a dim view of Fortinbras's ascendancy, that it also anticipates twentieth-century experience: "the play concludes without deciding between a corrupt government by consent on the one hand, and a military government by force on the other. *Hamlet* is most profoundly a political play in setting against one another the two modes of government that have predominated in Western history, and . . . the limitations of both are revealed."[55] Yet it is not at all clear that Fortinbras will govern any differently from Hamlet's father, about whose reign we know almost as little. Foakes's reading reflects

---

[55] R. A. Foakes, *"Hamlet" versus "Lear": Cultural Politics and Shakespeare's Art* (Cambridge: Cambridge University Press, 1993), 147, 178. See also Barbara Everett, *Young Hamlet: Essays on Shakespeare's Tragedies* (Oxford: Clarendon, 1989), 7–8.

a late twentieth-century conviction, generally pessimistic, that history does repeat itself—so much so that Fortinbras is cut in the same image as later military dictators. There is a more marked difference between Shakespeare's way of thinking about historical time and that of the nineteenth century, though even there we can find a range of views.[56] Scott's novels do not anticipate history repeating itself. The past of Scott's historiography—like the past generations of Redgauntlets—recedes for good.

Scott was not much of a theorist of history. If asked, he would probably say—as in the first chapter of *Waverley* or the dedicatory epistle to *Ivanhoe*—that human nature is the same in all ages. It is, rather, the practice of history in the Waverley Novels that accounts for his great influence: one should consult, in the last chapter of *Waverley*, his crisp summary of the changes that have occurred in Scotland in the past half century, most of them in his lifetime. In the eyes of Scott and his readers, these developments are not likely to be undone; and the representations of change in the novels encouraged the serious study of history in the nineteenth century.[57] There was also a deeper reason for giving credence to the history delineated by Scott: the improvement of political institutions, in particular, comes to be portrayed as one-directional. The concrete renderings of past British history testify to the triumph of Locke's two treatises on government over Filmer's *Patriarcha*, to the principle of consent over a polity analogous to family, and to the settlement of 1688. As Carole Pateman reminds us, the principle of masculine authority has not been abandoned, but the new covenant or contract "is a specifically modern tale, told over the dead body of the father."[58] This was not a narrowly Anglophone view in the nineteenth century. Augustin Thierry and Jules Michelet, who admired Scott's novels as much as British historians did, interpreted modern history in much the same terms. In Lionel Gossman's summary, "the history of England, as Thierry writes it, and as Michelet was to see it after him, is a history of sons rising up against their fathers."[59] A hundred years later,

[56] Coleridge, for example, could interpret Scott's historical subject as "the contest between the two great moving principles of social humanity; religious adherence to the past and the ancient, the desire and the admiration of permanence, on the one hand; and the passion for increased knowledge, for truth as the offspring of reason—in short, the mighty instincts of *progression* and *free-agency*—on the other." See *Coleridge's Miscellaneous Criticism*, ed. Thomas Middleton Raysor (London: Constable, 1936), 341–42.

[57] See A. Dwight Culler, *The Victorian Mirror of History* (New Haven: Yale University Press, 1985), 20–34, 57–58.

[58] Carole Pateman, *The Sexual Contract* (Stanford: Stanford University Press, 1988), 88.

[59] Lionel Gossman, *Between History and Literature* (Cambridge: Harvard University Press, 1990), 143; see also 95.

writing the essays that became *Totem and Taboo*, Freud could still be enchanted by this thought. *Redgauntlet* is that modern tale, eschewing violence and retelling the story of Hamlet as a gentleman of modern times, not in some supercilious sense, but in the sense that Blackstone and Burke endow the independent gentlemen of the land with political power.

Darsie, Alan, and the other heroes of Scott are creatures of the social contract; if they seem helplessly subject to the rule of law, that is because they have in theory brought it into being by their own free consent. Their renewed and burnished sense of male honor commits them to the present constitution of laws, for honor itself has become prudential and pacific, as can be seen in this contrast of the views of nephew and uncle:

> "Alas!" said Darsie, "and is it upon such vague hopes as these, the inconstant humours of a crowd, or of a disbanded soldiery, that men of honour are invited to risk their families, their property, their life!"
>
> "Men of honour, boy," replied Redgauntlet, his eyes glancing with impatience, "set life, property, family, and all at stake, when that honour commands it!"[60]

Despite the intended rebuke, Redgauntlet's argument is circular, and what honor arbitrarily commands will no longer pass scrutiny. Fergusson contends that Shakespeare's Hamlet is already dissatisfied with "the simple soldierly code of honor," and adduces the differences between Hamlet and Laertes, Hamlet and Fortinbras.[61] But Scott is describing and instructing the manners of a different era. His heroes are almost religiously spared from ever killing; anyone who struck through the arras as Hamlet did would duly have to stand trial and risk conviction, on violation of his contract.

If critics of Shakespeare are sometimes troubled that Hamlet should "get away" with killing Polonius, critics of Scott often forget that one of the reasons his celebrations of the polity need to be historical is to allow a space for violence that will be pacified, or a space for any social change whatsoever. His key novels specialize in actions of recent British history that were formative of the contract or that display the origins of what was coming to be called the British Constitution—not a document but a commitment to the way things are done. A double fable of history is thus implicit in the novels and in their immense success: that many actions were possible in the past, but scarcely any in the foreseeable future. History is

---

[60] Scott, *Redgauntlet*, 19.319.
[61] Fergusson, *Idea of a Theater*, 140.

irreversible, and happily in Britain it has arrived upon a tolerable plateau. Perhaps it is this confidence in a new social order rather than local color that was on Goethe's mind when he offered this jibe in 1823:

> Scott's charm . . . rests on the splendour of the three British Kingdoms and the inexhaustible variety of their history, while nowhere in Germany from the Thuringian Woods to the sandy deserts of Mecklenburg is a fruitful field for the novelist to be found; so that in *Wilhelm Meister* I had to choose the most appalling material that can be imagined—travelling actors and poor gentry—only in order to get some movement into my picture.[62]

For nearly a century, the fortunes of the Waverley Novels rested upon the plateau of history they helped to create. Literary historians today make much of the ethos of "capitalism" in that century, as if the economic system that had come into being monopolized the myths of a people or its leaders. Yet all over Europe and America, though only a tiny fraction of novel readers were rentiers, people happily took satisfaction in reading something more near Darsie's—one should say, Sir Arthur Redgauntlet's—allegiance to family, property, and security. True, the ideal of the society of landed gentlemen was precarious; in the decade that saw the publication of *Waverley*, the landed interest was already being challenged by James Mill and David Ricardo, and the theories of rent and labor value began to take hold in intellectual debate. But even those who like Karl Marx envisioned a further revolution to come were fortified by their belief that history would then arrive at a suitable resting place. Scott's novels spoke to this faith in history; it is entirely understandable that the Marxist Lukács should champion them. Scott's readership and his influence on nineteenth-century realism were thus considerable. Goethe was not so fortunate as to live in a country where historical change was thought to be achieved and done with—though his insight that Hamlet might be equated with a poet or writer would be revived many times. Scott on his part paid the penalty for being so alertly historical in 1814 by going abruptly out of fashion around 1914.

The ghost of Hamlet—the son and not the father—frequented the nineteenth century so often and so freely that it is difficult to imagine the course of literary history without him. Goethe advanced the idea of a youth who was special, set apart by his art or his studies or his feelings—a Hamlet

---

[62] Conversation with Friedrich von Muller, 17 Sept. 1823. Quoted by Reiss, *Goethe's Novels* (note 12 above), 108.

undeniably like Goethe himself. Wilhelm Meister, after all, not only performs the part of Hamlet on the stage but shelters behind the precedent that hero affords in apartness and resistance to others. Scott, with this example before him, also conceived of Hamlet as a contemporary, but without this singularity. In *Redgauntlet*, a novel that surely bears the impress of the *Lehrjahre*, he sets to work autobiographically but soon adapts Hamlet's case to his wider project; he gives body, if you will, to Hazlitt's belief that it is we who are Hamlet. Scott enlists Hamlet among the heroes of society— privileged young gentlemen, to be sure, but invested by history with shared political power. A persuasion that history has left fathers and uncles behind is the mark of civil society and faith in the future.

Hamlet's Expectations, Pip's Great Guilt

Iɴ ᴛʜᴇ ᴘᴏʟɪᴛʏ of Shakespeare's plays, expectations tend to be royal. Expectations that matter most and absorb the interest of all ranks are those of princes for the ensuing kingship. In Ophelia's distraught summary of what Hamlet seemed to be before his mind was overthrown, he was "th' expectancy and rose of the fair state" (3.1.146). This notion of succession and inheritance is a far cry from the private dream of improving his lifestyle that teases the imagination of Dickens's young hero even before the lawyer Jaggers—"as the confidential agent" of someone—announces that Pip has "great expectations."[1] Those Victorian expectations, quite apart from the irony that plays about them and the narratives of crime and resentment that eventually explain them, are of nothing more than money and gentility, and so much like the prospect of winning a lottery that they emphatically confirm the opinion of the players in *Wilhelm Meisters Lehrjahre* that chance—"guided and controlled by the sentiments of the personages," to be sure—will hold sway in a novel, as contrasted to fate in a drama.[2] Since there is little likelihood that Pip will inherit anything of value, he overinvests in luck.

Scott's heroes inherit property, which entitles them to a managing interest in the state of which their real estate is a portion. The sense of history afforded by their experiences accommodates the past by mourning it and thereby grows confident of a future. But Pip's expectations originate in private longings in the first instance, unknown benefaction in the second, and criminal connections in the end. *Great Expectations* would seem to be about individual advancement and accompanying repression rather than a role in history. Its mourning ritual has to do with a personal case, the case from which Pip longs to escape all the more when he meets his secret benefactor. As in *Hamlet*, the most sensational revelation is closely guarded by the hero, and the discovery that finally matters seems wholly interior. One feature that distinguished the action behind Shakespeare's play and

---

[1] Charles Dickens, *Great Expectations*, ed. Margaret Caldwell (Oxford: Clarendon, 1993), 1.18.136–37. Citations of the novel by "stage" of Pip's expectations (or volume in the 1861 edition), chapter, and page number will be given in parentheses; but to facilitate reference to most other editions, I have supplied continuous chapter numbering rather than renumbering chapters for each stage or volume.

[2] See above, chapter 3, note 16.

other English revenge tragedies from such older stories as Feng's exercise of brute force against his brother Horwendil was secrecy. Secret poisoning, Claudius's weapon of choice, is especially effective if the death can be made to seem natural, or accidental like that of Hamlet's father. That no one but the ghost and his brother are certain that any crime has been committed already accommodates, one may think, a nineteenth-century fondness for the coverup of any unpleasantness, hence a general pervasiveness of repression. Indeed the mystery of the business anticipates both nineteenth- and twentieth-century detective fictions, for which murder provides the favorite plot, and depth psychology in the same era.

Curiously, in Shakespeare's play Hamlet seems less concerned with the succession to power than Ophelia and—according to Claudius—"the distracted multitude" or "the general gender" seem to be (4.3.4; 4.7.18). Only as the last scene gets under way does Hamlet allude directly to his expectations of ruling. After justifying to Horatio the sending of Rosencrantz and Guildenstern to their deaths, he offers four quick justifications for doing away with Claudius, the third of which addresses his own political future in a single line:

> He that hath killed my king, and whored my mother,
> Popped in between th'election and my hopes,
> Thrown out his angle for my proper life,
> And with such cozenage—is't not perfect conscience
> To quit him with this arm? (5.2.64–8)

Earlier he is too sickened with grief and angry with his mother to think of his prospects; even now he waits for his uncle to angle for his life a second time before striking back.

When Guildenstern and Rosencrantz first arrive on the scene, they seem prepared to cope with a Hamlet frustrated of his expectations. Whether from loneliness or from craftiness—or from both—Hamlet shares his thoughts with them directly in that encounter. He forces them to admit they were sent for, but nonetheless confides his melancholy state and delivers his troubled world view, with Montaigne-like reflections on the state of man.[3] In the folio text, Hamlet welcomes these sometime friends to his "prison":

GUILDENSTERN: Prison, my lord?
HAMLET: Denmark's a prison.
ROSENCRANTZ: Then is the world one.

---

[3] See Harold Jenkins's notes to the lines, in his *Hamlet*, 468–70.

HAMLET: A goodly one, in which there are many confines, wards, and dungeons; Denmark being one o'th'worst.

ROSENCRANTZ: We think not so my lord.

HAMLET: Why then 'tis none to you, for there is nothing either good or bad but thinking makes it so. To me it is a prison.

ROSENCRANTZ: Why then your ambition makes it one; 'tis too narrow for your mind.

HAMLET: O God, I could be bounded in a nutshell, and count myself a king of infinite space, were it not that I have bad dreams.

GUILDENSTERN: Which dreams are indeed ambition, for the very substance of the ambitious is merely the shadow of a dream.

HAMLET: A dream itself is but a shadow.

ROSENCRANTZ: Truly, and I hold ambition of so airy and light a quality that it is but a shadow's shadow.

HAMLET: Then are our beggars bodies, and our monarchs and outstretched heroes, the beggars' shadows. Shall we to th'court? for by my fay I cannot reason. (2.2.233–52)

Not even Hamlet seems to grasp the last point (he "cannot reason"), but since his friends will not let go of the subject, he puts an end to it. Both parties concur as to "thinking makes it so"—namely, that mood can influence our judgment as to what is good or bad, tolerable or intolerable. To Hamlet, Denmark is a prison. His "bad dreams" have an independent reference that goes unexplained: possibly he refers to his father's murder, to the ostensibly innocent arrival of his friends, or to both. A moment later, he chooses to pursue the immediate matter with "Were you not sent for?" and, after more prodding, is successful: "My lord, we were sent for" (2.2.261,277). To these spying friends, at any rate, Hamlet is ambitious: he feels confined because he is ambitious; get rid of those dreams, they tell him, and you'll feel better. Everything will be all right.

Rosencrantz and Guildenstern reach first for the theme of ambition because they have been brought in, after all, as political agents; but they are willing to adopt Hamlet's psychology of "thinking makes it so" to give him a way out. The subject of investigation resists this interpretation of his dreams, however, and turns the spies off with the cryptic words that frame their dialogue: "Then are our beggars bodies, and our monarchs and outstretched heroes the beggars' shadows." In other words, let us accept for now your cautions about ambition; then it will be evident that beggars, who must ask before they receive anything, are mere bodies without dreams. Bodies and only bodies cast shadows; and if "the very substance of the ambitious" is a shadow, then monarchs and their rivals—the out-stretched heroes—must be beggars' shadows, less than beggars themselves. What people have in common, so to speak, is just bodies. In act 4, Hamlet will pointedly tell Claudius to his face "how a king may go a progress through the guts of a beggar" (4.3.28–9)—another way of saying that we are all bodies, and even more like one another when dead and decomposed. Here in act 2, he is content to play along with his buddies from former times and put them off with his antic disposition, only half-caring for logic. They have picked up on his welcoming them to "prison," so he'll let them have their "shadows."

On the evidence of the play, Hamlet has no great expectations. His ob-jection that his uncle has "popped in between th'election and my hopes," spoken in the last scene, seems little but an afterthought. At the conclusion of the scene and of his life, he remarks almost matter-of-factly that For-tinbras has "my dying voice"—or vote—to succeed Claudius (5.2.335). The exchange with Rosencrantz and Guildenstern earlier mainly serves notice that they, and not he, raise the matter of ambition—though no doubt Ham-let knows better than to confess to the same, even supposing he is ambi-tious. In the assumed culture of the action, the difference between a beggar and a king is a given, not a certain social distance that beggars may occa-sionally work their way across. Claudius has elevated himself to the king-ship, but he is brother of a king to begin with and has married a queen; he could be a natural to succeed the older Hamlet, and if it were not for murder and sex, he would not be an obvious usurper. Some of the same assumptions about rank and position still hold for Scott's novel, *Redgaunt-let*. It cannot be said that Darsie Latimer and Alan Fairford, the two heroes, are ambitious in the sense that Rosencrantz and Guildenstern try to tease Hamlet into admitting. Scott was so bold as to give history into the hands of his Hamlet-like heroes, but never to spark them with ambition. Rather, they are the just inheritors of property and the power that accompanies property; the succession to property is deemed as essential to stability and authority in the contractual state as succession to the throne is in a monar-chy. Ambition perversely characterizes the uncle, Hugh Redgaunt-let, who would willfully turn back history to a time before the settlement of 1688—a vain ambition in the eyes of his nephew, inheritor of the baron-etcy and his mother's fortune.

But in the culture of *Great Expectations* things are not so clear. A whiff of capitalism is in the air, and a self-conscious class society is readily apparent. Instead of inherited rank and position, society is divided between those who have and those who have not the goods; and some remarkable social mobility is in evidence. Except for some quick real-estate dealing in Australia, property in land is of no account in the novel. According to the law clerk Wemmick, one should trust to portable property—often, it would seem, a portion of the direct proceeds of crime. Power is generally identified with money and gentility—the latter, a set of appearances supposed to accompany wealth. And frightening power resides in the law—which is scarcely noticed in *Hamlet*, championed over the old regime in *Redgauntlet*, but as ubiquitous as crime itself in *Great Expectations*. If Denmark is a prison because thinking makes it so, real prisons abound in Dickens's novel, from the hulks in the Thames estuary that hold much of the convict population to Newgate in the heart of London, and to the unnamed prison where Magwitch, under sentence to be hanged with thirty-one other newly convicted persons, dies in Pip's company at the end.

The prisons of *Great Expectations* are not metaphors, or at any rate not merely metaphors. Closer to Hamlet's usage in "Denmark's a prison" is the novel's "Little Britain," the street and place of business of Jaggers the criminal lawyer, which comes to stand for Britain itself as well as serving as the center of the novel's actions. And ambition? In such an economy it is manifestly possible to move from one sphere of life to another, and thus ambition is accounted for, and ambition ought to pay off. Yet as everyone knows, the title of the novel is ironic, the hero is as wary of expectations as he is drawn by them, as guilty about leaving the forge and going up to London as he is ashamed of staying where he is. Ambition continues to be just as much a dream as Hamlet's friends imply it is, and when Pip's convict returns—"my convict," as the narrative identifies him—the dream transforms itself to nightmare. Strangely, neither of the avenging ghosts of the novel—Miss Havisham and Abel Magwitch—nor the true criminal types—Compeyson, Orlick, Drummle—are as troubled by guilt as the hero himself is. In Shakespeare, Rosencrantz and Guildenstern presumably raise the matter of ambition because they are looking for sedition; but if so, they fail as far as Hamlet is concerned. In Dickens, the hopeful young Pip, craving he knows not what, becomes a perfect study in guilt.

THE INNOCENT HERO OF A REVENGE NOVEL

What is the warrant for supposing that *Great Expectations* owes any very significant feature to *Hamlet*, or indeed that the novel reflects at all seriously upon the play? Certainly the novel alludes to *Hamlet* noisily enough to pose the question. In the second stage of Pip's expectations, he and Herbert Pocket attend a laughable performance as Hamlet by the would-be actor and impresario Wopsle, appearing in London under the stage name of Waldengarver. This chapter of the novel (2.31) was the second of two published in *All the Year Round* for 6 April 1861: it cannot be entirely a coincidence that the actor Charles Albert Fechter's *Hamlet* opened in London on 20 March.[4] Yet that actual performance was generally well received, despite Fechter's foreign accent. Dickens knew the man and later became his friend. About a year later he described Fechter's performance to an older friend as "by far the most coherent, consistent, and intelligible Hamlet I ever saw."[5] George Henry Lewes also admired the performance, as "the nearest approach I have seen to the realization of Goethe's idea, expounded in the celebrated critique in *Wilhelm Meister*, that there is a burden laid on Hamlet too heavy for his soul to bear."[6] It has to be said that there is nothing in *Great Expectations* of the deliberation with which *Hamlet* is discussed and then produced in *Wilhelm Meisters Lehrjahre*. On the contrary, Wopsle's performance and the production are so bad that, in Pip's account, the rebellion of the audience drowns out everything else. This interlude in the novel has about the weight of the performance of *Hamlet* in *Tom Jones* a century earlier, and on that occasion the joke was on the naïve reaction of Partridge in the audience: the performance, supposedly by David Garrick, is so real-to-life that Partridge imagines he could do Hamlet himself. For reasons that I shall return to, despite the seriousness with which *Hamlet* has been received upon the world stage—to say nothing of the classroom—the play is frequently subject to variations of this jokey treatment.[7]

Whether because of Wopsle's performance or in spite of it, a critical literature has determinedly sought out other connections between Dickens's novel and Shakespeare's play. In a published dissertation, Robert F. Fleissner saw that both Magwitch and Havisham are ghost-like characters desirous of revenge; he noted, as well, a rough resemblance of Uncle Pumblechook to Polonius, the reading of the tragedy of George Barnwell as a play within the novel, and the Christmas season celebrated at the beginning

---

[4] See *The Letters of Charles Dickens*, ed. Graham Storey et al. (Oxford: Clarendon, 1965–), 9:405n. Wopsle's playing of Hamlet is first alluded to by Joe Gargery (2.27.220–21) two weeks earlier (i.e., *All the Year Round* of 23 March) and thus had to be conceived and drafted by Dickens just before Fechter's opening in London.

[5] To W. W. F. de Cerjat, 16 March 1862, *Letters*, 10:53.

[6] G. H. Lewes, "Fechter in Hamlet and Othello." *Blackwood's Magazine* 40 (Dec. 1861), 746. Lewes's *Life of Goethe* appeared in 1855.

[7] See Henry Fielding, *The History of Tom Jones*, bk. 16, ch. 5. One thinks also of the Shakespearean performances by the King and Duke in Mark Twain's *Adventures of Huckleberry Finn*, ch. 21.

of both works.[8] Different critics have called attention to still other features: that Magwitch swears Pip—subsequently Pip and Herbert—to secrecy and that, like Hamlet, Pip berates himself for not behaving the way he knows he ought to.[9] And the list might be extended to include the graveyard or the canon fire this Christmas season, the early allusions to pirates or the grappling between two boats near the end—not with pirates, to be sure, but with the river police. That encounter is a bad moment for Pip, but one in which he gets off safely and returns home in the other boat as smoothly as Hamlet tells us he did.

In both Goethe's and Scott's renderings of Hamlet's story, fathers have already been sharply curtailed. In the first few sentences of *Great Expectations*, Pip mentions "my father's family name" a couple of times and also his tombstone before coming to the man himself with the following negations: "I never saw my father or my mother, and never saw any likeness of either of them." He consistently declines to use the family name and famously imagines that his parents and brothers too resembled "their tombstones" (1.1.3). Dickens nevertheless creates another novel in which older people use the hero for their own purposes. By devoting the early chapters to childhood, as he had in *David Copperfield* (1849–50), he can adapt a fairy-tale mode in which parents have been exchanged for radically opposed figures of oppression on the one hand and gratification on the other. Thus Pip's sister—never called anything but Mrs. Joe—and the somewhat more lightly handled Pumblechook are monstrous stepparents, whereas Joe and Biddy, who love Pip and eventually marry one another, protect and guide him as they can. If Shakespeare endowed medieval Amleth with a modern family and put in Polonius's family for good measure, Dickens strips the family away except for these surrogates. As narrator, Pip sometimes refers to Mrs. Joe—"more than twenty years older than I" (1.2.8)—as "my sister" but never alludes to himself as her brother or records anyone else naming him her brother. The asymmetry, with its refusal of responsibility for Mrs. Joe, is merely the least of the narrator's ways of striking back.

The title *Great Expectations* presupposes a passive desire for money and gentility; the actions of the novel, however, tell repeatedly of revenge—so

[8] Robert F. Fleissner, *Dickens and Shakespeare: A Study in Histrionic Contrasts* (New York: Haskell, 1965), 193–94, 198.

[9] William A. Wilson, "The Magic Circle of Genius: Dickens' Translations of Shakespearean Drama in *Great Expectations*," *Nineteenth-Century Fiction* 40 (1985), 159; George J. Worth, "Mr. Wopsle's Hamlet: 'Something Too Much of This,' " *Dickens Studies Annual* 17 (1988), 40. Worth provides a survey of such criticism but remains skeptical of the whole issue. See also Valerie L. Gager, *Shakespeare and Dickens: The Dynamics of Difference* (Cambridge: Cambridge University Press, 1996), 271–95.

much so, that it is surprising Dickens's novel is not featured in John Kerrigan's compendious survey of *Revenge Tragedy*, ancient, medieval, and modern.[10] The representatives of the older generation most obviously seek revenge. One may think that the extraordinary Magwitch and Miss Havisham have not the clear-cut reason that the murdered Hamlet senior has to call upon the younger generation to act for them, yet both bitterly plot revenge. Imprisoned for crimes initiated by Compeyson and serving longer sentences than that supposed gentleman, Magwitch has resolved to get back at Compeyson *and* class privilege by creating in Pip a gentleman of his own. Moreover, in the first and last episodes of the novel, he is so determinedly revengeful that he physically assaults Compeyson and—public spiritedly, as it were—attempts to apprehend him even though he knows more severe penalties will fall upon his own head as a result. Havisham, on her part, is so furious at being betrayed and deserted by her bridegroom—the same scheming Compeyson, as it proves—that she has turned first against herself, shutting out the sun and stopping time, while she adopts and educates another young person, Estella, to enact revenge on all or any of the male sex. William A. Wilson argues that both Magwitch and Havisham are oddly self-defeating, because of the way they emulate the class or other characteristics of their oppressors.[11] That observation goes partly to the nature of most revenge and may even help in thinking about Hamlet's father's ghost.

The character "Old Orlick," as he calls himself, is not especially old but most distinctly revengeful. Within a few pages of his introduction in the novel, he has had an altercation with Mrs. Joe and a fight with Joe that trigger his murderous assault on the former the same evening. By the last third of the novel, Old Orlick has fixed most of his anger on Pip himself, mastered all of the hero's secret anxieties, and plotted to take his life at the abandoned lime kiln. Once or twice Pip has warned others about Orlick and thus indirectly acted against him, but that scene is so overly melodramatic that it can scarcely be read as anything but a bad dream. Orlick's expressed motive is revenge, inflamed by a burning resentment: "Oh you enemy, you enemy!" and "You was always in Old Orlick's way since ever you was a child. You goes out of his way, this present night. He'll have no

---

[10] See above, chapter 2, note 6.

[11] Wilson, "The Magic Circle of Genuis," 163: "So ideologically bound are both parents [*sic* for Magwitch and Havisham] to bourgeois culture that their idea of vengeance is not an heroic putting things right but social assimilation born of an unconscious identification with their oppressors. That is, Dickens portrays Havisham and the convict as social products who self-defeatingly embrace the ideology of the class that has unjustly destroyed their innocence and happiness."

more on you. You're dead." Also, "You was favoured, and he was bullied and beat. Old Orlick bullied and beat, eh? Now you pays for it. You done it; now you pays for it" (3.53.421–3). Yet another representative of the older generation—an actual parent, this one, the mother of Estella—has been tamed by Jaggers but is a former client and murderer. Pip learns some things about her from Wemmick, and Herbert learns enough more from Magwitch (while Pip is away) to make the identification with Molly, Jaggers's present housekeeper. As Herbert retells the story to Pip, "it seems that the woman was a young woman, and a jealous woman, and a revengeful woman; revengeful, Handel, to the last degree." Or as we might say, revengeful in the first degree, for when Pip has to ask, "To what last degree?" his friend replies, "Murder" (3.50.403).

A novel in which so much resentment leads to violent death does seem to bear some relation to revenge tragedy. If it is also an especially *Hamlet*-like novel, it is fair to ask what young Hamlet is up to; and though Pip himself is not actively engaged in revenge, by the end he has achieved something very like it in a number of quarters, without even trying. It so happens that Wopsle's performance in *Hamlet* occurs just after Estella's return to the action as an elegant woman and Pip has confessed to Herbert that he loves her: "I love—I adore—Estella" (2.30.247). After Wopsle's prating about his acting career has kept the friends late into the night, comes this, the only passage linking the performance directly to Pip:

> Miserably I went to bed after all, and miserably thought of Estella, and miserably dreamed that my expectations were all cancelled, and that I had to give my hand in marriage to Herbert's Clara, or play Hamlet to Miss Havisham's Ghost, before twenty thousand people, without knowing twenty words of it. (2.31.258)

While the passage has its interest—the true intimation of the ground Pip stands upon, the aggressive identification with Herbert, the anxious identification with Wopsle and his embarrassing performance of the part—it confirms very little beyond the hero's passivity. In the next possible allusion to the play, the ghost has become that of Mrs. Joe, his sister. The news of her death opened "a grave . . . in my road of life. . . . The figure of my sister in her chair by the kitchen fire, haunted me night and day. . . . I had now the strangest ideas that she was coming towards me in the street, or that she would presently knock at the door." Pip actually thinks of revenge for her death, it seems, but like Hamlet he also thinks of proof: "I was seized with a violent indignation against the assailant from whom she had suffered so much; and I felt that on sufficient proof I could have revengefully pursued Orlick, or any one else, to the last extremity" (2.35.277). "To the last extremity" is a little like Herbert's expression later, "revengeful . . . to the last degree": it is murder Pip has in mind.

As Wilhelm Meister remarks of *Hamlet*, "the hero has no plan, but the play has."[12] So indeed does *Great Expectations* have a plan. The hero's expectations will turn out to be funded by the transported criminal Magwitch and not, as Pip believed, by Miss Havisham. The plan also calls for the end to his hope to marry Estella, though this hope was restored in the printed texts of the novel.[13] Most potently, the plan entails the deaths not only of Compeyson, whose nefarious actions have affected both the true and false grounds for Pip's expectations, but of three ghostlike characters who have used Pip for their own purposes: Magwitch, Havisham, and Mrs. Joe. With Magwitch, the generous ghost, Pip comes to sympathize once the man is dying; in the case of the two women, he has the gratification of some slight signs of their repenting the wrongs they have done to him before they die. Through the poetic justice meted out at the end of the novel, Pip surely has his revenge. Though the hero himself escapes the carnage (Hamlet does not), it is still the case that the original plan refused him any domestic happiness other than a saddened bachelorhood.

One can stop there, with the novel's plan, or accept—as I always have—Julian Moynahan's reading that Orlick and Drummle are doubles for the hero, whose very reason for existing in the novel is to act out his revenge and sexual interests.[14] Orlick, most particularly, materializes on the scene to hand Mrs. Joe her death blow with the convict iron that Pip has supplied, in effect, by stealing a file for Magwitch in the opening chapters; Orlick also administers a comic punishment to Pumblechook, the uncle who has plagued Pip's childhood only less than his sister has; and Orlick lusts after Biddy and Estella, the very two women who attract Pip. Drummle, on his part, gets to marry Estella and to demonstrate her folly and the futility of Havisham's scheme by beating her. If that demonstration seems a harsh reading of Pip's revenge, one may recall the equally unpleasant fate of Pet Meagles in *Little Dorrit* (1855–57), who is beaten by the man she marries after ignoring Arthur Clennam. In that novel, also, the paralysis of Mrs. Clennam anticipates the fate of both Mrs. Joe and Miss Havisham. To be sure, Orlick in *Great Expectations* also turns upon Pip, penetrates his secrets,

[12] See above, chapter 3, note 10.

[13] In her edition, Margaret Cardwell prints the proof of the original ending as appendix A, 481–82.

[14] Julian Moynahan, "The Hero's Guilt: The Case of *Great Expectations*," *Essays in Criticism* 10 (1960), 60–79.

and means to kill him. They trade accusations back and forth in the scene at the lime kiln: "It was you as did for your shrew sister," versus "It was you, villain" (3.53.423). What reverberates in the relationship is the possibility of guilt, real or imagined.

That the hero shares in the murderousness of the novel is corroborated in lesser ways. Pip may be awed and terrified by his first visit to Satis House, for example, but he does not depart without a sudden hallucination of Havisham "hanging there by the neck" and "trying to call to me" (1.8.65). Though this incident is as ambiguous as his connection with the attack upon his sister, his feelings about Orlick and Pumblechook are more explicit. Orlick he would pursue and murder if he could prove that Orlick was Mrs. Joe's assailant; Pumblechook he would do away with secretly: "I really do believe . . . that if these hands could have taken a linchpin out of his chaise-cart, they would have done it" (1.12.96). So may our hero's thoughts be bloody or be nothing worth! Elsewhere Pip's narrative takes a ruthless, supposedly humorous, stand against the lives of those who stand in the way of youth. Thus the death of a person scarcely noticed before is registered this way: "Mr. Wopsle's great-aunt conquered a confirmed habit of living into which she had fallen, and Biddy became part of our establishment" (1.16.122). Pip subsequently generalizes the case, by "recalling what a drudge [Biddy] had been until Mr. Wopsle's great-aunt successfully overcame that bad habit of living, so highly desirable to be got rid of by some people" (1.17.125). With similar callous humor, the narrator anticipates the death of another old person waited upon by a young woman, this time the father of Herbert's Clara: "I felt that Herbert's way was clearing fast, and that old Bill Barley had but to stick to his pepper and rum, and his daughter would soon be happily provided for" (3.52.413). No doubt Pip as narrator can count on our siding with the young against any such old people, about whom he tells us very little else. So also does the hero will the death of Magwitch in the end, though with guilty anguish rather than humorous generality: "It was dreadful to think that I could not be sorry at heart for his being badly hurt, since it was unquestionably best that he should die" (3.54.443). Once the returned convict has been sentenced to be hanged—the eventuality that recalls Pip's strange vision of Miss Havisham—a sort of race against time commences, in the hope that he will die first of the injuries sustained on the river. "I earnestly hoped and prayed that he might die," and "I was suspected of an intention of carrying poison to him." The guard and other sick prisoners comfort Pip on his visits to the prison by assuring him that Magwitch is "worse" each day (3.56.454–5).

Every death in *Great Expectations*, even this gradual death of Pip's un-wanted stepfather, can be construed as revenge. Revenge is not only the issue in the schemes of Havisham and Magwitch, in the treatment of Pip and his sister by Orlick, and in the punishments authorized by the criminal code, but reveals itself as an incidental motif in the novel. The first thing we learn about Wopsle's literary tastes, well before we encounter him playing Hamlet, stems from his contribution to what passes for school in Pip's village:

> There was a fiction that Mr. Wopsle "examined" the scholars, once a quar-ter. What he did on those occasions, was to turn up his cuffs, stick up his hair, and give us Mark Antony's oration over the body of Caesar. This was always followed by Collins's Ode on the Passions, wherein I particularly venerated Mr. Wopsle as Revenge, throwing his blood-stain'd sword in thunder down, and taking the War denouncing trumpet with a withering look. (1.7.45)

Here we may get a glimpse of Dickens's working-in of the revenge motif, since in the manuscript he featured Wopsle's reciting of the part of "Fear, whistling to keep his courage up"—consistent with the clerk's feelings in the previous chapter during the hunt for the escaped convicts. Whether in order to address a passion in Collins's ode suited to the role of Antony in Shakespeare's *Julius Caesar* or in anticipation of Wopsle's production of *Hamlet*, Dickens altered the passage in proof to read, as at present, "Re-venge," etc.[15] The motif is then repeated on the occasion of Pip's appren-ticeship to Joe, an occasion dominated by Pumblechook's accusatory be-havior, which—apart from the apprentice's feelings—leads Pip to be mistaken for a criminal taken in custody. All the narrator remembers fur-ther is that "rather late in the evening Mr. Wopsle gave us Collins's ode, and threw his blood-stain'd sword in thunder down" so loudly that the other patrons of the Blue Boar complain (1.13.105–6). These light touches are akin to designating, in the second stage of Pip's expectations, the wholly unnecessary servant whom he hires as "the Avenger."

Though *Great Expectations* first appeared in Dickens's weekly *All the Year Round*, the action was carefully divided into three stages corresponding to

---

[15] See Cardwell's textual note to 1.7.45. Whereas Fear, in Collins's *The Passions* (1750), "back recoil'd he knew not why, / Ev'n at the Sound himself had made," Revenge "threw his blood-stain'd Sword in Thunder down, / And with a with'ring Look, / The War-denouncing Trumpet took, / And blew a Blast so loud and dread, / Were ne'er Prophetic Sounds so full of Woe," etc. Text from Thomas Gray and William Collins, *Poetical Works*, ed. Roger Lonsdale (Oxford: Oxford University Press, 1977), 161–62.

the three equal volumes that would constitute the first bound edition of 1861. In the first stage, the hero's nearly relentless sense of guilt actually precedes any account of his expectations. No doubt Pip already suffers from survivor's guilt when he visits the family tombstones in the opening pages, but the first guilty sensations that he narrates have to do, plausibly enough, with the aid and comfort he has been terrified into extending to the convict. Bringing the convict food and drink and the file to use on the leg iron involve the child in some daring deceptions and petty theft, and these actions are amplified by all the scariness of the graveyard and the prison hulks offshore, not to say the loneliness of the marshes at this season of the year. But fear alone cannot produce guilt feelings. Dickens's psychology is acute: the constant blame and threats of punishment to which this child is subjected by Mrs. Joe and Uncle Pumblechook are sufficient to induce a lifetime of guilt feelings. Hamlet is merely scolded by his mother and uncle for persisting in mourning. Pip's sister both threatens and uses violence against him, and both his warders cast him often enough in a criminal light that it is hardly surprising that he fears the punishment of the law or avenging relatives after he fights with the pale young gentleman (Herbert Pocket). Watched over by such a sister and such an uncle and with no one he is willing to trust with his most secret thoughts, Pip puts on an antic disposition like Hamlet or Amleth, and tells fantastic lies about the fantastic things he has witnessed at Satis House.

Retrospectively Pip attributes most of his snobbery and discontent to the days with Miss Havisham. "What could I become with these surroundings? How could my character fail to be influenced by them? Is it to be wondered at if my thoughts were dazed, as my eyes were, when I came out into the natural light from the misty yellow rooms?" (1.12.96). As he recalls his consciousness of being ashamed of his life and home, however, he at least once points toward Mrs. Joe as well: "How much of my ungracious condition of mind may have been my own fault, how much Miss Havisham's, how much my sister's, is now of no moment to me or to any one. The change was made in me; the thing was done" (1.14.106–7). It is a shrewd guess that his sister—and that uncle, again—are partly responsible for his torturing snobbery as well as his guilt feelings, and for the pained class consciousness of these moments. In a typical tirade, for example, Pip's sister can exclaim, "It's bad enough to be a blacksmith's wife . . . without being your mother" (1.2.10); and, notoriously, she and Pumblechook are the ones who envy most Pip's admission to Satis House and who desperately want to know, even at second hand, what the well-to-do brewer's daughter, Miss Havisham, is like.

The best demonstration of the hero's guilt feelings at this stage of his expectations coincides with the assault upon his sister. Quite by chance on that same evening, Wopsle runs into Pip returning from a disappointing call on Miss Havisham (hoping to find Estella), and quite by chance Wopsle has just purchased "the affecting tragedy of George Barnwell"—the apprentice who murdered his uncle—and is delighted to find a live apprentice to read it to along with Pumblechook.[16] As usual with Wopsle's performances, the narrator relentlessly makes fun of this one. But more than that:

> What stung me, was the identification of the whole affair with my unoffending self. When Barnwell began to go wrong, I declare that I felt positively apologetic, Pumblechook's indignant stare so taxed me with it. Wopsle, too, took pains to present me in the worst light. At once ferocious and maudlin, I was made to murder my uncle with no extenuating circumstances whatever; Millwood put me down in argument, on every occasion; it became sheer monomania in my master's daughter to care a button for me; and all I can say for my gasping and procrastinating conduct on the fatal morning, is, that it was worthy of the general feebleness of my character. Even after I was happily hanged and Wopsle had closed the book, Pumblechook sat staring at me, and shaking his head, and saying, "Take warning, boy, take warning!" as if it were a well-known fact that I contemplated murdering a near relation, provided I could only induce one to have the weakness to become my benefactor. (1.15.116–7)

The popular tragedy, *The London Merchant* (1731), becomes the perfect play within the novel for *Great Expectations*. George Lillo's drama was already remarkable in theater history for its moralizing tragedy adapted for the bourgeoisie. It is identified in Dickens's text only by the name of the wicked apprentice, who is tempted by the woman Millwood first to theft and then to the murder of his uncle Barnwell. This is George, nephew to his benefactor. He stabs him in the garden for Millwood's sake. The merchant's name is Thorowgood. The story is extant, written in indifferent English. You shall see how the apprentice gets the love of his master's daughter. Dickens ingeniously adapts all this revised Gonzago business to narrative. In Pip's account of the reading of the play "Wopsle" modulates first to "he," the character Barnwell, and then, after the explicit "identification of the whole affair with my unoffending self," to "me"—young Pip.

---

[16] Wopsle himself "appeared to consider that a special Providence had put a prentice in his way to be read at" (1.15.116). Valerie Gager, *Shakespeare and Dickens*, 274, picks up the echo of *Hamlet* (5.2.129).

The device, for all its fun and arbitrariness, follows from Hamlet's sudden announcement that the poisoner in his play within the play is "nephew to the king" (3.2.221); but instead of objectifying Claudius's guilt by displaying his reaction to the murder of Gonzago, the play within the novel objectifies the guilt of the narrator himself. This play's the thing wherein Pip catches his own conscience, howsoever "unoffending" he may be.

That this performance, or reading, of the play within the novel works is attested by the sudden confession with which the following chapter begins, after the discovery of the assault on Mrs. Joe:

> With my head full of George Barnwell, I was at first disposed to believe that *I* must have had some hand in the attack upon my sister, or that at all events that as her near relation, popularly known to be under obligations to her, I was a more legitimate object of suspicion than any one else. But when, in the clearer light of next morning, I began to reconsider the matter and to hear it discussed around me on all sides, I took another view of the case, which was more reasonable. (1.16.119)

Of course, the confession itself—the first sentence—is triply hedged against the possibility that it could be true: the emphasis on "*I*" registers first of all surprise; a "head full" of something is an idiom generally reserved for imagination or improbable dreams; and having been represented as guilty by the Barnwell play that night, Pip was but "disposed to believe" he had something to do with the attack. The very idea that Pip might have done it himself is clothed in pleasing sarcasms. The boy who has been lucky to survive being brought up by hand is "popularly known" to be obliged to her; the near relationship (brother, not nephew) makes him a "legitimate object of suspicion" only if there is something to inherit; and ingratitude, the old charge, is somewhat beside the point. Ingratitude is not the same thing as murder. Yet Pip, should he be suspected, has longer-lived reasons for revenge upon Mrs. Joe than Orlick has, as represented by the narrative of his childhood. The second sentence above withdraws the playful confession of guilt before such motives can be examined and serves to introduce seven further paragraphs of facts and inferences about the crime that mainly exonerate Pip by pointing to Orlick. As in a detective novel, too, the police are far less likely to know what to think than is the hero: "They took up several obviously wrong people, and they ran their heads very hard against wrong ideas, and persisted in trying to fit the circumstances to the ideas, instead of trying to extract ideas from the circumstances" (1.16.121). For all that, the playful little confession of a guilty conscience has been tendered by our hero. As Gertrude speaks aside in *Hamlet* (the last she speaks of herself before she too is poisoned), "So full of artless jealousy is guilt, / It spills itself in fearing to be spilt" (4.5.19–20).

The second stage of Pip's expectations then introduces him to London, to financial means, and to gentility. The novel is another bildungsroman with *Hamlet* connections, but one that is henceforth urban-centered. Pip does not yet know, though he thinks he knows, who his benefactor is. The important thing is that he has moved on and left his surrogate parents behind, one of them paralyzed and muted by Orlick's attack. In this new stage of life and fortunes, the day-to-day functional relations will be with friends of the hero's own age: Herbert Pocket, Estella herself, and the school chums Startop and Drummle. The clerk Wemmick is another frequent companion: though older, he is marked as of the younger generation by the presence of a father, the Aged, and a fiancée. Pip's first dinner with Herbert alone acquires "additional relish from being eaten under those independent circumstances, with no old people by, and with London all around us" (2.22.177). The old people, including Jaggers, have become subjects of observation and conversation rather than moral judges. Pip accepts lessons in gentility from Herbert and polishes his mind, somewhat, by going to school to Matthew Pocket, whose younger children are still tumbling up. In Mrs. Pocket, Pip has before him an extreme example of the debilitating effects of snobbery—at least in women. Together, Pip and Herbert begin to practice gentility by living in debt.

"Love her, love her, love her," Miss Havisham incites Pip, and he does love unreservedly the now womanly Estella. Yet to an extraordinary degree Estella remains the eroticized icon of his expectations. "Truly it was impossible to dissociate her presence from all those wretched hankerings after money and gentility that had disturbed my boyhood—from all those ill-regulated aspirations that had first made me ashamed of home and Joe. . . . impossible for me to separate her, in the past or in the present, from the innermost life of my life" (2.29.240,236). Money and gentility mutate, however, toward criminality and greater guilt. With very little regard to the hero's wishes, Estella becomes associated with the criminal element. Soon after Pip and his friends have dinner with Jaggers and thereby get a glimpse of his housekeeper, the resemblance between that sometime murderer and Estella begins to tease Pip's mind, even though he cannot penetrate to their relation as mother and daughter until much later. Similarly, when he eagerly awaits Estella for the first time at the coach office near Little Britain, Wemmick persuades him to have a look at Newgate, where young Barnwell was taken in less auspicious circumstances in the play. With still three hours to wait for Estella's coach, this prison visit becomes the occasion for Pip's longest meditation on his own experience of convicts. He wishes Wemmick had not encountered him that day and tries to "beat the prison dust" away as he waits; but when he glimpses Estella's features in the coach at last, he asks melodramatically at the chapter's close, "What *was* the nameless shadow which again in that one instant had passed?" (2.32.263).

All of the explicit allusions to *Hamlet* belong to this stage of Pip's expectations, but curiously Shakespeare's play intrudes without being explicitly named, as if it could be taken for granted at some point. Pip receives a letter from Biddy that precedes Joe's trip to London, and he digresses to explain to the reader that he has hired a servant—"this avenging phantom"—who then announces Mr. Gargery's arrival. From Joe, Pip learns immediately that Wopsle has "had a drop": that is, "he's left the Church, and went into the playacting," and has accompanied Joe to London. Joe takes a playbill from his hat and hands it to Pip, as requested by Wopsle; but if the playbill gives the name of the play, it is suppressed in the narrative. Pip quotes from it words about the actor, "whose unique performance in the highest tragic walk of our National Bard has lately occasioned so great a sensation in local dramatic circles." Then Joe's report of the play that he has seen reveals that it must be *Hamlet*:

> I put it to yourself, sir, whether it were calc'lated to keep a man up to his work with a good hart, to be continiwally cutting in betwixt him and the Ghost with "Amen!" A man may have had a misfortun' and been in the Church . . . but that is no reason why you should put him out at such a time. Which I meantersay, if the ghost of a man's own father cannot be allowed to claim his attention, what can, Sir? Still more, when his mourning 'at is unfortunately made so small as that the weight of the black feathers brings it off, try to keep it on how you may. (2.27.218,220–1)

Four chapters on—after the news of Estella's return, a visit to her and Miss Havisham, encounters with two convicts, Orlick, Jaggers, and Trabb's boy—Pip and Herbert attend a performance of the play, and still it is not named. "On our arrival in Denmark," the chapter begins, "we found the king and queen of that country elevated in two arm-chairs on a kitchen-table, holding a Court." The role of Mr. Waldengarver is named "Hamlet" only by his dresser, after the show, and indirectly by Pip referring to his dream, later that night, of his own playing "Hamlet to Miss Havisham's ghost" (2.31.252,257,258)—though the performance and behavior of the audience have been travestied at some length.

If Orlick and Drummle are to be taken seriously as doubles of the hero—figments, that is, of his least acceptable desires—then Wopsle may be thought of as a different sort of alter ego, or alter ego in a different mode. The killer and the wifebeater have parts to play that are too reprehensible to countenance except melodramatically, and so far from being recognized as kindred spirits, they are loathed by Pip. Dickens takes care that these two oppose the hero even as they oppose those who have crossed him, such as Mrs. Joe, Pumblechook, and Estella. Wopsle's ambitions, however, are open for anyone to see; he has to be mocked and differentiated from the hero as too self-important and absurd. Yet Wopsle is the other man from the provinces in the novel, who is setting his sights on London and a wholly new sphere of life, and who has his own misguided expectations to tempt him. Wopsle's commitment to theater is finally no more believable than his commitment to the church. He is an actor and nothing but, with such an inflated idea of his merits that he is totally oblivious of his audience. Yet the narrator is at some pains to exorcise that actor in all of his appearances.

Dickens himself was a talented amateur actor and, in the last decade of his life, was supremely good at public readings from his own works. The theatricality of the novels themselves has often been noticed, both pejoratively and appreciatively.[17] Another piece of stock wisdom about Dickens is that *Great Expectations* is a remake, with greater self-criticism, of the autobiographical *David Copperfield* ten years before. Ever since the publication of John Forster's *Life of Charles Dickens* (1872–74), after the novelist's death, readers have had no difficulty in identifying Murdstone and Grimby's wine business in *Copperfield* with the blacking warehouse in which Dickens was set to work as a child, to his defeated hopes and deeply wounding embarrassment.[18] He felt not only abandoned by his parents but thrown in with working-class boys and a marginal existence from which he might never emerge. In *Great Expectations* there is an explicit reference to the blacking warehouse that seems to link it to Wopsle's fortunes, or Wopsle's career. When Pip asks Joe what he has seen of London, he elicits the reply that "me and Wopsle went off straight to look at the Blacking Ware'us. But we didn't find that it come up to its likeness in the red bills at the shop doors; which I meantersay . . . as it is there drawd too architectooralooral" (2.27.222). Whatever this in-joke is supposed to signify, it is the self-deluding Wopsle who has led the pilgrimage to the blacking

[17] See Robert Garis, *The Dickens Theatre: A Reassessment of the Novels* (Oxford: Clarendon, 1965); Paul Schlicke, *Dickens and Popular Entertainment* (London: Allen and Unwin, 1985).

[18] See John Forster, *The Life of Charles Dickens*, 2 vols. (London: Everyman's Library, 1948), 1:19–33.

warehouse. I like to believe that Dickens now finds his own emotional construction of that episode in his life was too architectooralooral. Through Wopsle, Pip has first been associated with George Barnwell. Now, in the second stage of Pip's expectations, Wopsle has moved on to London and the role of Hamlet.

Pip's own most Hamlet-like experience concludes this stage: Magwitch turns up in the night at Barnard's Inn while Herbert is away. The return of "my convict" has the dramatic force of the appearance of the ghost to Hamlet himself in the fifth scene of Shakespeare's play.[19] Of all the ghost-like appearances in the novel, this is the one that conveys hard information by word of mouth and places a new and unexpected burden on the hero. The apportioning of the action in the dramatic and narrative texts differs, but the order of exposition is similar. In *Hamlet*, the ghost appears in the first scene and is tentatively identified as the former king; then he reappears at the end of act 1 for an explicit dialogue with his son that reveals the true situation and calls for revenge. More particularly that ghost asks to be remembered, "If thou didst ever thy dear father love" (1.5.23). In *Great Expectations*, the convict appears in the opening scenes and displays a nobility of sorts; then about sixteen years later he reappears in the night, with the purpose of informing Pip in person of his identity, the source of the young man's expectations, and his own apparent intention of remaining in Britain. He has remembered, all these years, the assistance rendered him by the seven-year-old boy; he has loved and expects to be loved in return; and as for revenge, making a gentleman of Pip is the convict's revenge against Compeyson in particular and society in general.[20] In the remaining four acts of the play, Hamlet confronts not just his father's death and his mother's remarriage but murder and the demand for revenge. In the remaining third of the novel, Pip struggles with disillusionment and the problem of how to consort with his convict.

Guilty Ambition's Unwanted Stepfather

If anything, the exact division of the novel into thirds confirms the importance of Magwitch's role, even though, like Hamlet's father's ghost, he is for the most part absent from the scene. The action commences with a

[19] Cf. A. L. French, "Beating and Cringing: *Great Expectations,*" *Essays in Criticism* 24 (1974), 147–48.
[20] For the interval of time and ages of the characters, see Dickens's working notes, appendix B of *Great Expectations*, ed. Cardwell, 485. Magwitch the author calculates to be about sixty on his return to London.

small boy "beginning to cry" near the place where his family is buried and very little preparation else (that it is Christmas eve is deferred to the second chapter). "'Hold your noise!' cried a terrible voice, as a man started up from among the graves" (1.1.4). In the second stage Pip sojourns in London and imagines Miss Havisham to be his benefactor, but this stage begins with Little Britain and the intimations of crime that persist throughout and ends with the revelation that the source of his income and expectations is indeed the convict: "Magwitch . . . chrisen'd Abel," as he whispers the following day (3.40.328). The last third of the novel is not referred to as a stage of expectations, of course, because it is concerned with repudiating those expectations, while if possible saving Magwitch from the death that the law will exact for his return. Just as Hamlet finds himself only half-surprised to learn that his uncle murdered his father, so Pip has had occasion to wonder why his expectations and Estella herself seem linked to his acquaintance with criminals. He has wanted to believe a different, still less plausible story about why he should be blessed with good fortune, as if money and gentility could be his merely by longing for them—"Which dreams are indeed ambition," as Guildenstern claims, "a shadow's shadow," according to Rosencrantz.

The late king of Denmark—slain by his brother—and Abel Magwitch return to tell tales that are both specific to their own cases and fraught with news about death.

> But that I am forbid
> To tell the secrets of my prison house,
> I could a tale unfold whose lightest word
> Would harrow up thy soul, freeze thy young blood,
> Make thy two eyes start . . .   (1.5.13–17)

Hamlet's father is all but driven from his purpose by what he might tell of his experience of purgatory. Such forbidden matter may simply be designed to increase the dramatic impact, now that a ghost is at hand; yet in some ways *Hamlet* is easier to comprehend as a play about coming to terms with a father's death than about an uncle's wickedness. *Great Expectations* also speaks to concerns beyond the immediate situation of its characters, and when Magwitch returns he too has news about life and death. He speaks not of purgatory, but meaningfully of the criminal code and its current administration:

"Because, look'ee here, dear boy," he said, dropping his voice, and laying a long finger on my breast in an impressive manner, "caution is necessary."

"How do you mean? Caution?"

"By G—, it's Death!"

"What's death?"

"I was sent for life. It's death to come back. There's been overmuch coming back of late years, and I should of a certainty be hanged if took." (2.39.319)

This is the news that shapes the remaining action of *Great Expectations*, and not merely as it affects Magwitch. His is rather an extraordinary perspective: to observe that "there's been overmuch coming back of late years" implies current knowledge and an almost appreciative understanding of how the criminal justice system responds. For any such ghost, sent to an official purgatory, it's death to come back. Less self-pitying than Hamlet's father, he justly foretells the revenge of the state.

"What's death?" Young Pip's emphasis is on the *what*. He has some acquaintance with death. His account of himself opens with reference to the tombstones of his father, his mother, and his five little brothers. He has recently attended the funeral of his sister, Mrs. Joe. And the same account of himself that has dwelt on snobbery and class difference, and his removal from the marshes to the city, has from the beginning touched on the criminal class and its punishment. Since arriving in London he has become familiar with capital punishment, particularly through Wemmick's casual acceptance of hangings and the occasional favors to be accrued from them. Now, in the company of a convict who has returned in person to make his acquaintance, Pip will learn what it is to be threatened and then condemned to die by hanging. His immediate reaction is far from simple:

Nothing was needed but this; the wretched man, after loading wretched me with his gold and silver chains for years, had risked his life to come to me, and I held it there in my keeping! If I had loved him instead of abhorring him; if I had been attracted to him by the strongest admiration and affection, instead of shrinking from him with the strongest repugnance; it could have been no worse. On the contrary, it would have been better, for his preservation would then have naturally and tenderly addressed my heart. (2.39.320)

"Nothing was needed but this": that is, after the short conversation in which Magwitch proves indisputably that he is Pip's benefactor and has in effect adopted him—"Look'ee here, Pip. I'm your second father. You're my son—more to me nor any son" (2.39.317)—he urges caution, since he has risked his life for this reunion. The man who has plumped himself down in Pip's sitting room is "wretched" in all sorts of senses—in appearance, in his history, and in his near total misunderstanding of his welcome. But it is "wretched man . . . wretched me," and Pip mostly wants his readers to understand the latter. The metaphor for Magwitch's generosity—"loading . . . me with his gold and silver chains for years"—beautifully expresses their topsy-turvy relations. The man held in iron chains for years, whom Pip once helped to free for a few hours, has managed to transform iron to gold and silver; the quarterly income that Pip has been receiving has now become *his* sentence, a chain of indebtedness that he has never seriously acknowledged, let alone correctly traced. And note how swiftly, in the same sentence, Pip comes to reflect that Magwitch's life is now in *his* keeping, since he could betray the returned convict to the crown—at one extreme—or carelessly give him away. Pip's rapidly moving imagination attaches guilt to himself as readily as it did when he was a small boy, but in this case proleptically and for doing a mean instead of a kind deed. Get rid of him! is nearly his first thought, immediately checked by guilt but also by shame that is strictly social. If he "had loved" Magwitch, "it would have been better." As it is, just for form's sake he has to suppress his longing to be rid of the man.

The effect on Pip of this ghost's announcement is as ratiocinative as that of the ghost on Hamlet and reaches no certain conclusion until Magwitch dies for good. The narrated snatches of the hero's thought are like recovered soliloquy; narrated as well are dialogues with his friend Herbert, as the last third of the novel begins to unfold. If Hamlet's underlying problem has seemed to generations of interpreters to be whether or not he ought to revenge his father's murder, Pip's problem is the distinctly more passive one of whether or not he can possibly accept this putative father's generosity. Hamlet's instinctive response is yes:

> Haste me to know't, that I with wings as swift
> As meditation or the thoughts of love
> May sweep to my revenge.   (1.5.29–31)

Pip's instinctive response is no, he must have nothing to do with an ex-convict's fortune. Note that both responses are unselfish, but neither can possibly put an end to the matter.

Herbert Pocket is not so certain. "Too stunned" by the news of the source of Pip's expectations to think at this point, Herbert hesitates:

"You mean that you can't accept——?"

"How can I?" I interposed, as Herbert paused. "Think of him! Look at him!"

An involuntary shudder passed over both of us.

"Yet I am afraid the dreadful truth is, Herbert, that he is attached to me, strongly attached to me. Was there ever such a fate!"

Remember that Pip is rejecting not only the money and attachment but Magwitch's extravagant plan to avenge society's treatment of himself by creating a gentleman son. Moments later, in the continuing dialogue of the two friends, the very love and calm purpose of the older man are construed as coercive, a sort of moral blackmail of the adopted son:

"See, then," said Herbert; "think of this! He comes here at the peril of his life, for the realisation of his fixed idea. In the moment of realisation, after all his toil and waiting, you cut the ground from under his feet, destroy his idea, and make his gains worthless to him. Do you see nothing that he might do, under the disappointment?"

"I have seen it, Herbert, and dreamed of it, ever since the fatal night of his arrival. Nothing has been in my thoughts so distinctly, as his putting himself in the way of being taken."

"Then you may rely upon it," said Herbert, "that there would be great danger of his doing it. That is his power over you as long as he remains in England, and that would be his reckless course if you forsook him." (3.41.340,341).

Magwitch has hinted nothing of the kind, but Pip has "dreamed of it," and since his thoughts have coincided with Herbert's on the possibility, he may "rely upon it." By this compounded logic, Magwitch will turn himself in to the authorities if balked by his young man! As it is, Dickens has softened this conjecture of the two friends by replacing the word "revenge" in his draft of the novel—" that would be his revenge if you forsook him"—with the words "reckless course."[21]

Such revenge on the part of a revenger at present content with setting up a boy from the blacksmith shop by the marshes as a gentleman would be extraordinarily indirect. By turning himself in to be hanged, he would make Pip *feel* bad—guilty or ashamed again. On numerous occasions Pip is careful to inform his readers that he cannot accept Magwitch's fortune, which in the event is forfeited to the crown. So much scrupulosity, however,

---

[21] Textual note, *Great Expectations*, ed. Cardwell, 341.

is common with Scott's and other British heroes of the time, though seldom expressed by the Rastignacs and Rubemprés who arrive in the city
from the provinces in the French novel.[22] It is the British hero's way of
demonstrating that, no matter what, he must not have anything to do with
money touched by criminal hands—sometimes even merchant hands. Pip's
shrinking from his benefactor's love, and not merely the money, seems of
a different order. I find it hard to believe that Dickens is ascribing Magwitch's fantastic behavior to a homoerotic crush on the small boy or the
young man, though the possibility cannot be altogether ruled out. Magwitch's frequently addressing Pip as "my dear boy" anticipates the characteristic address of Jasper to his nephew in *The Mystery of Edwin Drood*
(1870), where there may well be homosexual overtones. There was also the
example of Balzac, whose arch-criminal Vautrin does have a crush on Lucien de Rubempré. In the erotics of *Splendeurs et misères des courtesanes*
(1839–47), Vautrin seems vicariously to enjoy Lucien's affair with the de-
lectable Esther; but Magwitch, all unknowingly, is the father of Pip's great
love, Estella. It is just possible that Dickens was remaking Vautrin for a
different readership.[23]

Magwitch fancies himself a second father to Pip, and for any number of
reasons the young man hates the very thought of it. The former convict's
love makes the plan all the more threatening. In recounting his conversations with Herbert, the narrator manages to suppress something of the
moral delicacy of Magwitch himself, a delicacy not unlike that of Joe the
blacksmith. True, Magwitch boasts that he has labored and saved to make
the boy who befriended him "get rich" and "live smooth"; but he has also
checked himself with the words, "Do I tell it, fur you to feel a obligation?
Not a bit." Expressions of this kind have only made the younger man
squirm; or as he tells it, "the abhorrence in which I held the man, the dread
I had of him, the repugnance with which I shrank from him, could not
have been exceeded if he had been some terrible beast" (2.39.317). The
reaction is unfair to beasts and to Magwitch. The reciprocal love anticipated by this second father is simply not forthcoming, and the burden Pip
experiences from these unexpected revelations could be said to resemble
Hamlet's burden as interpreted by Harold C. Goddard.[24]

[22] Balzac's young heroes seem almost licensed to revenge themselves on society; because
they start with nothing, they will seek to reverse the disadvantages that weigh against them.
[23] The relation of *Illusions perdues* (1837–39, 1843) and *Splendeurs et misères des courtisanes*
to *Great Expectations* may be merely generic. Nowhere to my knowledge does Dickens explicitly refer to the novels, but he was increasingly acquainted with France and French culture.
[24] Harold C. Goddard, *The Meaning of Shakespeare*, 2 vols. (1951; rpt. Chicago: University
of Chicago Press, 1960), esp. 1:339–42.

In *Great Expectations* it is easier for Pip to cope with the hatred of Mrs. Joe or the deviousness of Miss Havisham than with the love of Joe or Magwitch. In the last third of the novel, he attempts to reconcile himself to the person if not the wealth of his benefactor but is notably less troubled by the man's love once he is dying. The prisoner himself observes the alteration in his young gentleman: "And what's best of all . . . you've been more comfortable alonger me, since I was under a dark cloud, than when the sun shone." And with true love he repeats, "That's best of all." Even the novelist seems finally unable to cope successfully with this ghost of a criminal, for either he or Pip gets wrong the words of the gospel that the latter applies to the situation: "Mindful, then, of what we had read together, I thought of the two men who went up into the Temple to pray, and I knew there were no better words that I could say beside his bed, than 'O Lord, be merciful to him, a sinner!' " (55.456–7). But the words of the publican that Jesus singled out, and which give the parable its point, were "God be merciful to *me* a sinner."[25] For all of Pip's chiding of himself, a blind egotism still seems to protect him from self-knowledge.

The novel permits Magwitch to die a natural death before his sentence to be hanged can be carried out, but the judgment against him and the retaliation of the state for his crimes are never questioned. The narrator, in fact, indirectly compliments the prisoner for never trying "to bend the past out of its eternal shape." Though no fewer than thirty-two prisoners are sentenced to die at the same sessions, these sentences are placed in a wider perspective that subordinates innocent and guilty alike to divine judgment.[26] A shaft of sunlight across the courtroom is said to link the judge to the condemned and suggest "how both were passing on, with absolute equality, to the greater Judgment that knoweth all things and cannot err" (3.56.452,454). So there is poetic justice and, more imposingly, divine justice to come. But absolute equality? That claim would seem to obliterate the very deprivations, aggrandizements, and expectations that the novel tries to sort out, along with the morals and manners of its characters. In truth, *Great Expectations*, like so many novels, proposes a compromise. For all the horror and alarm of the discovery of the source of his unearned expectations, Pip holds on to the income long enough to ensure his passage from the working class and rural way of life to the bourgeoisie; and by a fortunate act of generosity—"the only good thing I had done, and

[25] Luke 18:13; my emphasis.

[26] Dickens at the time opposed public executions but not the death penalty as such: see Philip Collins, *Dickens and Crime*, 2nd ed. (London: Macmillan, 1964), 220–55.

the only completed thing I had done, since I was first apprised of my great expectations" (3.52.413)—he has put aside some of his money to purchase a place for Herbert in the firm of Clarriker's. The deed was done secretly, without Herbert's knowledge, and as a result Pip gains for himself a place and an eventual partnership in the Eastern branch of the firm. A prudent investment of Magwitch's money has been laundered by an act of Christian charity.[27]

A different compromise with criminal earnings takes place every working day in Little Britain. Unlike the divine judgment that sees everything, a principle of the criminal defense business is to know only what one needs to know and to admit to knowing only that which is legal. It is necessary for Jaggers to know that "Provis" is Pip's benefactor but improper for him to know that the former convict is in England. Or Jaggers can routinely employ false witnesses, but not if they tell him they are willing to testify whatever he pleases. He carefully instructs Pip from time to time about what he may or may not ask about his income. Yet he always knows, or seems to know, the secrets that young man most needs to share. If there is a character remotely like him in *Hamlet*, it is Claudius. Jaggers is not, of course, a criminal, but in his two-sidedness—his ability to play the uncontaminated power-broker and adviser to youth—he is like Claudius the earnest stepfather and older friend. Jaggers' clerk Wemmick leads a more quaintly divided life and is similarly circumspect. The "portable property" that he all but solicits from criminals condemned to death, along with his salary and Jaggers' own fees, recirculate from Little Britain to the nation at large. Thus, however much Pip protests that he cannot accept any of Magwitch's fortune, he has progressed a considerable distance by its means and his world is supplied with no less dubious means wherever he might care to look.

A compromise, or deep connection with criminal activity has been written into the very plot of the novel, planted in the erotics of Pip's expectations and therefore inseparable from "the innermost life of my life" (2.29.236). The longing for a different estate in life that Pip associates most vitally with Estella culminates in an irony that would have weighed more heavily with readers if Dickens had not altered the ending. In the midst of Magwitch's return and discovery of himself to Pip in London, the narrator compresses soliloquy as apostrophe—"O Estella, Estella!" (2.39.318). Pre-

---

[27] Dickens's working notes also conclude with the thought, "The one good thing he did in his prosperity, the only thing that endures and bears good fruit." See appendix B, *Great Expectations*, ed. Cardwell, 486.

sumably her name escapes from his lips at that moment because, in his imagination, she was part of a plan that Havisham rather than Magwitch was funding. But far from being unrelated to Magwitch, as Pip soon learns, Estella is the daughter of his convict and an unconvicted murderess. In Herbert's words about that murderess, "on the evening of the very night when the object of her jealousy was strangled as I tell you, the young woman presented herself before Provis for one moment, and swore that she would destroy the child" (3.50.403). Pip and Estella, it might be said, were made for one another: he is the tool of Abel Magwitch's revenge upon society and Compeyson; she is the tool of Miss Havisham's revenge upon mankind and Compeyson, and "for one moment" she was the tool of her revengeful mother. Estella is the biological daughter, Pip the adopted son of one sire. In Magwitch's dying moments—a prelude to either ending of the novel—Pip at long last tells him what he has learned of Estella: "She is living now. She is a lady and very beautiful. And I love her" (3.55.456). That she is a lady should be important to Magwitch, of course, as it is to Pip. For the latter to love Estella and lose her, or to marry her after her stint with the punishing Drummle, affects very little this tracing of the "money and gentility" she represents to criminal origins. But the new ending relieves Pip's and his reader's immediate disappointment by promising a kind of incest between the only begotten and the chosen child.

The ghost in *Hamlet* charges that a horrible crime of parricide and incest underlies the present Danish state and has deprived young Hamlet of his proper father and mother. But once the ghost has addressed the hero personally, he departs, with the words "Adieu, adieu, adieu. Remember me" (1.5.91). Except for prodding Hamlet to swear his friends to secrecy by growling beneath the stage and a few anxious moments of concern for Gertrude in the closet scene, he keeps out of the way for the rest of the action and notably does not return to express satisfaction at the play's end. The principal ghost in *Great Expectations* returns personally to deliver his stunning revelation of the facts to Pip—"more to me nor any son"—and apparently moves in to stay. For the rest of the novel Pip wishes in vain to be rid of him, or at the very least to get him out of Britain so that the burden of his being arrested and hanged will not be on Pip's conscience. In the play and in the novel, the ghost is never fully exorcised until the very end of the represented action, but two important differences need to be stressed. First, Pip survives the ending and profits from his experience. He learns something about snobbery, and his modest business success— "we had a good name, and worked for our profits, and did very well" (3.58.476)—would not have been possible without the benefaction from his convict. But second, Pip has been haunted by guilt from the very first scene without his having done anything wrong or been asked to do something he did not perform. An element of unjustified guilt in Hamlet's makeup can be traced to mourning and is a temporary state; Pip's guilt is endemic and is associated throughout with criminality, or kinds of behavior that are thought to violate the social contract, the very nadir of which is Compeyson's behavior over his lifetime. Dickens's notion of guilt is a nineteenth- and twentieth-century invention of the sort that colors formal interpretation of *Hamlet* in the same era.

MODERN HAMLET AND PSYCHOANALYSIS

A liability to guilt feelings in the well-meaning hero is already evident in Scott's novels, but most often in limited episodes. Scott's emphasis is on mourning the patriarchy while establishing a new polity of consent, and even so—or because of the commitment to a self-governing nation of gentlemen—there are times when his heroes all but place themselves under arrest.[28] With *Great Expectations*, Dickens gives the entire novel over to trespass and its punishment: innocent trespass accompanied by guilt feelings, criminal trespass met with imprisonment, transportation, and death. In this revenge novel, as it may be called, there is none of Dickens's usual satire of government. The polity that lies behind the criminal justice system is simply assumed. Criminals abound, yet seemingly more ubiquitous are the institutions and personnel devoted to suppressing crime. Significantly, the criminals one meets are mostly convicts, who nevertheless retain invisible means of communicating among themselves. The protagonist, his sister and uncle, and others dream idly of social advancement; with varying degrees of self-consciousness they are subject to a terrible class snobbery. But underlying these ostensible themes of the novel are criminal connections that the plot drives home, the steadfast punishment awaiting crime—"it's Death!"—and the hero's abiding sense of guilt. The newness—the currency—of social advancement *is* the concern that attaches the superficial and underlying themes of *Great Expectations*. Whereas Scott's novels relegate violence to the past and celebrate a peaceable polity founded on prop-

---

[28] See Alexander Welsh, *The Hero of the Waverley Novels* (1963; rpt. Princeton: Princeton University Press, 1992), 22–24, 101–4, 118–24; and *Strong Representations: Narrative and Circumstantial Evidence* (Baltimore: Johns Hopkins University Press, 1992), 76–99. Daniel Born, *The Birth of Liberal Guilt: Dickens to H. G. Wells* (Chapel Hill: University of North Carolina Press, 1995), credits Dickens with first writing of so-called liberal guilt in *Little Dorrit*.

erty in land, this novel confronts an entrepreneurial economy and notes the suppressed violence that attains in the present. Both *Redgauntlet* and *Great Expectations* tell of the modern society that Carole Pateman characterizes as "told over the dead body of the father," but Dickens's *Hamlet*-inspired novel exposes the psychic costs.[29]

The novel stops short of asserting a direct connection between commerce and crime, as if to engage in business were to take money without providing goods or services in return. Yet the modesty of the business Pip engages in at the last is instructive. Pointedly, the Eastern branch of Clarriker's to which he and Herbert devote themselves does not make "mints of money" or do business "in a grand way" (3.58.476). Their small business contrasts with the Australian wool and mutton trade and perhaps real-estate dealing on the side that have amassed a fortune for Magwitch in a few years. None of the funding of Pip's expectations appears to have been unlawful: the Australian fortune must be rejected because it was made *by* a former convict and made in a hurry, or by sheer luck, without due attention to the suspicion that attaches to large profits. The distinction seems very much a matter of appearances: too active a pursuit of wealth is to be avoided. Passivity of income remains an ideal, even though one of Pip's mistakes was to believe he could achieve money and gentility with no work at all. Nineteenth-century gentility still posits a certain ease: on the assumption that just having something is better than making it.

Dickens had plenty of experience with these Victorian mores, which contributed greatly to a downplaying or concealment of ambition, hence to the state of repression assumed by depth psychology at the end of the century. Regardless of what Pip says, it would be unlikely—even unproductive—for him to be "content to be partners with Joe in the honest old forge" (2.34.271). Indeed, "forge" is such a precarious term in the novel that it is hardly surprising that this one has to be named both honest and old. Forging in another sense is Compeyson's way of making something by taking it away from someone else. When Dickens read proof of the second chapter of his novel, to Mrs. Joe's explanation in the manuscript— "People are put into the Hulks because they murder, and because they rob, and do all sorts of bad"—he added after "they rob," the words "and forge" as they now appear in the text, no doubt in anticipation of Compeyson's criminal career.[30]

[29] For Pateman, see above, chapter 3, note 58.
[30] Textual note, *Great Expectations*, ed. Cardwell, 1.2.15.

In yet another sense, Dickens forged with words the fictitious representation of his or another man's life known as *Great Expectations*. The successful novelist, be it said, had long before this set himself up in a style nearer to that imagined for Pip by the fast-working Magwitch than to that quietly adopted by Pip with Herbert Pocket in foreign lands. Old Orlick obscurely alludes to the two sorts of forging with words, when at the lime kiln he boasts of his "new companions" and suddenly understands more about the ongoing action than the hero himself does. His new companions almost certainly include Compeyson: "Some of 'em writes my letters when I wants 'em wrote—do you mind?—writes my letters, wolf! They writes fifty hands; they're not like sneaking you, as writes but one" (3.53.424). Naturally Orlick's idea of sneakiness is all askew. Whereas law-abiding persons fear that anyone who writes in fifty hands is capable of emptying their bank accounts and estates, Orlick finds something suspicious in sticking to just one signature. But either he is angry because everything the reader knows about him is set down in Pip's hand, or smug because his new friend Compeyson has as many hands as the practicing novelist.

Still more evidently, Dickens's novel anticipates psychoanalytic readings of *Hamlet* itself. Late eighteenth-century and Romantic criticism, including Goethe's and Coleridge's opinions, already featured Hamlet's character: instead of revenge posing a problem for the young hero, his delay became symptomatic of his character and his character the problem for interpretation. Thenceforth Hamlet's delay would be the starting point for virtually all criticism until the mid-twentieth century—"the central mystery," as Ernest Jones would put it, the hidden "cause of his delay" or "specific aboulia."[31] The classic psychoanalytic solution to the mystery rapidly whittles away to guilt: "Hamlet's own sense of guilt—what the Freudian explanation makes central," according to C. L. Barber and Richard P. Wheeler.[32] The very word *guilt*, in twentieth-century parlance, has come to stand first for guilt feelings and only secondarily for criminal accountability. Psychoanalytic interpretations regularly reduce the figure of Claudius to a personification of the hero's guilty wishes to do away with his father and make love with his mother—usually as these wishes were fixed in infancy and then repressed. The revenge play becomes a sort of bildungsroman with opportunity for therapy awaiting its interpretation. But *Great Expectations* is also about a child's encounter with crime as narrated by the

[31] Ernest Jones, "The Oedipus-Complex as an Explanation of Hamlet's Mystery," *American Journal of Psychology* 21 (1910), 74, 86.

[32] C. L. Barber and Richard P. Wheeler, *The Whole Journey: Shakespeare's Power of Development* (Berkeley: University of California Press, 1986), 266.

child when an adult. Already in Dickens's novel the emphasis has shifted from the crime of the several criminals to the guilt of the hero: from the perspective of psychoanalytic readings of *Hamlet*, it cannot be surprising that the Barnwell play-within-the-novel serves to reveal Pip's own guilty conscience or that his telling of his life's story achieves a degree of self-understanding.

"It is *we* who are Hamlet," according to Hazlitt. In the same era, Scott's heroes were not just anyone, perhaps, but any law-abiding young gentleman of property. Hazlitt believed that the passivity of Hamlet and of Scott's heroes made it relatively easy for readers to identify with them, a process that may further diminish their individual particularity.[33] Yet the hero of Shakespeare's play—*The Tragedie of Hamlet, Prince of Denmarke*, as the folio has it—was not such a cipher as that. He may be a prince of an earlier time, but he is a prince of an identifiable nation, with existing diplomatic relations to England. As James VI of Scotland, James I had married Anne of Denmark in 1589, and in 1603 her sons became heirs apparent in England. Princes have this notoriety, and in one way or another Hamlet's particular inheritance has been an issue for many readings of the play spanning four hundred years. In marked contrast, and far more in accord with Hazlitt's observation, the hero of *Great Expectations* has no historical identity and little personality other than that implied by the humor and sentiment of his narrative. Pip really might be anyone at all. His formal name, Philip Pirrip, never appears after the first page; his friend Herbert calls him Handel, because "there's a charming piece of music by Handel, called the harmonious Blacksmith" (2.23.177)—a whimsical way of bridging the class difference of the two friends. Pip's unique experience of the convict class is so thoroughly assimilated to a psychological narrative that it leaves no other record—no famous trial, no newspaper account or memorial for Magwitch, no public distinction for Pip. A comparison with David Copperfield, Dickens's earlier hero, is telling. Just as modest as Pip—even more so, in proportion to his achievements—Copperfield becomes a famous novelist like Dickens, with the initials of their names reversed.[34] Pip goes abroad into obscurity and greater anonymity: presumably Herbert goes on calling him Handel, but what do his other business associates call him? In British novels, such removal to foreign parts is most often reserved for characters who *have* broken the law or infringed some moral standard and are heard from no more. After the departure of Orlick and the deaths of

[33] See above, chapter 3, notes 20 and 21.
[34] See Forster, *The Life of Charles Dickens*, 2:78.

Compeyson and Magwitch, in short, an ordinariness descends over the representation and makes everything that has gone before seem like a dream.[35] What remains is a famous story: but not the fairy story of success, the favorite story of the nineteenth-century that it travesties; more like a model therapy for the shadow of ambition, a story of shame converted to guilt that is assuaged by the telling of it.

According to Freud, it is we who are Oedipus. But if everyone has an Oedipus complex, the determination of a particular identity is clearly not the issue that it was for Sophocles' hero. To have an Oedipus complex, one does not need to be the respected leader of Thebes or the son of anyone in particular. If there is such a complex, all one need be is male, ambitious, and still wary of fathers. In short, the middle-class culture of Dickens and Freud's time supplied the conditions for guilty expectations, which then could be ironized as Great or Oedipal. The projection at work in Pip's narrative of his own life, the displacement of partially entertained motives upon other characters, the wish fulfillment apparent in events supposedly beyond his control are effects contrived by the novelist, even if not always with the same degree of conscious deliberation. Pip could be any young man of his time, but all one has to do is ask how representative was his experience and the dreamlike components of his story will come to the fore, quite as they do in *Hamlet*. The events told of in the novel may be unusual, but the dreams are still representative. Pip's is a story of upward mobility and astounding guilt, with some of that guilt dissipated in telling and still more of it displaced on others. The narrative devices of *Great Expectations*—and Dickens had become a master of such devices—are the very means of fiction making that Freud discerned in *The Interpretation of Dreams* (1900) and called dreamwork.

For many readers, the most attractive parts of Freud's dream book are those numerous passages in which he writes of his own dreams and so reverts to autobiography. The theme of most of those dreams is indeed ambition, as Freud plays tendentiously with the latent matter of his own expectations. In some pages added to the book in 1911, for instance, Freud tells of a recurrent dream by another self-made Austrian writer, Peter Rosegger, who testified, "I have for many years dragged around with me, like a ghost from which I could not set myself free, the shadow of a tailor's life." The founder of psychoanalysis then compares this shadow to that

---

[35] The infused criminality of the novel evaporates. Compare the "malady of Denmark" that Francis Fergusson traces in *Hamlet*: "with the end of Claudius and his regime it is gone like a bad dream." *The Idea of a Theater* (1949; rpt. New York: Anchor, n.d.), 122.

of his own earlier days in a chemical laboratory, "without ever becoming proficient in the skills" required for that sort of analysis, and avers that he too has suffered disagreeable dreams taking him back to the laboratory. If in the daytime he feels "inclined to boast to myself how successful I have become," Freud continues,

> my dreams remind me during the night of those other, unsuccessful analyses of which I have no reason to feel proud. They are the punishment dreams of a *parvenu*, like the dreams of the journeyman tailor who had grown into a famous author. But how does it become possible for a dream, in the conflict between a *parvenu*'s pride and his self-criticism, to side with the latter, and choose as its content a sensible warning instead of an unlawful wish-fulfillment? . . . We may conclude that the foundation of the dream was formed in the first instance by an exaggeratedly ambitious phantasy, but that humiliating thoughts that poured cold water on the phantasy found their way into the dream instead.[36]

Freud struggles to fit such punishment dreams to his claim that all dreams must fulfill a wish, but to anyone persuaded that the text has more to do with nineteenth-century homiletics than with science, that argument is less telling than the correctness of the writer's attitude toward ambition. *Great Expectations* is about such an "exaggeratedly ambitious fantasy," similarly qualified by the apprentice blacksmith's subsequent self-criticism, not least by the exposure of his pride and thoughtlessness. Just as Pip's narrative—his wretched mistakes, his poor treatment of Joe and Biddy, his snobbery altogether—displays an awareness of the crassness of his youth, Freud's laboratory dreams and his interpretation of their latent meaning testify to his modesty; that he repeatedly discovers to the reader, as to himself, the unconscious aggression of his dreams shows that he knows very well how to behave when conscious.[37] Like Pip, he likes to refer his most outrageous secret longings to childhood or to a phase of behavior outgrown. Pip does not really have it in for Wopsle's great aunt or Clara Barley's unseen parent when he wishes them dead; even Pumblechook, whose demise is hastily planned at one point, is too choice a butt for the narrator's humor to do away with. Freud writes with similar good humor about the professional scene in *The Interpretation of Dreams*. In the so-called specimen dream itself, he cheerfully claims to have "revenged" himself on

---

[36] Freud, *The Interpretation of Dreams, Standard Edition*, 5:473–76.
[37] For a fuller account of this argument, see Alexander Welsh, *Freud's Wishful Dream Book* (Princeton: Princeton University Press, 1994), 51–78.

his patient Irma and his colleagues as well. Especially one poor colleague suffers, but only amusingly so in the dream: "Otto had in fact annoyed me by his remarks about Irma's incomplete cure, and the dream gave me my revenge." Needless to say, Freud would not deliberately hurt anyone more than Pip would. Later in the book he will dryly deny "avenging myself on my friend Otto, whose fate it seems to be to be ill-treated in my dreams."[38]

Hamlet himself is featured in the long footnote to the paragraphs on Oedipus that was raised to Freud's text in 1914. At this key juncture he is examining dreams such as one might have of the death of loved ones. Though Freud does not put it quite this way, the dreamer is in a state of anticipatory mourning. The wish behind the dream is unconscious, of course. The dreamer does not consciously wish to be rid of a loved one, any more than the waking Freud would get rid of Otto or Dickens permit his hero actually to murder Pumblechook. But fatefully—at least for the duration of the twentieth century—the targeted loved one of this "typical dream" is the father of a dreaming son. For psychoanalytic criticism of *Hamlet*, the assumed unconscious aggression of son against father makes Claudius's responsibility pale. For social history, the presumed eagerness to surpass the father figures a personal motive of commercial and industrial progress for which ambition is surely requisite. These same psychological assumptions and social conditions are implicit in *Great Expectations*. The hero's parents—already diminished in the fables of Goethe and Scott—are tucked underground by the first few sentences. But there is nothing unconscious in Pip's loathing of his appointed stepfather, whose criminal aspect reflects traditional doubts about economic gain more than any direct family connection.

The nineteenth century came to want it both ways: respect for the older generation but surpassing its representatives with increasing speed and energy every day—the shadow of a dream and the shadow's shadow, in the doublespeak of Rosencrantz and Guildenstern. Freud is almost disingenuous about the unconsciousness of what he soon came to call the Oedipus complex. He lets the cat out of the bag when he writes frankly in these same pages of *The Interpretation of Dreams* of the conscious hostility of father and son:

> The more unrestricted was the rule of the father in the ancient family, the more must the son, as his destined successor, have found himself in the position of an enemy, and the more impatient must he have been to be-

---

[38] Freud, *The Interpretation of Dreams*, 4:115, 118, 271.

come ruler himself through his father's death. Even in our middle-class families fathers are as a rule inclined to refuse their sons independence and the means necessary to secure it and thus to foster the growth of the germ of hostility which is inherent in their relation. A physician will often be in a position to notice how a son's grief at the loss of his father cannot suppress his satisfaction at having at length won his freedom. In our society to-day fathers are apt to cling desperately to what is left of a now sadly antiquated *potestas patris familias*.[39]

Nothing of the unconscious here, and nothing doubted of the now waning power of fathers: rendering the "hostility" or "satisfaction" unconscious is more like a sop to lingering respect for elders. Thus it might be more conscionable to speak outright of mourning for fathers rather than defer familiarly to the Oedipus complex and insist that it is both universal and infantile in origin. Shakespeare had already suggested in *Hamlet* that this mourning could be deeply uncomfortable, conflicted, and finally insincere in the young while they are young. Admittedly not all thoughts expressive of mourning may be presently conscious to the mind, but a state of melancholy can summarize much that is unspoken. It would still be foolish to underestimate the range of fully conscious thought in a state of mourning, or to ignore the range of Hamlet's thinking in the play.

"Which I meantersay, if the ghost of a man's own father cannot be allowed to claim his attention, what can, Sir?" asks Joe (2.27.220–1). Since Dickens's novel and Freud's dream book both trade upon *Hamlet*, it may be asked whether Shakespeare did not anticipate a psychoanalytic narrative and the sort of critic prepared to conduct the analysis. In *Hamlet*, Polonius is as confident as any nineteenth-century construer of the play that the problem lies with the hero himself, and Polonius assiduously seeks a solution to that problem.[40] He does not succeed with this case before he is killed behind the arras, but he does not give up easily either; he never quite surrenders his notion that thwarted love is the cause of Hamlet's hysteria, as it might be called. Three times Polonius urges that his follow-up plan, to eavesdrop on Hamlet's conversation with his mother, be adopted. This conviction that words overheard are more revealing than words purposefully addressed to one runs deep in Polonius and may usefully be compared

---

[39] Ibid., 4:256–57.

[40] Fergusson, *The Idea of a Theater,* 154, suggests that Shakespeare's representation of Polonius anticipates "the rationalism of the next age." He has in mind the Enlightenment rather than the nineteenth century, but the sort of reasoning involved bridges both ages. See Welsh, *Strong Representations,* esp. 121–50.

to the dependence on a patient's free associations in psychoanalysis. His practice is still more like that of well-meaning detective work, but Freud himself reflected on the similarity of psychoanalysis to the methods of criminal investigation.[41] In the heyday of detective fiction—Dickens and Poe are thought to be the originators of the form—*Hamlet* too has often enough been called a detective story.[42] It was hardly that, but if there is a would-be detective running about, he is Polonius:

> If circumstances lead me, I will find
> Where truth is hid, though it were hid indeed
> Within the centre.   (2.2.155–7)

He is the play's true believer in circumstantial evidence, the distruster of persons and of direct evidence. The method, like that of psychoanalysis, is to collect any small and seemingly unrelated clues and organize them into a fresh narrative of what has taken place, as critics since Bradley have reconstructed the story behind *Hamlet* or as I have just done with *Great Expectations*.

Yet the play surely mocks Polonius: the effect is partly due to the bias toward youth throughout, partly to dramatic irony—Polonius does not know what the ghost has told Hamlet—and partly because the hero mocks him so mercilessly, alive and dead. The investigating psychologist in Polonius also betrays himself, by rushing to complete his narrative of the case without sufficient evidence. Thus—"a short tale to make"—he contends that Hamlet, his love repelled by Ophelia,

> Fell into a sadness, then into a fast,
> Thence to a watch, thence into a weakness,
> Thence to a lightness, and by this declension
> Into the madness wherein now he raves,
> And all we mourn for.   (2.2.144–9)

Prepared "by indirections to find directions out," eager "to define true madness," and persuaded that any "effect defective comes by cause" (2.1.64;2.2.93,103), Polonius reminds one most of the young Ernest Jones who, in service to Freud, is confident that he has found Hamlet out, though he is baffled by what the young man says for himself. In truth Shakespeare's

---

[41] "Psycho-analysis and the Establishment of the Facts in Legal Proceedings" (1906), *Standard Edition*, 9:99–114.

[42] Peter Alexander amended this commonplace by likening *Hamlet* to the American-style crime story that by the mid-twentieth century could be said to supplant the fiction of detection as such. See his *Hamlet: Father and Son* (Oxford: Clarendon, 1955), 170–85.

believer in snares to catch woodcocks managed to snare Freud's disciple before the latter was through with *Hamlet*.

When Jones wrote "The Oedipus-Complex as an Explanation of Hamlet's Mystery" (1910), he was thirty, or about Hamlet's age, though from the tone of the essay one would imagine that he was much older. That early elaboration of Freud's idea scarcely mentions Polonius. But appropriately, when Jones at seventy came to write the well-known *Hamlet and Oedipus* (1949), he took more notice of the assiduous counselor. In his book Jones urges the reader to consult for an understanding of Hamlet's mental disorder "above all, Polonius," and his footnote supplies the same "short tale" given above. Another footnote protests productions of the play that "seem to accept Hamlet's distorted estimate of Polonius." Jones praises the man and remarks, "After all, his diagnosis of Hamlet's madness as being due to unrequited love for Ophelia was not so far from the mark, and he certainly recognized that his distressful condition was of sexual origin." Thus Polonius had the right idea though the wrong woman—a compliment that might be extended further by recalling that when his diagnosis of the case was rejected by Claudius, the counselor's next move was to try to overhear some conversation of the patient with Gertrude. Finally, in an addendum on the acting of *Hamlet*, Jones testily complains again of productions that turn Polonius into a "buffoon" and direct his children "to snigger at him" when attending his advice in act 1. In the play as Jones reads it, only the hero "takes an unfavorable view" of Polonius, "and that for reasons of his own which are far from objective."[43] This last reproof of Hamlet reverts to the tone of the original article, on which the book is closely based.

Even a scolding tone may have been contagious. Polonius in the play dares not scold Hamlet: on the contrary, his deference is so marked that the prince scorns and mocks it. But the counselor is not nearly as careful with his daughter when she speaks of Hamlet's love: "Affection? Puh! You speak like a green girl, /Unsifted in such perilous circumstance. /Do you believe his tenders as you call them?" (1.3.101–3). And he continues in this vein for thirty lines. If there is a Polonial figure of this mode in *Great Expectations*, it is undoubtedly the uncle of Pip and Mrs. Joe, one Pumblechook by name. A great advantage of the autobiographical form, in which the adult writer looks back from a healthy perspective of years, is that Pip too can indulge in a fit of scolding: "that fearful Imposter, Pum-

---

[43] Ernest Jones, *Hamlet and Oedipus* (1949; rpt. New York: Norton, 1976), 67 and n2, 87n1, 159. For an important corrective to Jones, see Dan Jacobson, "Hamlet's Other Selves," *International Review of Psycho-Analysis* 16 (1989), 265–72.

blechook," "that abject hypocrite, Pumblechook," "that basest of swindlers, Pumblechook." How he loves the name! These excoriations are but preamble to that man's officious patronizing of the narrator when he was articled to Joe as an apprentice—a patronizing somehow indistinguishable from criminalizing of the child:

> The Justices were sitting in the Town hall near at hand, and we at once went over to have me bound apprentice to Joe in the Magisterial presence. I say, we went over, but I was pushed over by Pumblechook, exactly as if I had that moment picked a pocket or fired a rick; indeed, it was the general impression in Court that I had been taken red-handed, for, as Pumblechook shoved me before him through the crowd, I heard some people say, "What's he done?" and others, "He's a young 'un, too, but looks bad, don't he?" (1.13.103–4)

Moreover, in the larger narrative Pumblechook is but one more servant of the demonstration that the hero is both innocent and awash with guilt. As in Romantic readings of *Hamlet* generally and Freudian readings especially, the hero's guilt has grown out of proportion to that of uncles and stepfathers. In the novel, at least, Dickens allows Pip to fight back—displace some of the blame on Pumblechook—much the way Hamlet went after Polonius.

Hamlet Decides to Be a Modernist

MINDFUL PERHAPS of the correlation between analysis and synthesis in chemical engineering, Freud toyed with the idea of dream synthesis in his own work of analysis, *The Interpretation of Dreams*. "I cannot disguise from myself," he rather wistfully remarks, "that the easiest way of making these processes [condensation and displacement] clear and of defending their trustworthiness against criticism would be to take some particular dream as a sample . . . and then collect the dream-thoughts which I have discovered and go on to reconstruct from them the process by which the dream was formed—in other words to complete a dream analysis by a dream synthesis." But for his omission of this synthesis in the dream book, he then offers the rather lame excuse that confidentiality forbids such an attempt.[1] In any event, the synthesis of a narrative suitable for analysis is probably better left to a novelist, that of a tragedy to a dramatist—more especially when a career of writing is itself the object of representation. Of the latter sort of action, *Hamlet* became a model in the nineteenth and twentieth centuries.

More than one novel by Dickens can attest to his ability to synthesize materials for analysis. *Great Expectations*, with its "taint of prison and crime" verging upon unconscious guilt "starting out like a stain that was faded but not gone," is just one of the best.[2] Condensation and displacement prepare a narrative that, once the different characters find their places, cannot help but provide grist for Freudian analysis like that of dreams. That strain of modernism whose underlying stories are of unconscious meanings could almost be said to have been invented by Dickens, with a little help from Shakespeare. Another strain, a modernism of doubtfulness and loose ends, at once serious and parodistic, often faithful in its way to *Hamlet*, is distinctly less amenable to psychoanalysis, however many times it is subjected to it. Just nine years before Dickens was composing his novel for weekly publication in his own magazine, Herman Melville was writing *Pierre; or, The Ambiguities* even while *Moby-Dick* was still in press, so needful was the

---

[1] Freud, *The Interpretation of Dreams* (1900), *Standard Edition*, 4:310.

[2] Charles Dickens, *Great Expectations*, ed. Margaret Cardwell (Oxford: Clarendon, 1993), 263.

meager income from his fiction making. Though a disaster with the public in 1852, a century later *Pierre* rapidly earned a reputation as a psychological novel.

Great Expectations rewards—even demands—analysis because of the deliberately buried connections, the questions these pose, and the resolution of various lines of suspense by the ending. The synthesis of the protagonist's feelings, conscious and unconscious, seems very nearly complete. In contrast, the synthesis provided by *Pierre* is incomplete: psychology finally bows to mystery, especially as to Pierre's half sister Isabel, whose most meaningful communications are said to be musical rather than linguistic. Among other preachments, some psychological analysis is offered directly by the narrator, but neither he nor the hero seems fully to understand where the action is headed or its significance. Whereas *Great Expectations*, *David Copperfield*, and half of *Bleak House* are Dickens's only novels trusted to first-person narrators, *Pierre* is Melville's only novel in the third person. Critics sometimes complain that the roles of Ishmael as narrator and Ahab as tragic hero in *Moby-Dick* have become awkwardly confused in its sequel. One passage of exceptionally smooth collaboration between narrator and hero repudiates the kind of synthesis supplied by other literary fictions:

> Like all youths, Pierre had conned his novel-lessons; had read more novels than most persons of his years; but their false, inverted attempts at systematizing eternally unsystematizable elements; their audacious, intermeddling impotency, in trying to unravel, and spread out, and classify, the more thin than gossamer threads which make up the complex web of life; these things over Pierre had no power now. . . . By infallible presentiment he saw, that not always doth life's beginning gloom conclude in gladness; that wedding-bells peal not ever in the last scene of life's fifth act; that while the countless tribes of common novels laboriously spin vails of mystery, only to complacently clear them up at last; and while the countless tribe of common dramas do but repeat the same; yet the profounder emanations of the human mind, intended to illustrate all that can be humanly known of human life; these never unravel their own intricacies, and have no proper endings; but in imperfect, unanticipated, and disappointing sequels (as mutilated stumps), hurry to abrupt intermergings with the eternal tides of time and fate.[3]

---

[3] Herman Melville, *Pierre or The Ambiguities*, ed. Harrison Hayford, Hershel Parker, and G. Thomas Tanselle (Chicago: Northwestern University Press and the Newberry Library, 1971), 7.8.141. Subsequent citations of book, section, and page number of this edition are given in parentheses.

When Sacvan Bercovitch observes that *"Pierre* registers the shock of modernism," he presumably accepts Melville at his word here. The novel will eschew conventional wish fulfillments and actually prefer ambiguities to reassuring certainties. The manner of it might be summed up as parodistic, deliberately rude to complacency and even self-defiant.[4]

Bercovitch also takes due note that *Pierre* is a bildungsroman. Moreover, "it is essential to the psychodrama of *Pierre*—fundamental to Melville's revision of the bildungsroman as a tale of the ambiguities of mind—that this is a book about books, and more broadly a book about art."[5] In truth, the novel is another *Künstlerroman*, and while very different from *Wilhelm Meisters Lehrjahre* in its modernist tendencies and its pessimism, it owes something to Carlyle's translation of that novel.[6] The self-conscious reflection on the novel form may recall the discussion among Goethe's players about the differences of novel and drama, which singled out *Hamlet's* likeness to a novel. Significantly, Wilhelm's explanation of Hamlet's behavior—since famous as Goethe's own—began by citing the same two lines that trigger Pierre's thoughts on the play: "The time is out of joint: O cursed spite, / That ever I was born to set it right" (1.5.189–90).[7] When Pierre has opened his copy of *Hamlet* to these lines, "he dropped the too true volume from his hand; his petrifying heart dropped hollowly within him" (9.2.168). Pierre's premonition is sound: the ending of Hamlet's life in act 5 will supply the model for the ending of his own. For the present, he tears his copy of the play in shreds, along with his copy of Dante's *Inferno*.

With this futile gesture, Melville's hero sums up the characteristics of other nineteenth- and twentieth-century artist heroes—a group irreverent on the whole, disdainful of fathers, contemptuous of others, yet sheepishly aware of their weakness. Their very existence admits the inadequacy of Romantic Hamlets. If you cannot act, they seem to tell themselves, write! But then they fail, or seem poised to fail, as writers too. They are a tiresome lot, these Hamlets, as even their authors seem to acknowledge by portraying them in such isolation. Melodramatically, Pierre departs from this life and from the novel exclaiming, "the fool of Truth, the fool of Virtue,

[4] Sacvan Berkovitch, *Rites of Assent: Transformations in the Symbolic Construction of America* (New York: Routledge, 1993), 283.

[5] Ibid., 262.

[6] See Merton M. Sealts, Jr., *Melville's Reading: A Check-list of Books Owned or Borrowed* (Madison: University of Wisconsin Press, 1966), entry 230. Melville borrowed a copy of Goethe's novel from Evert Duyckinck in 1850.

[7] See above, chapter 3, notes 6 and 16.

the fool of Fate, now quits ye forever!" (26.4.358). We have seen how the story of Amleth has attracted autobiography, especially after Shakespeare's treatment of it. Goethe and Coleridge, Hazlitt and Scott in their different ways confirmed the tendency, and *Pierre* has generally been read as an auto-biographical fiction, notwithstanding the surprisingly belated discovery of the hero's vocation in book 17. In Richard Poirier's judgment, "*Pierre* is an allegory of Melville's thwarted career as a novelist. It is a totally self-absorbed performance wherein failure is attributed to the nature of litera-ture itself and to language as a necessary betrayer. The claim in all this to a lonely cultural heroism was to become familiar to readers of 20th-century Modernist literature."[8]

The running head of F. O. Matthiessen's chapter on *Pierre* in *The Ameri-can Renaissance* was "An American *Hamlet.*" Matthiessen summed up the parallels as follows: "Lucy's pale innocence fails Pierre as Ophelia's did Hamlet; the well-named Reverend Falsgrave's cushioned voice of worldly policy is not unlike the platitudinizing of Polonius; Charlie Millthorpe plays a kind of Horatio; Glen Stanly confronts Pierre's seemingly mad violence with the decisiveness of Laertes. But the crucial relation here as in *Hamlet* is that of son and mother." The last is crucial, that is, because Melville as well as Shakespeare anticipated "Freud's investigation of the Oedipus-complex."[9] To be sure, there is a sort of closet scene in *Pierre* that might be compared to the one in *Hamlet*. The opening pages of the novel describe what seems to be a daily flirtation of mother and son, including the whimsy that they are siblings. But the primary investment in this rou-tine proves to be that of Mary Glendinning, a widow who has been using her attractiveness to command her teenage son's allegiance. In *her* solilo-quy, which concludes book 1, she repeats the words "docile" and "docility" ten times to express the quality she finds most attractive in Pierre (1.6.19–20). She has been fully in command, in short, and becomes furious when he breaks his approved engagement with Lucy and runs off to the city with his newly discovered half sister. It is the latter, Isabel, who is conspicuously absent from Matthiessen's list of parallels to *Hamlet*.

It so happens that this is one alteration in Pierre's life for which Melville offers his own analysis. As he puts it, the brother-and-sister game of Pierre and Mary Glendinning has mentally prepared the hero—"it is somehow hinted to us, to do thus or thus"—to embrace his half sister:

---

[8] Richard Poirier, "The Monster in the Milk Bowl," *London Review of Books*, 3 Oct. 1996, 22.

[9] F. O. Matthiessen, *American Renaissance: Art and Expression in the Age of Emerson and Whit-man* (New York: Oxford University Press, 1941), 477–78.

possibly the latent germ of Pierre's proposed extraordinary mode of executing his proposed extraordinary resolve—namely, the nominal conversion of a sister into a wife—might have been found in the previous conversational conversion of a mother into a sister; for hereby he had habituated his voice and manner to a certain fictitiousness in one of the closest domestic relations of life; and since man's moral texture is very porous, and things assumed upon the surface, at last strike in—hence, this outward habituation to the above-named fictitiousness had insensibly disposed his mind to it as it were; but only innocently and pleasantly as yet. . . . and in sport he learnt the terms of woe.

Freudian interpretation, needless to say, is fond of opposite and surprising meanings—surprising in that they are unintended or unlikely or both. But patently Melville and Pierre abandon Mrs. Glendinning on the "surface" of this represented life, where she is associated with "those arbitrary lines of conduct, by which the common world, however base and dastardly, surrounds thee for thy worldly good" (10.1.176–7). Dark Isabel, on the contrary, lives in the depths, as the mysterious object of male transgression of the lines of conduct.

In *Pierre* the ghost of the father returns in the shape of this illegitimate daughter, whose existence has been unknown to Pierre and remains unknown to his mother. Isabel it seems was born in the father's bachelor years, to a French woman who immediately and permanently vanished. In a fraught decision, Pierre feels he must live with this sister but conceal his father's sin: hence his abrupt and offensive lies to Lucy and his mother that he has married Isabel. But he is also liberated by knowledge of his father's waywardness and pleased that his mother did not enjoy a monopoly of his father's attentions. Now he, like his father before his marriage, is free of the exclusive direction of his love by Mary Glendinning; he will have a sister with whom that play-sister has nothing to do. Lastly, Isabel, the product of the compliant mother who bore her and then disappeared, is free for the taking. These motives, the reader may surmise, lie behind the heroics of Pierre's fall from innocence. Who calls him coward? He shall defy the "base and dastardly" world and carry off Isabel to New York as his wife. For good measure he takes along Delly, a fallen representative of the working class disdained by his mother and discarded by Falsgrave.

In *Hamlet*, just before the ghost intervenes for the last time, the son presents his mother with two portraits: "Look here upon this picture, and on this, / The counterfeit presentment of two brothers. . . . This was your husband. . . . Here is your husband, like a mildewed ear / Blasting his

wholesome brother" (3.4.53–65). And Hamlet continues with the comparison, with a bullying tone sometimes echoed in *Pierre*. But two portraits in
this uncle-free novel afford a different contrast: they are of the one father,
before and after marriage.[10] The former—the so-called chair portrait, smil-
ing and free—Mrs. Glendinning hates, and it hangs in Pierre's closet; the
latter, "taken in the prime of life; during the best and rosiest days of their
wedded union; at the particular desire of my mother; and by a celebrated
artist of her own election, and costumed after her own taste," hangs in the
drawing room. In this long meditation on the paintings, the chair-portrait
speaks as the ghost of the father:

> Pierre, believe not the drawing-room painting; that is not thy father; or,
> at least, is not *all* of thy father. Consider in thy mind, Pierre, whether we
> two paintings may not make only one. Faithful wives are ever over-fond
> to a certain imaginary image of their husbands; and faithful widows are
> ever over-reverential to a certain imagined ghost of that same imagined
> image, Pierre. Look again, I am thy father as he more truly was. In mature
> life, the world overlays and varnishes us, Pierre; the thousand proprieties
> and polished finenesses and grimaces intervene, Pierre; then, we, as it
> were, abdicate ourselves, and take unto us another self, Pierre; in youth
> we *are*, Pierre, but in age we *seem*. Look again. I am thy real father . . .
> (4.5.82–3)

The drawing-room portrait never addresses Pierre at all, in his meditation,
let alone at such length, of which this extract is about one-fifth. The "real"
ghost, furthermore, antedates Pierre's own fathering: along with his
mother, her marriage, the world (so disparagingly described), the very conception of the son has been elided. In a mystery of purely male inheritance,
Pierre is being invited to replicate the deceased.[11]

Whatever one thinks of the closet scene in the play, Gertrude's loyalty,
judgment, and behavior really matter to Hamlet. Melville's novel attracts
the focal misogyny of *Hamlet* like a magnet and adapts it to a metaphysical
principle. That principle—call it originality—does not elude Pierre en-

[10] Henry A. Murray, in his edition of *Pierre* (New York: Hendricks House, 1949), 454–55,
identifies the portraits with two painted of Melville's father in 1810 and 1820. These are now
in the possession of the Metropolitan Museum of Art and the Henry E. Huntington Library
respectively. Hershel Parker, *Herman Melville: A Biography*, vol. 1 (Baltimore: John Hopkins
University Press, 1996), 266ff, reproduces the portraits as illustrations 5 and 7. Parker also
discusses (62–65) the evidence that Allan Melvill may have fathered an illegitimate daughter.

[11] In current gay studies, one critic has gone so far as to claim that Pierre has a homosexual
crush on his deceased father: see James Creech, *Closet Writing / Gay Writing: The Case of
Melville's "Pierre"* (Chicago: University of Chicago Press, 1993).

tirely, but the quest for it proves tragic in the end.[12] Melville can effectively use *Hamlet* because originality, whether as artistic achievement or self-conscious Americanism, has to be wrested from the course of generations. Shakespeare had already loaded the scales in favor of the younger generation; nineteenth-century reflections of his play seize upon the possibility that the ghost of the father is unwelcome to the hero. Ingeniously, Melville can change the significance of two portraits from which is the proper and desirable husband to which, if either, is the more manageable father—a question something like that which Joyce will pose in *Ulysses*. The relationships and tensions between *Pierre* and *Hamlet* are not confined to a set of roughly parallel characters by any means.

The first important redaction of Hamlet's fate, then, is this sudden incursion of a paternal past upon Pierre's exaggeratedly pastoral present and the elaborate game he is playing with his mother, which pretends that she is of his own generation. And even as Pierre sees his chance to emulate his deceased father's waywardness, he resists the incursion mightily—much as Hamlet resists and resents his elders but more so. (Only against Polonius, verbally and then impulsively with drawn sword, does Hamlet resist with abandonment like Pierre's.) When the hero packs his belongings to depart Saddle Meadows with Isabel and Delly, he takes the chair-portrait along; but when he arrives at the Black Swan, he determines to destroy it. "It shall not live. Hitherto I have hoarded up mementoes and monuments of the past; been a worshipper of all heir-looms; a fond filer away of letters, locks of hair, bits of ribbon, flowers, and the thousand-and-one minutenesses which love and memory think they sanctify:—but it is forever over now! . . . How can lifelessness be fit memorial for life?" In a ritual that he associates with classical funerals, he rolls the painting, ties it, and burns it in a flame kindled from its own frame. Then he throws all letters and other memorials on the fire. "Now all is done, and all is ashes! Henceforth, cast-out Pierre hath no paternity, and no past; and since the Future is one blank to all; therefore, twice-disinherited Pierre stand untrammeledly his ever-present self!—free to do his own self-will and present fancy to whatever end" (12.3.197–9). Thus ghostlike revelations result in self-determination—and trouble, for sure.

The funeral ceremony is one of dozens of motifs for death and mourning in the novel, whose inception can also be traced to *Hamlet*. The second scene in the play introduces Hamlet in black, continually—excessively, ac-

---

[12] For the theme of originality in *Pierre*, see Wai-chee Dimock, *Empire for Liberty: Melville and the Poetics of Individualism* (Princeton: Princeton University Press, 1989), 140–46.

cording to Gertrude and Claudius—mourning his father's death. Grief inexplicably descends over the idyllic world at the end of book 2 of *Pierre* and resounds as a threnody thereafter (twenty-six books in all). Merely the face of Isabel is its messenger, before she can be identified or has even exchanged a word with Pierre. "Grief;—thou art a legend to me," he soliloquizes. "Grief! art still a ghost-story to me. I know thee not,—do half disbelieve in thee." But he has met with grief in that face, which now haunts him, and which he associates with that of Francesca in Flaxman's illustrations of the *Inferno*. "Francesca's mournful face is now ideal to me. . . . Damned be the hour I read in Dante! More damned than that wherein Paolo and Francesca read in fatal Launcelot!" (2.7.41,42). Already one can guess why the *Inferno* will be shredded along with *Hamlet*, for Dante first opened to Pierre's "shuddering eyes the infinite cliffs and gulfs of human mystery and misery" (3.3.54). But grief and mournfulness do not reside merely in Isabel's person, her origin and experience, for they pervade the novel after her appearance; and it can be argued that grief rather than love serves to convert Lucy to Pierre's cause at the end.[13]

Initially the cause of so much mourning seems to be the knowledge that Pierre's father has fallen from grace—and into disgrace—since Isabel's existence is the evidence for it. But that explanation is rubbed away by the hero's increasing scorn for the world. Or it might be thought that the grieving is for Pierre's own fall from innocence and temptation to incest. The most general explanation, however, is that sorrow inevitably accompanies knowledge of the truth: for "now, now, for the first time, Pierre, Truth rolls a black billow through thy soul! Ah, miserable thou, to whom Truth, in her first tides, bears nothing but wrecks!" (3.6.65). This generalization builds most dramatically, not from Pierre's new knowledge of Isabel and his father, but from fresh contemplation of his mother's character.

> Oh, now methinks I a little see why of old the men of Truth went barefoot, girded with a rope, and ever moving under mournfulness as underneath a canopy. I remember now those first wise words, wherewith our Savior Christ first spoke in his first speech to men:—"Blessed are the poor in spirit, and blessed they that mourn." Oh, hitherto I have but piled up words; bought books, and bought some small experiences, and built me in libraries; now I sit down and read. Oh, now I know the night, and comprehend the sorceries of the moon, and all the dark persuadings that

---

[13] "Something of thy secret I, as a seer, suspect," Lucy writes in her letter. "Grief,—deep, unspeakable grief, hath made me this seer. I could murder myself, Pierre, when I think of my previous blindness; but . . . now I see it, and adore thee the more" (23.2.309).

have their birth in storms and winds. Oh, not long will Joy abide, when Truth doth come; nor Grief her laggard be.

This melancholy meditation is inspired by an "electrical insight" into the truth about his mother, whose love Pierre now realizes is but her own pride. "To her mirrored image, not to me, she offers up her offerings of kisses" (5.1.90–1).

The first explicit reference to *Hamlet* in the novel arises from the contemplation of a large rock in the forest that Pierre has long thought of as the Memnon stone, together with the legend that the monument to that young hero of the Trojan war emitted a mournful music each dawning day. Via this allusion Hamlet also is identified with "boyish and most dolorous death." "Herein lies an unsummed world of grief. For in this plaintive fable we find embodied the Hamletism of the antique world. . . . And the English Tragedy is but Egyptian Memnon, Montaignized and modernized; for being but a mortal man Shakespeare had his fathers too" (7.6.135). Aside from the reminder that even Shakespeare faced the problem of being original, the context shows that Melville is recalling, in this interval between Pierre's two interviews with Isabel, Hamlet's conversation with Rosencrantz and Guildenstern. Thus the next section describes how man delights not Pierre either:

> He could not bring himself to confront any face or house; a plowed field, any sign of tillage, the rotted stump of a long-felled pine, the slightest passing trace of man was uncongenial and repelling to him. Likewise in his own mind all remembrances and imaginings that had to do with the common and general humanity had become, for the time, in the most singular manner distasteful to him. (7.7.136)

As Shakespeare's play demonstrated, melancholia cuts to the bone and confronts reality most painfully. But what a difference in perspective Hamlet commands, compared to Pierre's despairings. "Indeed," he says, "it goes so heavily with my disposition that this goodly frame, the earth, seems to me a sterile promontory; this most excellent canopy the air, look you, this brave o'erhanging firmament, this majestical roof fretted with gold fire— why, it appeareth no other thing to me but a foul and pestilent congregation of vapours" (2.2.281–6). The balance struck by Hamlet's adjectives spells the difference between him and Pierre. Hamlet also, on this occasion at least, confides his thoughts to others.

Even before Pierre has exchanged any words with Isabel, he resolves to act. He feels "loudly called upon, not only to endure a signal grief, but immediately to act upon it"; he would not prove "entirely given up to his grief's utter pillage and sack" (5.1.87). Still, another five books of exposition and inward breast beating on the hero's part will pass before he does act, by announcing his supposed marriage and carrying Isabel and Delly off to the city. By taking action, Pierre imagines himself opposed to Hamlet's course. Ostensibly, the episode in which he deliberately tears his copy of *Hamlet* to pieces takes for granted the common perception of the play since Goethe and the Romantics, that the hero is incapable of avenging his father's murder. Yet Melville hedges on this interpretation even as he invokes it to show Pierre's determination:

> If among the deeper significances of its pervading indefiniteness, which significances are wisely hidden from all but the rarest adepts, the pregnant tragedy of Hamlet convey any one particular moral at all fitted to the ordinary uses of man, it is this:—that all meditation is worthless, unless it prompt to action; that it is not for man to stand shillyshallying amid the conflicting invasions of surrounding impulses; that in the earliest instant of conviction, the roused man must strike, and, if possible, with the precision and the force of the lightning bolt.
>
> Pierre had always been an admiring reader of Hamlet; but neither his age nor his mental experience thus far, had qualified him either to catch initiating glimpses into the hopeless gloom of its interior meaning, or to draw from the general story those superficial and purely incidental lessons, wherein the painstaking moralist so complacently expatiates.

Melville seeks both to justify all those extraordinary meditations that he and his hero have indulged in and to insist on his belief that the melancholy view of existence is the true one. "Wherefore have Gloom and Grief been celebrated of old as the selectest chamberlains to knowledge?" he asks once again. "Wherefore is it, that not to know Gloom and Grief is not to know aught that an heroic man should learn?" One point he is making is that Pierre cannot yet fully understand *Hamlet*; another, that the symbolic act of tearing the literary fiction is itself something short of taking action (9.3.169). "Eight-and-forty hours and more had passed. Was Isabel acknowledged? Had she yet hung on his public arm?" And, "did he, or did he not vitally mean to do this thing?" Book 9 concludes with Pierre still debating with himself. "Now indeed did all the fiery floods in the Inferno, and all the rolling gloom in Hamlet suffocate him at once in flame and smoke. The cheeks of his soul collapsed in him: he dashed himself in blind fury and swift madness against the wall, and fell dabbling in the vomit of his loathed identity" (9.4.170–1; phrases that have raised more than one reader's eyebrow).

Some of this extravagant language is to be attributed to the prospect of incest in *Pierre*. To act, on Pierre's wild plan, is not to acknowledge Isabel as his half sister and his father's illegitimate daughter, but to save her dignity, the reputation of their father, and the feelings of his (now despised) mother by asserting that Isabel is his wife; and that pretense, according to various hints in the text, some more heated than others, is but prelude to embracing her as a wife.[14] Such an act dares to go beyond the ethical, and is tantamount to outdoing Hamlet and Claudius both. In order to attest the primacy of the Oedipus complex, Freudian interpreters tend to regard the half sister as a displacement of the mother and generally assume that Melville's glances at the "wisely hidden" significance of *Hamlet* or "the hopeless gloom of its interior meaning" confirm some such reading. But the hero's dare to free himself and Isabel to incestuous desire, or to commit incest if he should so please, has more probably to do with the impossible quest for originality and Promethean heroics. Pierre seeks to make love to his own devoted mirror image and dreams of being the titan Enceladus, "the present doubly incestuous Enceladus within him" (25.5.347). Once it becomes clear that Pierre is also a writer, the act of tearing works of Dante and Shakespeare to shreds can be seen as indicative of similar strivings.

Improve on Hamlet or destroy *Hamlet* as he may, Pierre cannot avoid his fate. The fifth act of the inescapable modern play will impress its design on Pierre's own final days. No sooner has Lucy Tartan been impelled by her grief to join all chastely the hero and his supposed wife in New York, than she is pursued to the very door by her frustrated suitor Glen Stanly and her older brother Frederic, a naval officer, who both regard her as mad. The two men leap at Pierre, and the three of them skirmish in the stairwell. To their loud accusations he replies, "I render no accounts: I am what I am" (24.3.325). Pierre's "I am what I am" echoes an heroic line in Spanish honor plays, and this moment shapes the action of the rest of the novel.[15] It also corresponds to Hamlet's "This is I, / Hamlet the Dane (5.1.224–5); and Frederic makes a good Laertes, with the rival Glen thrown in for good measure, a more hateful adversary than the brother. (If there is a usurper in *Pierre*, it is this cousin with the name Glendinning Stanly—

---

[14] For the sexual bonding of the two, real or imagined, see *Pierre*, 7.8.142; 10.1.177; 12.1.188–92; and 19.2.272–74.

[15] The Latin influence may also be felt in Melville's description of "pride-horror . . . more terrible than any fear," which accosts a man when the chastity of his women folk is challenged (25.2.336).

a very minor character nonetheless.) Somehow in this short time Lucy has come of age, and thus there is no legal redress against her remaining with Pierre and Isabel and the disgraced Delly. A duel with these men is therefore in the offing, when Pierre will be called to account for Lucy's adherence to his household; but as respite from "the ambiguities which hemmed him in," he welcomes the chance to kill or be killed. His eagerness is an angry and despairing version of Hamlet's readiness—puzzling to Horatio, remember—to fence with Laertes. Whereas Hamlet's stoicism leaves him superior to whatever may happen, Pierre's exhaustion lowers him to a match with unequals: "the utmost hate of Glen and Frederic were jubilantly welcome to him; and murder, done in the act of warding off their ignominious public blow, seemed the one congenial sequel to such a desperate career" (25.2.336–7).

When Pierre receives in the mail an insulting challenge from these adversaries, a quite wonderful scene ensues: no courtly fencing match, but like the shootout in later westerns. He stalks north on Broadway (never named, but it has to be Broadway) with two borrowed pistols; Glen and Frederic scout for him from the other direction with a horsewhip. Fred the navy man holds back from a sense of fairness; and Pierre, struck on the face by Glen's whip, empties both pistols into his rival—"Tis speechless sweet to murder thee!" (26.5.359). The hero's two women come to him in the city prison that evening. Isabel bears the poison from which she and Pierre die, while Lucy apparently dies from the shock of hearing Isabel address Pierre as brother rather than husband. Of course, dueling is always already suicidal: the man of honor accepts the risk whenever he has recourse to a duel. Just so, many have regarded Hamlet's murdering end as a kind of suicide. Yet Melville is fully aware of the different historical epoch. As in Scott's and other nineteenth-century novels, dueling is treated as an archaic institution. But when a gentleman is placed on the defensive, he must abide by that archaism. The social contract, suddenly characterized as "arbitrary homage to the Law" (25.2.335), is in abeyance.

To focus on the end of this novel, however, scants a more important turning. Arguably the catastrophe of *Pierre* falls in book 16 when the hero escorts Isabel and Delly to the city. The anonymity, the dark streets, the nightly scene in the watch house, the helplessness of the three newcomers provide the truly scarifying scene of the novel.[16] Notoriously, after this

---

[16] Matthiessen, *American Renaissance*, 486, agrees that this is "the most powerful" scene in *Pierre* and suggests "a partial model in the flight of Clifford and Hepzibah" in Hawthorne's *The House of the Seven Gables* (1851).

point the bildungsroman itself takes a bizarre turn. Book 17 is entitled "Young America in Literature" and gives an hilarious, unexpected account of Pierre's juvenilia and letters from editors and publishers. But the reader, before now, has never been informed that Pierre has written anything but a letter. Melville scholars suspect that something has gone awry in the New York chapters. Perhaps the author had not earlier expected his hero to be a writer and was improvising, or protesting his own publisher's reception of the first part of this manuscript. But one way or another, after Pierre's father's ghost appeared in the shape of Isabel, our hero decided to be a writer. In book 18, the narrator is constrained to write:

> It may have been already inferred, that the pecuniary plans of Pierre touching his independent means of support in the city were based upon his presumed literary capabilities. For what else could he do? He knew no profession, no trade. Glad now perhaps might he have been, if Fate had made him a blacksmith, and not a gentleman, a Glendinning, and a genius. (18.2.260)

Great Expectations had not been written yet, so the alternative of Pierre being set up in life for a blacksmith cannot be traced to that novel. Yet Dickens, I suggest, may indirectly have been responsible for the belated announcement of Pierre's career as a writer. *David Copperfield* appeared from May 1849 to November 1850 and, like the other novels of Dickens, was freely pirated in the United States. Dickens's autobiographical novel gave no hint of the narrator's profession until an aside in the fifteenth of twenty monthly installments: "For I wrote a good deal now, and was beginning in a small way to be known as a writer."[17] Moreover, Copperfield is such a modest fellow that he never tells what the experience of writing is like, though by the end he is an immense success at it. That coyness alone might account for the facetiousness of Melville's revelation that Pierre is to be a writer. The profundity of Pierre's purpose thereafter, his suffering and tragic end, contrast markedly with Copperfield's career. Both writers attract the loves of two women, the earlier in each case associated with the mother. David's deeper attachment is to Agnes Wickfield, whom he calls "sister"; after Dora's death he comes to realize Agnes's love and remarries. He hasn't the fortune or misfortune to live with two at the same time, or to embrace a veritable half sister.

---

[17] Charles Dickens, *David Copperfield*, ed. Nina Burgis (Oxford: Clarendon, 1981), 551. Sealts, *Melville's Reading*, entry 181, records that "Miss Melville" borrowed *David Copperfield* from Duyckinck in late 1850. Parker, *Herman Melville*, 806—presumably on this same basis— writes that Dickens's novel was family reading in the winter of 1850–51.

The outrageous bit in the uncovering of the hero's vocation in *Pierre* is the line, "For what else could he do?" If you cannot do anything, write something! Such would seem to be the Romantic idea of Hamlet, and each Hamlet must write his own book. The surest way to do that is to engage in autobiography, and the heaviest matter to take up is the meaning of life and death. To be or not to be, that is the question. From slips of paper on the plank that serves as Pierre's writing table and other slips on the floor, we learn that he intends to compose an autobiographical novel. His "author-hero, Vivia . . . soliloquizes" as follows: "A deep-down unutterable mournfulness is in me. Now I drop all humorous or indifferent disguises, and all philosophical pretensions. I own myself a brother of the clod, a child of the Primeval Gloom. Hopelessness and despair are over me, a pall on pall" (22.3.302). From this and other fragments it is evident that Vivia can only mourn. His name seems bitterly ironic; his plight commands some sympathy because it is also Pierre's plight.

> That which now absorbs the time and life of Pierre, is not the book, but the primitive elementalizing of the strange stuff, which in the act of attempting that book, has upheaved and upgushed in his soul. Two books are being writ; of which the world shall only see one, and that the bungled one. The larger book, and the infinitely better, is for Pierre's own private shelf. That it is, whose unfathomable cravings drink his blood; the other only demands his ink. . . . He is learning how to live, by rehearsing the part of death. (22.4.304–5)

Unfortunately, terms like "primitive elementalizing of the strange stuff" do not convey any very definite idea, and the teasing thought that—analogous to Vivia's and Pierre's efforts—the bungled book is Melville's, now in the reader's hands, does not help matters. Melville is more successful in winning sympathy for his hero and getting readers to take him seriously when, in the same pages, he evokes the bodily strain under which Pierre works, his surroundings and the bitter cold of his room, and his estrangement from the women who are devoted to him. "One in a city of hundreds of thousands of human beings, Pierre was solitary as at the Pole." And yet Pierre, like other writers, hopes to reach those people, his potential readers. For all the peculiar need to write about the deepest truths, he hopes to be read. His failure to penetrate the gloom with insight that can be set to paper contributes to the wearing down of his health and the consciousness, however premature, that he will not live to know whether he has succeeded. "All panegyric, all denunciation, all criticism of any sort, would come too late for Pierre." Melville's insistence on this writer's heroism is not always convincing and is often parodic, as if conviction were despaired of in any case. But his descriptions of Pierre's deterioration can be moving.

> Much oftener than before, Pierre laid back in his chair with the deadly feeling of faintness. Much oftener than before, came staggering home from his evening walk, and from sheer bodily exhaustion economized the breath that answered the anxious inquiries as to what might be done for him. . . . His incessant application told upon his eyes. They became so affected, that some days he wrote with the lids nearly closed, fearful of opening them too far to the light. . . . Sometimes he blindly wrote with his eyes turned away from the paper;—thus unconsciously symbolizing the hostile necessity and distaste, the former whereof made of him this most unwilling states-prisoner of letters. (25.3.338,339,340)

Pierre is not necessarily a muddled thinker, even if readers might wish for more demonstration of his brilliance. Melville attributes the difficulty to the nature of truth and the limits of verbal representation. Putting experience to use in a book is bound to be a partial business, subject to the partialities of author and language both. Pierre is said to be assimilating this wisdom himself:

> For the more and the more that he wrote, and the deeper and the deeper that he dived, Pierre saw the everlasting elusiveness of Truth; the universal lurking insincerity of even the greatest and purest written thoughts. Like knavish cards, the leaves of all great books were covertly packed. He was but packing one set the more; and that a very poor jaded set and pack indeed. So that there was nothing he more spurned, than his own aspirations; nothing he more abhorred than the loftiest part of himself.

This seems a plausible description of the melancholic at his desk, perversely insisting on perfection so that he can disparage others' achievements and his own hopes. Books are ever approximations, but more than that they cheat, even the best of them, by forever falling short of the truth. Something like "infatuation" is required to go on writing. The "next morning—it was some few days after the arrival of Lucy . . . he returned to the charge. But again the pupils of his eyes rolled away from him in their orbits: and now a general and nameless torpor—some terrible foretaste of death itself—seemed stealing upon him" (25.3.339,341–2).

Lucy's arrival, in effect, saves him from this slow death from abhorrence of his own task. For one thing, she bucks him up; she is another sexual conquest, all the more so because she submits to Isabel, averring no expectations of love. Her bloom has gone, but has not been replaced by "sallowness"; rather, "a brilliant, supernatural whiteness now gleamed in her cheek" (24.4.328). Her shining presence is enough to set him doubting again about his determinate unHamlet-like decision to leave Saddle Meadows. "How did he know that Isabel was his sister?" (26.2.353). The uncertainty plagues him even after an encounter with two more signifying portraits would seem to confirm the relation.[18] But above all, Lucy's adherence brings on Fred and Glen; their insulting challenge arrives in the same post as an insulting letter from his publishers, "Steel, Flint & Asbestos" (26.4.356). Thus Pierre, instead of definitively failing as a writer, chooses to die honorably by fighting the nearest substitutes he has for Laertes and Claudius. Still, that choice is also of suicide, and the final action of *Pierre* would seem to argue that Hamlet's choice was similar: slow death from grief and self-doubt or a quick bout with poison.

Forgotten even in the United States until the mid-twentieth century, *Pierre; or, The Ambiguities* has since then been read as an allegory of American history or a camp autobiography of Melville himself. There can be little doubt that the author, like his hero, "directly plagiarized from his own experiences" (22.3.302), but it is far less certain that his particular purpose was to treat of an American identity or the problem of generations as confined to this country. Matthiessen admits that Pierre's "tragedy has really very little to do with political or social values."[19] Basically, the novel takes a character of Hamlet-like mourning, confuses it with Promethean suffering and Faustian ambition for unprecedented experience, and latterly superimposes on this figure a career of writing. If *Pierre* belongs to a tradition, it is principally a Hamlet-as-writer tradition. Yet as a *Künstlerroman* it does not much resemble *Wilhelm Meisters Lehrjahre*, still less the overtly self-depreciating *David Copperfield*. *Pierre* keeps inflating and deflating of its own accord. "I write precisely as I please," the narrator announces when he changes course midway (17.1.244); "Life's last chapter well stitched into the middle!" the hero begins his last speech (26.6.360). Bercovitch is surely

---

[18] "With both Isabel and Lucy bodily touching his sides as he walked" (26.2.353), Pierre in these remaining days of his life enjoys exclusive possession of two contrasting types of early nineteenth-century heroine. One of Lucy's namesakes is Lucy Edgermonde, in Madame de Staël's immensely popular *Corinne* (1807). Scott, Cooper, and Hawthorne all exploited the convention.

[19] Matthiessen, *American Renaissance*, 469. For a younger generation of writers on American literature, *Pierre* has served to anchor some inaugurations of their own: see Richard H. Brodhead, *Hawthorne, Melville, and the Novel* (Chicago: University of Chicago Press, 1973), 163–93; Eric J. Sundquist, *Home as Found: Authority and Genealogy in Nineteenth-Century American Literature* (Baltimore: Johns Hopkins University Press, 1979), 143–85; and Myra Jehlen, *American Incarnation: The Individual, the Nation, and the Continent* (Cambridge: Harvard University Press, 1986), 185–226. I have benefited from each of these chapters.

right to stress the parodic veering about of *Pierre*, and Poirier, its stubborn insistence on the artist as culture hero. That the fiction entertains both of these aims at the same time stamps it as a remarkably modernist text. And similarly *Hamlet* becomes that modernist text, particularly as its hero becomes at once honored and parodied in the later nineteenth century.

Among nineteenth-century novelists who are still widely read, one has to turn to Victor Hugo to match Melville's inflated rhetoric. Hyperbole and incantation, for these two, insist that writing itself is heroic business. The prose seems to boast that it can afford self-parody, if that is what it is. The cultural allusions and borrowings are never less than grand larceny. Hugo, both in his admiration and larcenous practices, might be said to be *the* champion of Shakespeare for all time; and for Hugo, Hamlet was the epitome of Shakespeare's achievement. To commemorate the three-hundredth anniversary of the poet's birth, and to accompany his son François-Victor's translation of the plays, Hugo published a book on Shakespeare in 1864. The hero of his *William Shakespeare* is something like the hero of *Pierre*, or perhaps of the book Pierre was writing before he was mercifully seized by the "pride-horror" of honor and could find relief by murdering Glen Stanly. "There is in 'Hamlet' all the majesty of the mournful [*lugubre*]. A drama issuing from an open sepulchre—this is colossal."[20] If Pierre sometimes seems as Promethean as he is Hamletian, that coupling is confirmed by Hugo's estimate of Prometheus and Hamlet as the two greatest literary types, one ancient and one modern (this after a brief apology to Dante as Dante, knocking on the door of the infinite).

According to Hugo, Aeschylus's hero embodies action, Shakespeare's inaction. The former is constrained by Zeus, however; the latter, by himself.

> In Prometheus the four limbs of incarnate Will are nailed down with brazen spikes, and cannot move: besides, it has by its side two watchers, Force and Power. In Hamlet the Will is still more enthralled: it is bound by preliminary meditation, the endless chain of the irresolute. Try to get out of yourself if you can! What a Gordian knot is our revery! Slavery from within, is slavery indeed. Scale me the barricade of thought! escape, if you can, from the prison of love! The only dungeon is that which immures the conscience. Prometheus, in order to be free, has but a bronze collar to break and a god to conquer; Hamlet must break and conquer himself. Prometheus can rise upright, quit with lifting a mountain; in order that Hamlet may stand erect, he must lift his own thought. If Prometheus

---

[20] Victor Hugo, *William Shakespeare*, trans. Melville B. Anderson (Chicago: McClurg, 1906), 236.

plucks the vulture from his breast, all is done; Hamlet must rend from his flank Hamlet. Prometheus and Hamlet are two livers laid bare: from the one trickles blood, from the other doubt.[21]

In pairing these two prodigious types, Hugo seems unable to help himself from making the hero of inaction still more heroic than he of action. Hamlet's struggle is clearly the harder one, and when Hugo's rhetoric—in the second person—appeals directly to his readers, it is exclusively in the cause of Hamlet. A few pages later he makes this implicit identification explicit: "His strange reality is our own reality, after all. He is the mournful [*funebre*] man that we all are in certain situations." Hugo does not quite imagine himself or his reader in the situation of Prometheus. And far from denigrating Hamlet, the comparison with Prometheus elevates him, as if he were a later development of the same greatness of striving and suffering. Not a word of revenging the death of a father: Hugo depreciates the usual comparison of Hamlet to Orestes. That "Hamlet walks behind Orestes, a parricide through filial love," is merely the learned idea of the Aeschylean analogy. Such an "easy comparison, rather superficial than substantial, is less striking than the mysterious confrontment of those two captives, Prometheus and Hamlet." The latter comparison, to be sure, is Hugo's own; he no more asks what good, corresponding to Prometheus's gifts of fire and knowledge, Hamlet brings to humanity than Melville asks what practical advantages Pierre will confer on his fellow Americans. No wonder a certain amount of posturing can be expected from this Hamlet, who "is incapable of governing a people, so wholly apart from all does he exist." But for Hugo, that is sufficient: "Take from him his family, his country, his ghost, the whole adventure at Elsinore, and even in the form of an inactive type he remains strangely terrible. This results from the amount of humanity and the amount of mystery in him."[22]

---

[21] Ibid., 228. The French reads as follows: "Dans Prométhée, la volonté est clouée aux quatre membres par des clous d'airain et ne peut remuer; de plus elle a à côté d'elle deux gardes, la Force et la Puissance. Dans Hamlet, la volonté est plus asservie encore; elle est garrottée par la méditation préalable, chaîne sans fin des indécis. Tirez-vous donc de vous-même! Quel noeud gordien que notre rêverie! l'esclavage du dedans, c'est là l'esclavage. Escaladez-moi cette enceinte: songer! sortez, si vous pouvez, de cette prison: aimer! l'unique cachot est celui qui mure la conscience. Prométhée, pour être libre, n'a qu'un carcan de bronze à briser et qu'un dieu à vaincre; il faut que Hamlet se brise lui-même et se vainque lui-même. Prométhée peut se dresser debout, quitte à soulever une montagne; pour que Hamlet se redresse, il faut qu'il soulève sa pensée. Que Prométhée s'arrache de la poitrine le vautour, tout est dit; il faut que Hamlet s'arrache du flanc Hamlet. Prométhée et Hamlet, ce sont deux foies à nu; de l'un coule le sang, de l'autre le doute." *William Shakespeare* (Paris: Flammarion, 1973), 192–93.
[22] Hugo, *William Shakespeare*, 238–39, 229, 239.

Just eight years later, in his first book, Friedrich Nietzsche rather abruptly identified Hamlet with the Dionysian man—not the god Dionysus, to be sure, but one who had experienced the reality of life in nature. Nietzsche is drawn to this identification through reflection on the lethargy and even nausea that he believed followed upon the rapture of a Dionysian state, and he writes in a context from which other modern heroes are simply absent. As in Hugo, the comparison is distinctly flattering to Hamlet.

> In this sense the Dionysian man resembles Hamlet: both have once looked truly into the essence of things, they have *gained knowledge*, and nausea inhibits action; for their action could not change anything in the eternal nature of things; they feel it to be ridiculous or humiliating that they should be asked to set right a world that is out of joint. Knowledge kills action; action requires the veils of illusion: that is the doctrine of Hamlet, not that cheap wisdom of Jack the Dreamer who reflects too much and, as it were, from an excess of possibilities does not get around to action. Not reflection, no—true knowledge, an insight into the horrible truth, outweighs any motive for action, both in Hamlet and in the Dionysian man.[23]

Nietzsche does not spell out what Hamlet has learned. Possibly it is that anyone of us may smile and be a villain; possibly, that everyone of us will be annihilated. But whether a moral truth or a truth about the natural man, Nietzsche's *wahre Erkenntnis* and *grauenhafte Wahrheit* have the generality and disagreeableness of Melville's Woe and Truth.

The proviso that finally makes sense of parallels to Prometheus or the Dionysian man together with the unique hero's representativeness is that, secretly or otherwise, Hamlet must be a writer. Only so can he be unique, isolated and suffering within, yet representative of modern humanity: as a Romantic writer he stands apart, but he takes as his subject humanity. Or to put it the other way around, he will deliver as a gift to humanity, the

---

[23] Friedrich Nietzsche, *The Birth of Tragedy* and *The Case of Wagner*, trans. Walter Kaufmann (New York: Vintage, 1967), 59–60. "In diesem Sinne hat der dionysische Mensch ähnlichkeit mit Hamlet: beide haben einmal einen wahren Blick in das Wesen der Dinge gethan, sie haben e r k a n n t, und es ekelt sie zu handeln; denn ihre Handlung kann nichts am ewigen Wesen der Dinge, ändern, sie empfinden es als lächerlich oder schmachvoll, daß ihnen zugemuthet wird, die Welt, die aus den Fugen ist, wieder einzurichten. Die Erkenntnis tödtet das Handeln, zum Handeln gehört das Umschleiertsein durch die Illusion—das ist die Hamletlehre, nicht jene wohlfeile Weisheit von Hans dem Träumer, der aus zu viel Reflexion, gleichsam aus einem überschuss von Möglichkeiten, nicht zum Handeln kommt; nicht das Reflectiren, nein!—die wahre Erkenntnis, der Einblick in die grauenhafte Wahrheit überwiegt jedes zum Handeln antreibende Motiv, bei Hamlet sowohl als bei dem dionysischen Menschen." *Die Geburt der Tragödie* (Leipzig, 1899), 55–56; first published in 1872.

knowledge of himself. One can be skeptical of such a figure, but as the nineteenth century wore to an end and Hamlets were often viewed ironically, transformed one after another into superfluous men or arrant knaves, it is surprising how many of them were also writers. In literary circles, at least, Hamlet's pessimism and even self-blame still proved infectious. The hero of Anton Chekhov's *Ivanov* (1887) can be discovered reading a book at the opening curtain. An intellectual who has never really advanced from being a student, Ivanov falls subject to melancholy at age thirty. Despising himself as a Hamlet or superfluous man does not prevent him from cruelly telling his wife that he does not love her and that she is dying. Rather than repeat this sad act with a younger woman who perversely loves him for being a failure, he shoots himself in the closing scene. Ivan Laevsky in Chekhov's long story "The Duel" (1891) similarly recognizes himself as a Hamlet. He ought to be studying and writing, but is wasting his life and betraying the woman who lives with him. Fortunately, unlike Pierre's duel, the one that Laevsky fights at the end brings him to his senses; we last see him married and working at his desk. In *The Sea Gull* (1896), the younger of the two writers—another Hamlet figure—shoots himself again.[24]

Such unlikely scions of Prince Hamlet are not completely without merit as writers or as human beings. They have the decency to berate themselves, at least, and each is attractive to one or more women. At the same time, identification with Hamlet permits authors to stand back from themselves and to appear self-critical, even as they underscore the importance of their calling. In Paris, where Shakespeare's play was popular in the theater, Hamlet was readily adopted or internalized by poets. Here is Stéphane Mallarmé on this theater of the mind in 1886:

> That adolescent who vanished from us at the beginning of his life and who will always haunt lofty, pensive minds with his mourning is very present to me now as I see him struggling against the curse of having to appear. For that is precisely, uniquely the kind of character that Hamlet externalizes on the stage, in an intimate and occult tragedy. . . . And now here comes *the prince of promise unfulfillable*, young shade of all of us; and therefore there is myth in him. The lonely drama that he plays! This walker in a labyrinth of agitation and grievance so prolongs its windings with his unfinishing of an unfinished act, that he sometimes seems to be the only reason for the existence of the stage and of the golden, almost moral, space which the stage protects. For remember! Here is the only plot in drama:

[24] See also Eleanor Rowe, *Hamlet: A Window on Russia* (New York: New York University Press, 1976), 107–25.

the struggle, in man, between his dream and the fates allotted to his life by evil fortune.[25]

Hamlet as the model for those too diffident to appear, the hero of those who inwardly cannot hope to succeed? The elusiveness of this shade makes the meaning it held for Symbolists and Decadents hard to define, but Hamlet certainly has become one of them. "They took the Prince of Denmark out of the theater, in the strict sense of the term, to make of him a symbolic figure undefined by time or space, a *potential* hero, haunted by the specter of the absolute, harassed by cosmic doubt."[26] These words of Helen Phelps Bailey could equally apply to Melville's hero, though it seems unlikely that *Pierre* was known in France. In an essay on the background of Jules Laforgue's "Hamlet," Peter Brooks ventures some reasons for the phenomenon: "Hamlet was a symbol of the inviolable mind of the artist. . . . He is a metaphysical dreamer whose renunciation is hyperconscious; he not only rejects the world of contingency, he causes its bloody demise; haunted by the corruption of generalization, he predicts a future state of androgynous creative beings; he is the exponent of pure theater, or monologue."[27]

Laforgue's "Hamlet ou les suites de la piété filiale" was first published a month after Mallarmé's words on *Hamlet* above.[28] The subtitle, the supposed moral of the tale, is of course a joke, signaling how not to read this prose travesty of Shakespeare's drama. Laforgue's Hamlet is the artist as narcissist and could hardly care less about his father's "irregular decease," which is never otherwise described; so "filial piety" is nothing but a cynical comment on the earlier Hamlet's "Haste me to know't, that I . . . may sweep to my revenge" (1.5.29–31). The hero impatiently awaits the arrival of the players so that they can perform his play about the king, the queen, and her brother-in-law Claudius. Hamlet's own father was Horwendill; his mother is Gerutha, and his uncle, Fengo. But this is not medieval Denmark: it is 14 July 1601. Thus Laforgue's parody superimposes *Hamlet* as first performed by Shakespeare's company upon the story in Saxo and Belleforest. Not too subtly (forget that it is also Bastille Day), Laforgue

[25] Stéphane Mallarmé, "Hamlet," in *Selected Prose Poems, Essays and Letters*, trans. Bradford Cook (Baltimore: Johns Hopkins University Press, 1956), 57. These reflections were first published in the *Revue indépendante*, 1 Nov. 1886.
[26] Helen Phelps Bailey, *Hamlet in France from Voltaire to Laforgue* (Geneva: Droz, 1964), 137.
[27] Peter Brooks, "The Rest is Silence: Hamlet as Decadent," in *Jules Laforgue: Essays on a Poet's Life and Work*, ed. Warren Ramsey (Carbondale: Southern Illinois University Press, 1969), 101.
[28] Bailey, *Hamlet in France*, 143n.

has repeated Shakespeare's moves in naming Claudius, inventing more of the action, imposing his own interpretation on events. To do the English playwright one better, his tale adheres more nearly to the classical unities: Hamlet has killed Polonius the day before, and Ophelia has been missing since last night; their funerals take place the same evening as Hamlet's play; and so will Hamlet be killed by Laertes this night, before he can get away to Paris with an actress. The latter's real name is neither "Ophelia, Cordelia, Lelia, Coppelia, [nor] Camelia" but Kate, and she is stunningly beautiful. Sadly, Hamlet will never get to read the rest of his writings to her in Paris.[29]

This Hamlet's immediate project, he tells us in soliloquy, was to stage the "horrible, horrible, horrible" circumstances of his father's murder, but he grew fond of the work and continued it for his own sake. It helps that Horwendill was a bit of a bounder and fathered more than one child out of wedlock—his reputation makes Pierre's father's premarital affair with a French woman seem puritanical. From the gravedigger, between funerals of Polonius and Ophelia, Hamlet learns that he is one of the bastards: the brother of Yorick the jester, in fact, by the same beautiful gypsy mother. In this version of the story there are also two portraits, hanging side by side in Hamlet's tower quarters, but they are of the father and the son: the roguish Horwendill "in beautiful new armor," and his son the dandy with "thumb tucked into his rawhide belt." Downplaying the ghost, obviously, has made this Hamlet's burden lighter; still, the attractiveness of the story as a whole depends on the greater absurdity of the hero. The cool nastiness of the young man is implicit in the casual, scarcely mentioned fact that not only his father but Polonius and Ophelia have become casualties before the action commences; yet his self-love is so incorrigible and his sadistic treatment of other living creatures so cowardly (he strangles a pet canary and mutilates insects, toads, and snails in the woods) that his actions evoke laughter at every turn. The reader is reassured—somewhat!—by Laforgue's transparent identification with his Hamlet, whose physical appearance resembles that of the author and whose snatches of verse are borrowed from the author's published poetry.[30] Mockery of this horrible, horrible Hamlet is thus deliberately mixed with self-mockery. When our decadent

[29] Jules Laforgue, "Hamlet or the Consequences of Filial Piety," in *Selected Writings of Jules Laforgue*, ed. and trans. William Jay Smith (New York: Grove, 1956), 110. For some passages below I have slightly modified this translation.

[30] Conversely, Laforgue's poetry was filled with allusions to *Hamlet*: see Martin Scofield, *The Ghosts of Hamlet: The Play and Modern Writers* (Cambridge: Cambridge University Press, 1980), 34–44.

hero is abruptly stabbed by Laertes and dies with Nero's words "Qualis ... artifex ... pereo" on his lips, the tale ends with the narrator's witty rejoinder, "And so order was restored. One Hamlet the less does not mean the end of the race, that's for sure."[31] The words register how commonplace Hamlet has become as a figure for the artist and the author's own wry acceptance of death.

Laforgue died at the age of twenty-seven shortly after this *moralité légendaire* was written. His parody shrewdly touches on the knowledge of death that Shakespeare's Hamlet comes to possess in the course of the play. Mourning has no predictable terminus; revenge is more satisfying as a thought than as an act of justice; the death of one's father implies nothing less than one's own death; and surely that death is murder. Laforgue's Hamlet does not want to die; he wants life and liberty that he does not know what to do with. He is seemingly more bored than grieving. "Eh bien," one of his soliloquies protests,

> "what am I waiting for? Death! Death! Ah, have I time to think about death, such a gifted being as I? ... My father is dead; that body of which I am the prolongation is no more. He is over there stretched on his back with his hands folded. And what can I do but lie there when my turn comes? And will people look upon me, properly stretched out with my hands folded, without laughing! ..."
>
> With his two hands Hamlet clasps the skull of his future skeleton and tries to force a shiver through all his bones.[32]

It seems ridiculous for Hamlet to die; his father's death should have freed him for a time from that succession. But what else can he do?

Laforgue scores many hits on Hamlet and *Hamlet* criticism, including the commonplace that perhaps Laertes should have been the hero (his Laertes is willing to let Hamlet off but kills him just to put an end to his talk). The funniest rewriting of Shakespeare may be the truncation of the

---

[31] "Et tout rentra dans l'ordre. / Un Hamlet de moins; la race n'en est pas perdue, qu'on se le dise!" Laforgue, *Oeuvres complètes* (Paris: Mecure de France, 1924), 3:69. Michelle Hannosh, *Parody and Decadence: Laforgue's "Moralités légendaires"* (Columbus: Ohio State University Press, 1989), 101–03, notes that "la race" is ambiguous as to the human race or the race of Hamlets.

[32] Laforgue, "Hamlet," 123–24. "Eh bien, qu'est-ce que j'attends ici?—La mort! La mort! Ah! est-ce qu'on a le temps d'y penser, si bien doué que l'on soit? ... Mon père est mort, cette chair dont je suis un prolongement n'est plus. Il gît par là, étendu sur le dos, les mains jointes! Qu'y puis-je, que passer un jour à mon tour par là? Et on me verra aussi, dignement étendu, les mains jointes, sans rire! ... Hamlet se prend son futur crâne de squelette à deux mains et essaie de frissonner de tous ses ossements." *Oeuvres complètes*, 3:46–47.

play scene: instead of Fengo calling for lights, Hamlet calls for music and remarks of the murder he has uncovered: "So it's true! And I still only half believed it!—Well, this has been punishment enough for them in my opinion." Underlying the parody, however, there is respect for Shakespeare's Hamlet and serious identification with him. Laforgue's Hamlet doubts all too little when it comes to doing as he pleases, but he also doubts philosophically. Until "someone proves that our speech has some connection with a transcendent reality," his motto must remain "Words, words, words."[33] This sort of doubt lingers, all the more so because young Hamlet is slain by Laertes before he can worry the question or write more in Paris.

James Joyce was certainly acquainted with Laforgue's moral tale. The Hamlet figure in *Ulysses* (1922)—from any number of considerations—is young Stephen Dedalus. Like Laforgue's hero, this writer is first encountered by the reader in his tower by the sea, and the mocking allusions to *Hamlet* commence immediately.[34] The use of Shakespeare by Joyce is far more ambitious than that of the French parodist and at the same time more diffuse. One count establishes 91 verbal echoes of *Hamlet* in *Ulysses*, of which 42 are Stephen's, 26 are Bloom's, 15 from other characters, and 6 unattributed to any personality.[35] These allusions, however, merely supplement analogous plotting and overt discussion of the play.

The design and dimensions of *Ulysses* are epic, and Stephen Dedalus corresponds to Homer's Telemachus as well as to Hamlet. His father is very much alive, though they live apart; his mourning dress is for his mother, whose ghost hovers near and fills him with guilt. Like other Hamlet figures since Goethe's, he resists the imposition of either parent's will; and like the others, he answers not to some unmediated interpretation of the hero but to the received ideas about him—most notably that he should be a writer. Joyce outdoes his predecessors by having his hero conduct a still more extensive analysis of Shakespeare's drama. Stephen's virtual lecture on the subject, augmented by dialogue and interior monologue, occupies the full library scene, the last of five episodes in *Ulysses* featuring the younger hero more than Leopold Bloom and adhering to the narrative conventions of the first half of the novel—the last that is Stephen's own show, so to speak. That episode—the Scylla and Charybdis in the Homeric

---

[33] Laforgue, "Hamlet," 133, 123.

[34] Hugh Kenner is persuaded that "the comic dimensions of Joyce's treatment of Stephen owe much to Laforgue": see "Joyce's *Ulysses*: Homer and Hamlet," *Essays in Criticism* 2 (1952), 100–104.

[35] William M. Schutte, *Joyce and Shakespeare: A Study in the Meaning of "Ulysses"* (New Haven: Yale University Press, 1957), appendix B.

scheme of the book—begins with a paraphrase of "those priceless pages of *Wilhelm Meister*," which tell of a Hamlet inadequate to the task before him, but the homage to Goethe pointedly comes from the reference librarian who walks in and out of the room. Stephen himself spins a far-out biographical reading of *Hamlet*, as outrageous in its way as the antics of Laforgue's hero; and when asked if he believes his own theory, he replies, "No."[36]

It can be argued that the project for Joyce's modernist epic was set by Plato at the end of the *Republic*. There, in one of his fictions of the afterlife, Plato tells of the souls of famous Greeks, some of them veterans of the Trojan war, choosing among lives available on earth for their incipient reincarnations. The great Odysseus comes last and effectively has no choice, since only one life remains, that of an ordinary man. But Odysseus welcomes this choice, affirms it as his, and will be reincarnated as an ordinary man. Joyce names this man Leopold Bloom, half Jewish and half Irish, and relates his journeyings about Dublin on a single day, 16 June 1904—the date chosen for autobiographical reasons, but like Laforgue's use of 14 July 1601 in its aggressive particularity. Yet Bloom is never openly compared to Odysseus—or Ulysses—on that long day. Joyce divided his novel into eighteen epic, or mock-epic, episodes, but he had to leak to his friends their specific correspondences to the adventures in Homer. Nor is Stephen ever compared to Telemachus. Only the title, *Ulysses*, openly refers to the epic design. In the tradition of many nineteenth-century invocations of *Hamlet*, however, the characterization of Stephen as a sort of Hamlet—the modern hero and writer—is more nearly overt and ironical, as if he were Pierre in America or some superfluous man in Russia.

As chief theorist and most opinionated among the several writers present in the library, Stephen starts by complaining that Aristotle "would find Hamlet's musings about the afterlife of his princely soul, the improbable, insignificant and undramatic monologue, as shallow as Plato's."[37] An attack, it is said, is the best defense: this attack calls attention, not just to Stephen's Aristotelianism, but to Joyce's consciousness of having robbed Plato and Shakespeare both. The mixture of quarrelsomeness and reverence, however, owes more to the extremes of *Hamlet* criticism in the previous century. Plato never had the good fortune to meet Hamlet, whose fame now matched that of Ulysses and whose reincarnations could be either high or

---

[36] James Joyce, *Ulysses*, ed. Hans Walter Gabler (New York: Vintage, 1986), 9.2, 9.1067. Citations from this edition are by episode and line number.

[37] Ibid., 9.76–78.

low. Joyce was not only acquainted with Hamlet but had grand nineteenth-century authorities for regarding him as *the* modern type. Hugo had compared, more than contrasted, Shakespeare's hero to Aeschylus's Prometheus; Nietzsche had nominated him, and no other modern, the Dionysian man; Mallarmé, *le seigneur latent qui ne peut devenir*. Laforgue's cartoon of the prince only made it safer, in a way, to invest in him. Above all, Joyce could employ two types of heroism, one ancient and one modern, for his modernist epic or novel. It seems odd that Richard Ellmann could initially find "the combination of Homer and Shakespeare" surprising.[38]

Even as Joyce diminished Ulysses and Hamlet for their new roles, he could exalt his older and younger Dubliners by identification with their forebears. What may be unexpected is the vehemence of Stephen's own analysis of *Hamlet*, though it is marked as problematic from the beginning when Buck Mulligan both ridicules the theory and boasts about it to the Englishman Haines. As Ellmann quips, the theory that Stephen expounds to John Eglington, George Russell, and Richard Best in the National Library is of "*Hamlet* without the prince."[39] Neither Hamlet's meditations, nor his smart talk, nor his bloody revenge dominates the play, according to Stephen; rather it is about the determined sexual jealousy of the ghost. As legend has it, Shakespeare played the ghost; by Stephen's account, he is the ghost, whose complaint of being murdered is a skewed fiction about real life: Ann Shakespeare has betrayed the playwright by committing adultery with one of his brothers in Stratford.[40] Just as disturbing to today's Shakespeare scholars is that Stephen and his interlocutors depend on the biographical speculations of the time by such as Sidney Lee, Georg Brandes, and Frank Harris. No one takes those biographies of Shakespeare seriously any more, though it should be said that Stephen conducts a form of biographical criticism on even less evidence than they.[41] Of course, his extravagance is not to be taken with complete seriousness: he himself claims not to believe his own theory. What is clear is that Stephen affects Joyce's methods as a novelist and attributes these methods to Shakespeare. *Dubliners*, *A Portrait of the Artist as a Young Man*, and *Ulysses* demonstrate

[38] Richard Ellmann, *The Consciousness of Joyce* (New York: Oxford University Press, 1977), 58.

[39] Ibid., 57.

[40] Joyce participates in the turn-of-the-century game that *Hamlet* is a conundrum to be solved. Ellmann, *Consciousness of Joyce*, 54, informs us that he owned a German translation of Ernest Jones's 1910 paper on Hamlet's Oedipus complex.

[41] For the contribution of these three biographies to Stephen's theory, see Schutte, *Joyce and Shakespeare*, appendix A; for the general phenomenon, Samuel Schoenbaum, *Shakespeare's Lives* (New York: Oxford University Press, 1970), 383–768.

beyond a doubt that Joyce's materials were cavalierly seized from his own experience, that of his acquaintances, and that of his city. Eglington, Russell, and Best are real persons; Buck Mulligan is the invented name for Oliver St. John Gogarty, whose verses appear in *Ulysses* much as Laforgue's do in his own "Hamlet." If co-optation is the true principle of literary production, it is not such a stretch to believe that Shakespeare turned two of his brothers—Edmund and Richard—into villains, or even reinvented his wife as Gertrude. "If others have their will Ann hath a way. By cock, she was to blame."[42] Still, the entire speculation is lightened and checked by the wit of the travesty—again like that of Laforgue, but more precisely calibrated. You are expected to recall that, in Ophelia's ballad, young men are to blame—"By cock, they are to blame"—and one of them tumbled the woman, not she him (4.5.60–1).

Bloom's unknowing identification with Homer's hero does not exclude his knowledge of Shakespeare's by any means. He is not as familiar with the play as Stephen is, but he has evidently read *Hamlet* as well as seen it, and he even has some theories about it (as he has about most things). A billboard that he passes in the morning reminds him that the American actress Millicent Palmer played Hamlet the night before—15 June 1904—in Dublin, which thought causes him to reflect: "Male impersonator. Perhaps he was a woman. Why Ophelia committed suicide."[43] A couple of times in the network of *Hamlet* allusions spun by *Ulysses*, Bloom is associated with the ghost in the play. It is no accident that, as Bloom muses about poetry, an hour before the library scene, he reflects that Shakespeare writes in blank verse and comes up with the following slight misquotation:

> *Hamlet, I am thy father's spirit*
> *Doomed for a certain time to walk the earth.*[44]

If Stephen is to be identified with Hamlet, then the older man who flits past him several times during the day, who joins in conversation with him and others at the lying-in hospital, who comes to his rescue in Nighttown,

---

[42] Joyce, *Ulysses*, 9.256–57. Joyce scholars puzzle over the degree to which he endorsed Stephen's ideas. The lectures he gave on *Hamlet* in Trieste in 1912–13 have not survived, but for some clues to their nature see William H. Quillian, *Hamlet and the New Poetic: James Joyce and T. S. Eliot* (Ann Arbor: UMI, 1983), 42–48.

[43] Joyce, *Ulysses*, 5.195–96. In the library subsequently, Eglington alludes to the same performance and notes Edward Payson Vining's solution to the "problem" in *The Mystery of Hamlet* (1881). Here and elsewhere I am indebted to Don Gifford, *"Ulysses" Annotated: Notes for James Joyce's "Ulysses,"* 2nd ed. (Berkeley: University of California Press, 1988).

[44] Joyce, Ulysses, 8.67–68; cf. *Hamlet*, 1.5.9–10, where both the folio and quarto read "a certain term to walk the night." For comparisons of Bloom to the ghost in *Hamlet* by two other characters, see 7.237 and 15.951–52.

takes him home and offers to be a substitute father to him, should be identified with Hamlet's father's ghost. And if one accepts Stephen's theory of why Shakespeare wrote *Hamlet*, the fit is closer: Bloom has been betrayed and is being cuckolded that very day. That crisis seems to be one of the reasons he requires a Hamlet-Stephen. He needs the company, and Stephen will minister to his Gertrude-Molly—tutor her and otherwise distract her from the usurper of his bed, the tenor Boylan.

> O Hamlet, what a falling off was there,
> From me whose love was of that dignity
> That it went hand in hand even with the vow
> I made to her in marriage, and to decline
> Upon a wretch whose natural gifts were poor
> To those of mine.   (1.5.47–52)

> Oh step between her and her fighting soul:
> Conceit in weakest bodies strongest works.
> Speak to her, Hamlet.   (3.4.112–4)

Stephen, in addressing his few listeners at the National Library, says nothing of the evident mourning of Hamlet for his father. That is because in the latent meaning of the play—as Freud might say if he held this theory instead of his own—no one has died. Silence on this point testifies instead to the sense of loss and helplessness induced by sexual betrayal, or betrayals of intimacy short of the sexual; and such experiences can be very wounding, akin for a time to the loss of someone to death.[45] The novel begins with Stephen's mourning for his mother, exacerbated by the claims she has made upon him that he has refused. Yet Bloom as well as Stephen is in mourning throughout the day. Though he has dressed for Paddy Dignam's funeral, the black suit is still more expressive of pain over his wife's affair. Because he condones the affair, it would also seem to hold a lesson for avenging heroes of other times.

According to Stephen's theory, Hamlet's father's ghost is also Shakespeare himself. Thus William M. Schutte could make a reasonable case that Joyce wished his readers "to associate Bloom with Shakespeare."[46] The poet's son Hamnet died when he was eleven years old; Bloom's son Rudy died at eleven days; and so forth. According to the (dubious) character Lenehan in the Wandering Rocks episode, "There's a touch of the artist

---

[45] Quillian, *Hamlet and the New Poetic*, 38–40, compares the attack of sexual jealousy Joyce suffered when visiting Ireland without Nora in 1909. See also Richard Ellmann, *James Joyce* (New York: Oxford University Press, 1959), 288–93.

[46] Schutte, *Joyce and Shakespeare*, 126–35.

about old Bloom."[47] Where does this leave Stephen Dedalus, the Hamlet figure and artist as a young man? By the time *Ulysses* was completed, Joyce was father to a son and daughter and roughly Bloom's age. The novel was to be meticulously true to life, and Joyce bestowed his experience of life on the ordinary man instead of, or as well as, the dedicated artist. Because of the continuity between the *Portrait* and *Ulysses*, we think of Stephen as far as authorship is concerned. But Stephen literally could not (and did not) write either of these novels any more than Bloom did. After Stephen departs from the garden at 7 Eccles Street in the early morning of 17 June 1904, he ceases to exist—and perhaps a good thing, too, since he has nowhere to go and no plans. In both novels he is very much the young man and son: more Icarus than Dedalus, finally. By interweaving the lives of three principal characters (Molly Bloom gets the last word), Joyce refuses the temptation of one more Hamlet-as-writer story as such.

Stephen's ambition and search for truth are no less than Pierre's; but whereas Melville retained from *Hamlet* a perfunctory duel and death for an ending, Joyce elected to make the action diurnal and adapted prudently the Homeric ending that reunited Odysseus with Penelope. In a sense, Stephen has not lived long enough to succeed; he has not, in Nietzsche's formulation of Hamlet's case, woken to reality and found it "ridiculous or humiliating . . . to set right a world that is out of joint." Bloom, on the other hand, has traveled; and now he rests. How?

> With circumspection, as invariably when entering an abode (his own or not his own): with solicitude, the snakespiral springs of the mattress being old, the brass quoits and pendent viper radii loose and tremulous under stress and strain: prudently, as entering a lair or ambush of lust or adders: lightly, the less to disturb: reverently, the bed of conception and of birth, of consummation of marriage and of breach of marriage, of sleep and of death.[48]

By returning to the story of a bereaved older man, Joyce gains the simple advantage that Kyd's *Spanish Tragedy* held over Shakespeare's *Hamlet*. Kyd may not be as great a poet, but the keenings of Hieronimo for the son who has predeceased him are more directly moving than the sufferings of Hamlet, tinged with insincerity, for his father's natural or unnatural death. Nietzsche would likely call Hieronimo's outbursts paeans of grief, Apollonian rather than Dionysian.

---

[47] Joyce, *Ulysses*, 10.582–83.
[48] Ibid., 17.2115–21.

In overlaying the Shakespearean play upon the Homeric narrative, then, Joyce steadily rings changes on the relations of fathers to sons, sons to fathers. In the library episode, Stephen is most moved and carried away by his thoughts when he generalizes about fathers and sons while aware of his own discomfort with Simon Dedalus. "A father, Stephen said, battling against hopelessness, is a necessary evil": the declamation that follows asserts that the playwright wrote *Hamlet* after his father's death but still insists that the play has nothing to do with John Shakespeare. The argument comes down to the uneven contribution of man and woman in sexual reproduction, and to some timeworn theological and legal compensations for this biological state of affairs. "Fatherhood, in the sense of conscious begetting, is unknown to man. . . . *Amor matris*, subjective and objective genitive, may be the only true thing in life. Paternity may be a legal fiction. Who is the father of any son that any son should love him or he any son?" Nor does Stephen neglect the father's point of view—"The son unborn mars beauty: born, he brings pain, divides affection, increases care. He is a new male: his growth is his father's decline, his youth his father's envy, his friend his father's enemy"—in order to reinforce his position that there can be no love between fathers and sons.[49] Joyce half agrees with Stephen, half disagrees. He enlists for his book the ghostly, problematic relation of father and son from *Hamlet* and compounds it with the simpler, though shrewdly described relation of Odysseus and Telemachus in Homer. John Joyce and Simon Dedalus do not loom as large in all this as the writer's literary ambitions. Joyce did entertain a love as well as utter distrust for his father; he was certainly his father's favorite. But modernism itself, of which Joyce's productions were such a significant part, could get along neither with nor without the literature of the past, from Homer to the Victorians.

Novelists will no doubt continue to have mixed feelings about Hamlet. The late Iris Murdoch wrote an ingenious novel called *The Black Prince* (1973), of which the central character is a writer easily old enough to be a father but distinctly childless. In the tradition of Wilhelm Meister and Stephen Dedalus, Bradley Pearson conducts an informal seminar on Shakespeare's *Hamlet*, but Murdoch seems shy of appointing him as the Hamlet figure. The black prince of her title would seem to refer to an epiphany of the dark Apollo, which anticipates and then is accompanied by the sexual act. Like Joyce in *Ulysses*, the author overlays classical and modern types in the action, but in this case the classical references are to the Greek mysteries, which Nietzsche identified with Dionysus and Murdoch with the dark

---

[49] Ibid., 9.828–57.

Apollo and dark Eros.[50] The theme of *The Black Prince* is the dedication of a life to art—specifically the art of writing—and behind the action is the myth of Marysas and Apollo. Marysas the flutist was flayed alive, literally taken out of himself, for daring to compete with Apollo.[51] And Hamlet? Superficially she must be the girl named Julian, the only signifying young person in the novel. Bradley falls desperately in love with Julian when she reveals that she once played Hamlet in a school production of the play; he is able to consummate the affair only when she dresses as Hamlet for him. The writer-hero of this novel, in short, is in love with Hamlet; and that, given the tradition, is tantamount to being in love with oneself.[52]

As in *Ulysses*, the classical matter in *The Black Prince* is largely hidden, whereas the discussion of *Hamlet* and the dressing as Hamlet are above-board. To begin to decode Murdoch's occult classical parallels, for example, one has to know that the cottage on the English coast where Bradley Pearson intended to write his great work, and where he takes Julian to make love, is named Patara because Herodotus tells us there was a temple of Apollo at Patara on the Lycian coast, and that a prophetess of the god attended in the temple.[53] The references to *Hamlet* are not this recondite. Shakespeare's play is also mysterious, but the middle-aged writer and the young woman talk about it. Though Julian is all unaware that she is a temple priestess of Apollo, she dresses as Hamlet for fun. The reasons that the Shakespearean allusions in such works come to the foreground are not far to seek. *Hamlet* is still very much current; allusions to *Hamlet* represent the modern. And *Hamlet* itself is about a certain self-consciousness: Harold Bloom is right to celebrate the "fiercest inwardness" and extraordinary "self-overhearing" of its hero.[54] Shakespeare dramatized the inwardness, and his Hamlet confides in the audience.

Hamlet is a tragicomic figure in the nineteenth century and after. Even as a writer, instead of a doer, he is prone to failure. Bradley Pearson in *The Black Prince* is such a figure, squarely in the tradition of Hamlet as writer.

[50] Peter J. Conradi, *Iris Murdoch: The Saint and the Artist*, 2nd ed. (London: Macmillan, 1989), 188.

[51] See Edgar Wind, *Pagan Mysteries in the Renaissance*, rev. ed. (Harmondsworth: Penguin, 1967), 172–73.

[52] As for Apollo, I note that he must inhabit both a very young women's body and a Hamlet costume before he can have his way.

[53] Douglas Brooks-Davies, *Fielding, Dickens, Gosse, Iris Murdoch and Oedipal Hamlet* (London: Macmillan, 1989), 161–62, 200n.

[54] Harold Bloom, *Shakespeare: The Invention of the Human* (New York: Riverhead, 1998), 401, 423.

His initials, like those of the elusive Black Prince, are B. P.[55] Though he would seem to share Murdoch's view of art as a high calling, the frame of the novel very much suggests that he is an unreliable narrator. Laforgue's very funny parody may be the best short introduction to the ways Hamlet can be made fun of by an author who at the same time identifies with him. Though serious autobiography and even history may draw on Hamlet for inspiration, as we have seen, humorous asides and sendups of the character abound, often in the same texts. A "Ghost of Hamlet" appears as the doctor attending the birth of David Copperfield, in the same novel that "Hamlet's aunt"—Mrs. Henry Spiker—"had the family failing of indulging in soliloquy."[56] Such jokes about an aunt and the ghost are at Hamlet's expense, and they continue in *Great Expectations*, a novel that is nevertheless profoundly engaged with Shakespeare's play. No doubt the facetiousness and contradictoriness of many Hamlet allusions can be put down to the character's own mischievous baiting of Polonius, his sour and vicious humor with Ophelia, or his consorting with the clowns he happens to find in a graveyard. But the uneasy Hamletizing of the nineteenth and twentieth centuries also resulted from the universalizing of the character, as in Hazlitt's criticism or implicitly in the novels of Scott. Perhaps the general case accounts for Murdoch's shyness of locating Hamlet in any one figure of *The Black Prince*.

Scott constructed a myth of the new polity around his heroes, but in a private letter he called the first of them, Waverley, "a sneaking piece of imbecility" and tried to explain his misgivings this way: "I am a bad hand at depicting a heroe so calld. . . . I am myself like Hamlet indifferent honest but I suppose the blood of the old cattle-drivers of Teviotdale continues to stir in my veins."[57] In other words, as an author, the poet turned novelist shares something of Hamlet's ambivalence. He is sufficiently virtuous to know what a proper hero should be, but he is descended from those drovers on the Scottish border who were little better than bandits. (This last connection was a favorite boast of the Edinburgh lawyer.) Scott's apology and accompanying boast recall Hamlet's speech:

[55] Elizabeth Dipple, *Iris Murdoch: Work for the Spirit* (London: Methuen, 1982), 110. Dipple also suggests that Bradley's name alludes to A. C. Bradley, whose two lectures on *Hamlet* in *Shakespearean Tragedy* (1904) are so well known; but see Conradi, *Iris Murdoch*, 306n9.

[56] Dickens, *David Copperfield*, 8, 319.

[57] Letter to John Morrit, July 1814, in *The Letters of Sir Walter Scott*, ed. H.J.C. Grierson, 12 vols. (London: Constable, 1932–37), 4:478–79.

Get thee to a nunnery—why wouldst thou be a breeder of sinners? I am myself indifferent honest, but yet I could accuse me of such things, that it were better my mother had not borne me. I am very proud, revengeful, ambitious, with more offences at my beck than I have thoughts to put them in, imagination to give them shape, or time to act them in. What should such fellows as I do crawling between earth and heaven? We are arrant knaves all, believe none of us. Go thy ways to a nunnery. (3.1.119–26)

The disparagement of Hamlet thus began with himself. The joke that he so often became has as much to do with his dialogue as it has with his inaction or supposed foot dragging. We kid about him and kid ourselves further to distance ourselves from his mournful self-opinion. But contrariwise our admiration for Hamlet is also rooted in his self-consciousness. Judge the accuracy of Scott's recollection: "I am myself indifferent honest, *but* ..." The ensuing accusations are as compounded with pride in the original as they are in Scott's application to his own case. One strongly suspects that Hamlet would rather, for now, be all those things. He will confess to everything, which includes the unthinkable, the unimaginable, and the undoable. If Hamlet is not boasting of his wickedness, he is at the very least taking credit for leveling the charges. His *but* claims an exception to indifference as well as to honesty.

Ophelia understands something of this. After enduring two more blistering speeches from Hamlet that are both rude and cruel to her personally, she responds with the speech that is our best evidence that Hamlet's present melancholy is a temporary state and not the foundation of his character. It is also the best testimony to his sometime promise as a hero, a set speech for act 3 of the tragedy:

> Oh what a noble mind is here o'erthrown!
> The courtier's, soldier's, scholar's, eye, tongue, sword,
> Th'expectancy and rose of the fair state,
> The glass of fashion and the mould of form,
> Th'observed of all observers, quite, quite down.

Ophelia can only conclude that Hamlet is mad—"Like sweet bells jangled ... Blasted with ecstasy" (3.1.144–54). Obviously she is being defensive and nursing her own pride in so classifying Hamlet's behavior. But she is also putting that behavior in perspective—the way Hamlet manages to keep things in perspective when he speaks of how the world seems to him lately. Ophelia has grounds for her view, not only because of the way Hamlet used to be, but in the way he harangues her. Hamlet will later take his feelings out on Gertrude, yet "that it were better my mother had not borne me" is an apology in its way—a boast as well, perhaps, but not a threat. Possibly the cruelest things Hamlet says to Ophelia are about himself.

In the nunnery speeches Hamlet addresses more or less directly the facts of generation, of sexual reproduction and the passing of generations: and what is consciousness if not the knowledge of this passing of every generation? As Jonathan Bate succinctly puts the matter, since the eighteenth century Hamlet the character in the play has mutated into "an icon of consciousness."[58] That iconography, burdened since the days of Amleth with an antic disposition, could scarcely have been established without Hamlet's intense mourning, his obsession with the before and after and with his own existence. It might be said of Melville's Pierre's last howl— "the fool of Truth, the fool of Virtue, the fool of Fate"—that all he is remarking is so much consciousness, bitterly mournful to the end. By the close of the nineteenth century, in literature and other areas of Western intellectual life, human consciousness often seemed more ripe for investigation than either human actions or the external world. H. Stuart Hughes, in a still valuable book, characterizes the modernist period as that "in which the subjective attitude of the observer of society first thrust itself forward in peremptory fashion." Though Hughes tracks mainly social theory in the period, he also places literary texts in evidence. Even when he generalizes about his "social investigators," it is hard not to think of Hamlet: their increasing attention to subjectivity tended to be "self-defeating"; and "the new self-consciousness could readily slip into a radical skepticism . . . or, alternatively, a desperate resolve to 'think with the blood.' "[59]

The Hamletism of modernism attests to the part mourning plays in consciousness. One wonders whether postmodernism—if that is where we are now—can be the better for not mourning the family, the polity, or the past and what Hamlet, the character in the play, will stand for in the fifth century of his Shakespearean being.

[58] Jonathan Bate, *The Genius of Shakesperare* (London: Picador, 1997), 257.
[59] H. Stuart Hughes, *Consciousness and Society: The Reorientation of European Social Thought, 1890–1930*, rev. ed. (New York: Vintage, 1977), 15–17.

❖ Index ❖